THE GREAT ESCAPERS

THE GREAT ESCAPERS

The Full Story of the Second World
War's Most Remarkable Mass Escape

Tim Carroll

WINDSOR
THORNDIKE

This Large Print book is published by BBC Audiobooks Ltd, Bath, England and by Thorndike Press®, Waterville, Maine, USA.

Published in 2005 in the U.K. by arrangement with Mainstream Publishing.

Published in 2005 in the U.S. by arrangement with Mainstream Publishing Company, Ltd.

U.K. Hardcover ISBN 1–4056–1063–8 (Windsor Large Print)
U.S. Softcover ISBN 0–7862–7213–9 (General)

The text of this Large Print edition is unabridged.
Other aspects of the book may vary from the original edition.

Set in 16 pt. New Times Roman.

Printed in Great Britain on acid-free paper.

British Library Cataloguing in Publication Data available

Library of Congress Cataloging-in-Publication Data

Carroll, Tim.
    The great escapers : the full story of the Second World War's most remarkable mass escape / Tim Carroll.
      p.   cm.
    Includes bibliographical references.
    ISBN 0–7862–7213–9 (lg. print : sc : alk. paper)
    1. Stalag Luft III. 2. World War, 1939–1945—Prisoners and prisons, German. 3. Prisoner-of-war escapes—Poland—çagaâ. 4. Large type books. I. Title.

D805.5.S745C37 2005
940.54'7243—dc22   2004060604

For Georgia and Patrick

Per Ardua ad Astra
(Through adversity to the stars)

Motto of the Royal Air Force

CONTENTS

ACKNOWLEDGEMENTS

I must start by thanking Roy Conyers Nesbit, the Royal Air Force editor at the Public Records Office (now renamed the National Archives) and prolific aviation writer. Roy has extended me endless help and guidance on all matters relating to the RAF, and I will not forget his kindness and generosity in entertaining me at the RAF Club in Piccadilly. Thanks to Roy, I have acquired an abiding interest in aviation and the RAF, and I hope this will not be my last book on the subject. I owe an equal debt of gratitude to Ian Sayer, the author and chronicler of Nazi misdeeds, who offered me access to his extensive Second World War archive and very kindly allowed me permission to reproduce letters written by some of the Great Escapers. Ian has been continuously generous with his advice on this book and others. I'd like to thank Hugh Alexander and Paul Johnson at the National Archive's Image Library, as well as all the staff of the Archive's reference library at Kew, the Imperial War Museum in Lambeth and the British Library. Over the years I have been given a great deal of assistance by the staff of the United States National Archives in Maryland, USA, providing material for this book and documentary films. I am particularly indebted to General Albert Patton Clark, late of the United States Air Force Academy in Colorado Springs, USA, and the Academy's archivist, Duane Reade. I recall with great fondness my visits to the Academy, and am grateful for Duane's invaluable assistance when I produced and directed a short documentary about the Great Escape in 1999. Duane also gave me a copy of Colonel von Lindeiner's (unpublished) memoirs, and British Air Ministry records of the post-war SIB investigation into the killings of the 50 airmen from Sagan. I must thank Jimmy James, one of the greatest of the Great Escapers, for his invaluable help, encouragement and advice, and the use of much of his private archive. Thanks too to his escape partner Sydney Dowse as well as the four of the other remaining officers who actually made it out of the tunnel that March night 60 years ago. Tony Bethell, now living in Canada; Les Brodrick in South Africa; Mike Shand in New Zealand; and Paul Royle in Australia were all kind enough to help me with their reminiscences of the escape, as was Desmond Plunkett although, sadly, he has subsequently passed away. Thanks to Peter Elliott at the Royal Air Force Museum, Hendon. Thanks to Halvor Sperbund in Bergen for providing me with help and assistance regarding the two Norwegian escapers, Per Bergsland and Jens Muller; and to the Dutch flier Bob van der Stok's son, also named Bob, in California, USA. Thanks to the Air Force Museum in Christchurch, New Zealand. Many thanks to Charlotte Bergsland for the photographs of her late husband; Elizabeth Carter for her help regarding her brother Roger Bushell; and Bushell's biographer, John D. Carr. I must not forget the other authors whose efforts have cast intriguing light on this amazing period of history and without which my task would have been much harder. In particular Arthur Durand's *Stalag Luft III: The Secret Story* is an incomparable and scholarly dissertation on the subject. Jonathan Vance's *A Gallant Company* is the most comprehensive study of each of the individual escaper's lives that I have ever read. Finally, I must mention Dick Churchill, the seventh Great Escaper, who is still with us. Dick says he doesn't want to think about what happened 60 years ago, and would rather concentrate on what his five grandchildren will be doing in the future. I think that's a very commendable attitude, but one that I hope doesn't deter those who still find this episode of military and Commonwealth history enduringly fascinating.

PREFACE

This book owes its origins to a 1999 television documentary series for the Learning Channel that I was a producer and director for. It included a short episode about the Great Escape that I felt had been inadequately illustrated—which, given the comical ineptitude of the team making it, came as no surprise. I was determined to produce a better account. In fact I had hoped to make a full-scale documentary for either the BBC or Channel 4 to accompany a book. I didn't get anybody to take up the idea, but am pleased to know that Mark Radice of Windfall Films succeeded where I failed. His programme, which I think pursues a highly intelligent 'angle', should be broadcast around the same time this book appears.

What intrigued me about the Great Escape was the sheer scale and complexity of the achievement. I grew up with the film *The Great Escape,* as did probably every child of my generation. One summer I set myself the task of producing an authentic British passport for myself. I reasoned that if some half-starved Allied officers could produce thousands of bogus identity papers amid the deprivations of a freezing Second World War prison camp, I could surely make myself a passport in the comfortable surroundings of my home and with all sorts of modern technology at my disposal. I was wrong, of course, and the final product of my summer's efforts was lamentable.

The question that comes up time and again about the Great Escape is: how on earth did they do it? By simplifying the story I don't think the Hollywood version of events casts much light on this question. I've discovered that the answer is a complicated one. On the one hand it was not quite so difficult as it seemed. The officers imprisoned in Stalag Luft III, the German Air Force camp from which they escaped, were a privileged bunch, probably better treated than any other POWs in the European or Asian theatre. They were the elite of the Allied air forces and were treated as such. Their rations were good, and they were supplied with sporting equipment, books and materials to put on theatre productions that would have been the envy of many a regular soldier, whose treatment at the hands of the Germans was appalling.

It was not extraordinarily difficult for the officers to obtain the materials necessary for producing false identity cards. Their privileged status helped because the war, by the time of the Great Escape, had been going against Germany for some time and it was apparent to everybody that the Allies were going to win. Most of the German staff of Stalag Luft III were anxious to stay on the right side of the officers, many of whom had connections in high places and might reciprocate the favour in the post-war world. Many of the German security staff were impoverished and starving. It did not take a lot to win them over.

But, on the other hand, the Great Escape was an extraordinary achievement, far more so than it appears in the film. The figures who were involved in the prisoners' clandestine escape activities were extraordinary men; some, admittedly, because they came from wealthy and well-connected backgrounds, but most because they were an indomitable clan of adventure- and life-loving characters who all refused to accept captivity and were prepared to do anything to cock a snook at those who would oppress them.

It may come as a surprise to readers to learn that there were not just three tunnels, the famous Tom, Dick and Harry. There were 100 tunnels constructed in Stalag Luft III alone, and easily that amount in other Luftwaffe camps across occupied Europe. I've tried in my account to show just how indefatigable these men were in their desire to get out of these camps at any cost. And the extraordinary number of tunnels they constructed is surely testimony to this.

There is a tragic side to the Great Escape, of course, but I don't think the tragedy should be exaggerated and I think those contemporary writers who strike a mawkish pose about 'the 50' who were murdered by the Germans are letting the side down. They were brave men and their murders were dreadful. But they were in the middle of a brutal war in which many millions suffered far more heinous crimes. They were fighting men who had chosen to continue the war with the Germans from behind the barbed-wire confines of their camps. They were officers who were treated, for the most part, with extraordinary leniency by the enemy. They would be the last to complain about their treatment, I suspect.

In this book, I haven't succeeded in writing the comprehensive and definitive account that I had hoped for. But then I've discovered that there are so many stories associated with the Great Escape and Stalag Luft III, so many different angles and so many interesting avenues to go down, that it's an impossible task. I hope, though, that this is an interesting account that casts just a little light on this remarkable episode of our history.

PROLOGUE

THE LAST OF THE GREAT ESCAPERS

Today, in March 2004, sixty years after the Great Escape, there are only seven men still living who escaped out of the tunnel from Sagan on that fateful night. These are they, and their thoughts about the adventure that possibly shaped the rest of their lives.

Tony Bethell
Anthony Bethell was shot down flying a Mustang over Holland in December 1942.

> My greatest thought about the Great Escape is one of admiration for the genius of so many people whose work made it possible. I started on it by spreading sand and looking out for goons before graduating to digging. When I first went down I thought I'd be claustrophobic but being surrounded by competent people put my mind at rest. I was stuck once, at Leicester Square, one of the halfway houses in the tunnel, and I've never been so terrified in my life. I was sweating with fear. I was pulled out after 30 minutes but it seemed like a year.
> On the night of the escape my

1

overriding thought was that I had a job to do. I had to lead ten people away from the tunnel to the forest. Once that was done and we finally got away ourselves there was a wonderful feeling of freedom in the forest, and sucking in the beautiful cold air. But it was very difficult country made terribly muddy with melting snow. We broke our own rule of not walking in daytime and got caught by a couple of goons who came out with the classic line, 'For you the war is over.' We had only made it 40 or 50 miles.

I was in the cooler at Sagan when I found out about the 50. I listened to the news in stark disbelief. It's a ghastly statistic: three people home and fifty shot. But it was a wartime situation and that sort of thing happens in war. You have to do what you have to do. Roger Bushell said the whole idea was to 'harass, confuse, and confound the enemy'. And that's exactly what we did.

Now aged 82, Tony lives in Canada with his second wife, to whom he has been married for 30 years. They have eight children between them and fourteen grandchildren.

Les Brodrick
Lesley Charles James Brodrick's Lancaster was shot down on the way back from a

bombing raid over Stuttgart.

On the night of the escape there were 200 people all in their heavy coats and crowded into one hut that was quickly getting pretty hot. Apparently you could see the steam billowing out of the windows but thankfully the Germans didn't notice it. It was very exciting at first but that soon wore off because we were sitting there for hours on end waiting to go.

It was scary in the tunnel, to be honest. The majority of us had never been in it before and there was a little bit of panicking when some of us realised we suffered from acute claustrophobia. Once out, to be perfectly frank, my first thought was how blooming cold and miserable it was. Three of us had decided to 'hard-arse' it overland to Czechoslovakia, where it was suggested someone might help us.

Unfortunately we stopped to ask for help at a house that turned out to be a German soldiers' billet. Four Jerries came out and that was that. I was sent back to Sagan and given two weeks in the cooler. When I got out I heard about the 50. My two companions were among them. Frankly the only feeling I had was of how lucky I had been. Was it worth it?

No, not really. Fifty men dead, and only a few months before the end of the war? No, it wasn't worth it.

Les returned to England and taught at a school in Canvey Island before moving to South Africa, where he now lives with his wife and two children.

Dick Churchill
Sidney Albion Churchill ended up in Sagan after his light bomber was shot down by a Messerschmitt 109 over Ludwigshafen in September 1940.

Unlike the film there were no Americans at all in the escape, which was a shame because they were actually very active in building the tunnel. But they were moved into the South Compound only a short time before we broke out. It was a shame for them. Roger Bushell was a man of great determination. And our senior officer, 'Wings' Day, was a man who commanded such respect that if he had told us to storm the wire, a hundred of us would have done so without the slightest hesitation—even if it would have been a suicide mission. But I'd rather not dwell on what happened nearly 60 years ago. I'd rather concentrate on what my five grandchildren are going to do in their

4

lives.

Dick, now 86, lives in Devon, England.

Sydney Dowse, MC
Nicknamed 'the laughing boy' for his jovial
and easy-going bonhomie, Spitfire pilot
Sydney Henstings Dowse was one of the chief
diggers on 'Harry' and had already made two
escape attempts.

> I was determined to get out and cause the
> Germans as much trouble as possible. I
> was in charge of one of the main digging
> teams and thoroughly enjoyed being in
> the tunnel; we were doing something
> useful to the war effort after all, though I
> know some of the others didn't like it
> quite so much. In the film, the character
> played by '60s pop idol John Leyton was
> probably based on me, and my escaping
> partner Stanislaw 'Danny' Krol was
> played by Charles Bronson.
> We were two of the first to get out. It
> was an absolutely fantastic feeling to be
> free. Danny was Polish so we headed
> towards Poland. But we were caught after
> 12 days. I was sent to Sachsenhausen,
> where I met Jimmy James and learnt that
> the 50 had been murdered, including
> Danny. It just made me want to escape
> again—which I did. The Great Escape

was worth it. We caused havoc to the Germans and tied up thousands if not millions of them in the search for us.

After the war Sydney was an equerry to King George VI and worked in the Colonial Service. Now, aged 84, he divides his time between London and Monte Carlo.

Bertram 'Jimmy' James, MC
Jimmy James was flying a Wellington bomber when it was shot down in June 1940. His real name is Bertram but someone started calling him 'Jimmy' during his time in the RAF and it stuck. After being captured he was involved in no less than 12 escape attempts, for which he was awarded the Military Cross and a Mention-in-Despatches.

When I got to the exit shaft I climbed up the ladder and the first thing I saw were stars. I thought of the RAF motto—*Per Ardua ad Astra* (through adversity to the stars). It was hard to imagine a more appropriate context for the motto at that moment. There had been much toil for all concerned, I thought, as I climbed the ladder to the stars. The cost was terrible. I lost some good friends in that escape. They were some of the finest men I've ever known. But then a lot of us lost our good friends in that war, didn't we . . . ?

Now aged 89, Jimmy lives with his wife, Madge, in the pleasantly pastoral surroundings of Shropshire, where he is a regular on the golf courses and a stalwart of the community.

Paul Royle
Paul Gordon Royle was in the Royal Australian Air Force when he was shot down over France in 1940.

I did a lot of different jobs on the tunnel. A bit of digging, a bit of soil disposal, and keeping an eye out for goons. My only memory of the tunnel itself is the escape—never-ending darkness then suddenly someone pulls you up and you were free! I headed off south on foot through the woods and was caught the very next night. I was eventually sent back to the camp and thrown in the cooler for a fortnight. When I got out I discovered 50 of our friends had not returned.

I suppose my overall feeling was one of luck really. But as far as the whole thing goes, it never seemed so important to those who took part in it as it does to others. There were millions of people doing all sorts of things in that war and we were just a small part of it.

Paul worked in mining all over the world

7

before settling down in Western Australia with his second wife. He has five children and five grandchildren.

Mike Shand
In the film, when the German guard stumbles on the open tunnel exit and catches the prisoners emerging, the one who distracts him before running off into the woods was in reality New Zealander Michael Moray Shand. A Battle of Britain Spitfire pilot, Mike was the last to get away.

I didn't really know what was happening but I knew we'd been rumbled. I don't think the goon knew what was going on either. We all froze. Then, the minute he looked the other way, I made a run for the woods. That was it: we were out.

I hard-arsed it for a couple of days, heading for Czechoslovakia. But the local police caught me trying to jump a train. I was thrown in jail with what seemed like everyone else from Sagan. Eventually I was sent back to camp, where I presumed everyone else already was. But when I got there I discovered what had happened. It was a bit of a shock but my overall feeling, I have to be honest, was how lucky I was not to have been shot.

It was worth it. I don't think any of us thought we'd make it back to England. It

8

was a ridiculous idea with police and Gestapo checkpoints on every other corner. In those conditions—the freezing nights, the bleak countryside—it was impossible to get across Germany without being noticed. But we had to do something. We did it to cause chaos behind enemy lines and that's exactly what we did.

After the war, Mike returned to his native New Zealand, where he lived as a farmer with his English wife, who died 14 years ago. Mike, 89, has two children.

CHAPTER ONE

FOR YOU THE WAR IS OVER

The first Allied officer to fall into German hands was a New Zealand RAF airman who was shot down over the North Sea on 5 September 1939—shortly after war was declared. Flying Officer Laurence Hugh Edwards was on a reconnaissance flight in an Anson aircraft of 206 Squadron when he fell prey to two German Bv 138 flying boats. The two other crew of the Anson were killed in the attack. The enemy aircraft landed alongside the wreckage floating in the sea and took Edwards prisoner. He was to be the first of a sprinkling of RAF officers to fall into enemy hands in the early days of the 'Phoney War'. By the end of the year, some 26 British and French officers and NCOs were quartered, first in a prison camp at Itzehoe near Hamburg, to which Edwards was dispatched, and shortly afterwards in Spangenberg Castle, a medieval fortress near Kassel which had been used to house prisoners since 1870. Itzehoe was a fairly comfortable camp with a relaxed regime, at which the officers all had their own rooms and were allowed to buy fresh fruit and produce from the locals. Spangenberg Castle, designated Oflag IXA/H

11

('Oflag' being a corruption of 'Offizierslager', meaning 'officers' prison'), was far more picturesque, with a moat, formidable stone walls and a cobbled courtyard; it was the quintessential medieval fortress. But the living conditions were hopelessly primitive. The officers shared a long dormitory equipped with little more than straw mattresses and a couple of oak tables. They were given miserable German Army rations, a far cry from the more generous (and healthy) helpings they had been accustomed to in the officers' mess in Britain. Matters were made worse by the arrival of the bitter German winter. As the weather worsened it became too cold to venture outside, and the men mostly stayed inside playing cards and amusing themselves—or not—with whatever distractions they could find. It was a bleak portent of things to come as the very first Kriegies (derived from the German word for prisoners of war, Kriegsgefangenen) adapted to a way of life that would ultimately ensnare some 44,000 Allied airmen taken prisoner in occupied Europe.

The experience of airmen who fall into enemy hands is profoundly different to those of seamen and soldiers. The latter might be taken prisoner after a long struggle after possibly months at sea, or drudgery in the field. But airmen usually find themselves in enemy hands only hours after enjoying the comfort of their familiar surroundings: the mess and the local pub; the company of their girlfriends, wives and families. Most airmen, and particularly those who arrived in Germany at the start of the war, came from the sort of backgrounds where comfort was taken for granted. Yet one minute they are in the safe cocoon of their aircraft, which when thousands of feet above the ground gives exactly the feeling of limitless freedom that airmen crave, then the next they are plunged into a strange and unfamiliar land and are at the mercy of unknown people and an uncertain fate.

'It was quite a shock to suddenly realise you weren't going home and you faced an uncertain future in the hands of the Germans,' recalls General Albert Clark, who was one of the first Americans to be taken prisoner in the Second World War. Clark, nicknamed 'Bub' thanks to his youthful looks, was a lieutenant-colonel and second-in-command of the 1st US Fighter Group when he was shot down in his Spitfire 5B in July 1942. 'Today there is elaborate preparation for airmen should they be shot down, but then there was nothing.'

Airmen as a breed are not temperamentally well disposed to endure captivity. Most of them choose to fly because fighting in the sky offers them a sense of individuality that other forms of warfare deny them. The Second World War airman-writer Richard Hillary was typical of the breed. For the Australian-born

13

Spitfire fighter, the war presented an opportunity to leave his distinctive mark on life. Even if it was in death. In an age of mechanised mass slaughter, his ambition was to fight 'with a maximum of individuality and a minimum of discipline'. In his classic account of aerial combat, *The Last Enemy*, Hillary wrote:

> In a fighter plane, I believe, we have found a way to return to war as it ought to be, war which is individual combat between two people, in which one either kills or is killed. It's exciting, it's individual and it's disinterested. I shan't be sitting behind a long-range gun working out how to kill people 60 miles away. I shan't get maimed: either I shall get killed or I shall get a few pleasant putty medals and enjoy being stared at in a nightclub.

In that single passage Hillary summarises the mentality of warrior airmen better than the millions of other words written on the subject since men took to the skies. Not for airmen the rank conformity of army barrack life or cramped conditions of a life on the ocean waves. (Indeed to many soldiers and sailors, drudgery and conformity become such a fact of life that they often feel lost without it.) For airmen, however, to be suddenly caged and robbed of most freedom of movement is a particularly onerous burden to bear. Airmen are further distinguished from their land- and sea-bound comrades in arms in that almost all of them are very valuable individuals indeed, usually the product of much expensive training in the art of flying and navigating, or any of the other highly skilled abilities flying requires.

In the Battle of Britain planes were not a problem. Britain had the industrial capacity to produce more than she needed. The big problem was the supply of pilots. Pilots are so valuable that their superiors will go to great lengths to get them back and, indeed, the British government created MI9, the clandestine escape and evasion organisation, in December 1939 with that purpose in mind.

Agents of MI9 were parachuted into occupied Europe to link up with the local resistance. Their task (initially) was to spirit downed airmen back to England before the Germans could get their hands on them. But fortunately few fighting men as a group can be more suited to escape than airmen. The sort of sharp mind it requires to understand the complexities of, for instance, astro-navigation is hardly going to be daunted by the prospect of building a simple tunnel. The sort of mentality that is happy fighting alone in the sky without the immediate support of comrades is not going to be oppressed by the long hours of solitude that are often the escaper's lot. Airmen are a clever and aggressive breed, who value their personal freedom above all else.

If airmen are highly individualistic creatures, they were at first treated in a highly individualistic fashion in the nascent conflict between Germany and Britain that had begun in September 1939. Two of the first RAF officers to be shot down over Germany in the Second World War were taken to meet air Reichsmarschall Hermann Göring himself. Squadron Leader Phil Murray and Pilot Officer Alfred 'Tommy' Thompson were on a leaflet-dropping raid over Berlin in a twin-engine Armstrong Whitley bomber of 102 Squadron when it crashed after its engines failed on 8 September 1939. (Thompson, a Canadian, was one of the first foreign fighters in the RAF, the son of an Ontario Member of Parliament. He went to England and joined the RAF in 1936, craving adventure and excitement.) One evening Thompson and Murray had been indulging in the usual light-hearted banter of aircrew on the tarmac of their base in Driffield, Yorkshire. The next morning they woke up in the care of a few German guards who didn't quite know what to do with them. The two men were duly astonished to be marched before the jovial figure of the air Reichsmarschall sitting, incongruously, behind a large desk on a raised platform in a forest clearing. The chief of the German Air Force was proudly displaying his medals on his barrel of a chest. The British officers saluted their superior officer, and Göring returned the compliment before politely engaging the men in small talk for 30 minutes or so. Göring was surprised to learn that Thompson was a Canadian, as Canada had yet to enter the war. It would not be the first time that the Germans would be taken aback by the multi-national coalition of countries and even races that seemed to be prepared to come to the support of the supposedly hated imperialist power of Great Britain. Indeed, if there was one thing that the Allied airmen of the Second World War shared more than a love of adventure it was their bewilderingly diverse ethnocentricity in an age long before the phrase 'multi-cultural' had been invented.

Göring made some high-minded references to chivalry displayed by Britain's Royal Flying Corps in what was still then called the Great War. He went on to make it clear that as long as Allied airmen were in Luftwaffe hands they could expect to be treated as gentlemen in this, the second major European conflict of the century. His extravagant display of gallantry was by no means unusual in the early stages of the war. In a Reich that was partly founded upon a series of bogus racial theories, British and later American airmen were seen as the sort of superior breed of human beings with whom Hitler would definitely like to stock his Aryan state. But as the war—and particularly the war in the air—was to progress, Allied airmen were not to be regarded quite as benignly when they fell into enemy hands. The Anglo–American aerial bombardment of Germany was to become unprecedented in scale. By the end of 1943 Allied airmen were thought of as Luftgangsters (terror fliers) and murderers of children and women, by many of the unfortunate victims of their bombs. It might have been a case of the pot calling the kettle black, but it would not be an overstatement to say that by the end of the war many British and American bomber crews were also beginning to have misgivings about their task. It was this dramatic shift in perspective towards Richard Hillary's noble warrior airmen that contributed to one of the most heinous crimes against RAF fliers by the Nazi regime.

After their slightly surreal meeting with Göring, Murray and Thompson were dispatched to Itzehoe, where they met the New Zealander Hugh Edwards, brought down in his Anson over the North Sea. There were also two French airmen in the camp and some 600 Poles. Shortly thereafter the decision was made to keep captured fliers in their own separate prison camps, and the RAF men found themselves on the way to Spangenberg

Castle, which was very quickly filling up with prisoners of war. (Among them were Gerry Booth and Larry Slattery, the first non-commissioned RAF prisoners of war, who had actually been shot down before Edwards the day after war was declared. The distinction is important because officers and NCOs would be kept separate from then on. Booth and Slattery met their fate in a bombing raid on Wilhelmshaven, which was more of a futile gesture than a serious military manoeuvre.) Among the new officers to arrive at Spangenberg was a congenial Irishman of the RAF's 57 Squadron of lumbering old Blenheim bombers that were mainly being used for reconnaissance duties. Mike Casey, who was just 21 when he was captured, spoke in a deep, attractive brogue but had been brought up in India, where his father had been a senior figure in the Indian Police. He was educated in England, where he mixed a love of sport with a devotion to religion. Sadly, but not untypically, Casey had been married less than a month when he was shot down by a German fighter over Emden in October 1939. The plane crashed into a field below. Typically, at that early stage of the war, the Blenheim crew did not harbour any ill-will towards their German adversaries. As the fighter that had shot them down circled above their wrecked Blenheim, the crew gave the German pilot a friendly wave.

Shortly after Casey arrived he witnessed the arrival in mid-October of a familiar face. Wing Commander Harry Day had been in 57 Squadron with Casey. At 41 years of age, Day was one of the oldest RAF fliers. He would spend much of his war in German captivity and be pivotal to the escape activities of the Allied prisoners. A tall, balding and congenial character, he was known universally to his men as 'Wings' Day (not because of his 'wings', but after the RAF's anniversary day). He was old enough to be thought of by the younger men as an 'Uncle'.

Harry Melville Arbuthnot Day was born and brought up in Borneo, but educated in England. He joined the Royal Marines in the First World War and was decorated for gallantry after he rescued two crew members from below decks on a battleship, HMS *Britannia*, that had been torpedoed by a German submarine. Following the war, he continued to serve in the Marines, but after conceiving a love for flying, joined the newly formed RAF in which he became an ace fighter pilot and a noted stunt flier (leading the aerobatic flight at the Hendon Air Display in 1932). By the time hostilities broke out the second time around, Day was already in his 40s, an elderly man to the youthful fliers of the Air Force. He was sent to France commanding 57 Squadron. When he was shot down in October 1939 (as fate would have it, on Friday the 13th), Wings was flying one of the ancient old Blenheims on a reconnaissance flight in broad daylight over south-west Germany. He was a sitting duck flying in clear blue sky when three Messerschmitt 109 fighters set upon him. After checking that his crew had safely baled out, Wings followed suit, narrowly avoiding being burnt to death as he threw himself out of the escape hatch.

From the very start of his arrival on enemy soil Wings was treated with great courtesy. He landed in open countryside. As he was unclipping his parachute harness in a field, a local man arrived on the scene. 'Englander,' said Wings. The man grinned, held out his arm and shook his hand. Later, local villagers helped him clean up and treated his burns. Wings was billeted with a young German Army officer at his home nearby. At that stage of the war the Germans had not thought through their policy of dealing with prisoners of war and Wings was moved from one makeshift jail to another, rarely guarded properly, before he arrived at Spangenberg, where he immediately took on the role of Senior British Officer (SBO), a function he was to occupy in various camps for much of his Second World War career.

Day was a naturally courteous and chivalrous man. He took the attitude from an early date that the Germans should be treated exactly as the British officers would expect to be treated. He always insisted on a sharp turn-out for roll-call (or Appell as the Germans called it) and he snapped to salute a senior Luftwaffe officer just as sharply as he would have done an RAF one. However, there was no doubt in which direction his steely nerves were directed. On 11 November 1939 the British and French prisoners held a small ceremony to commemorate the end of the First World War. Wings made a moving declaration to the French officers. 'Nineteen-eighteen may seem a long way off to some of you. At the beginning of that year it looked as though we had lost the war. It may seem to some of you now that you have already lost this one. But we beat the Germans in 1918 and what you have already done will help to beat them again. For you the war is not over. *Vive la France*—and England.' Wings's sentiments were gratefully acknowledged by the French, but it was not long before the two nationalities were separated by the Germans.

As the Germans evolved their prisoner-of-war strategy, the Allied prisoners were not to suffer the deprivations of Spangenberg for much longer. In the first two weeks of that December the Germans dispatched five Royal Air Force and French Air Force prisoners to a camp just beyond the outer suburbs of Frankfurt am Main. Wings Day was among them, as was Mike Casey. Dulag Luft, as it became known, was situated at the foot of the

Taunus Mountains. It was the place that from then onwards most shot-down Allied officers would find themselves in before being dispatched to permanent camps across Germany. Dulag Luft was an abbreviation for Durchgangslager der Luftwaffe (transit camp of the Air Force). A former experimental agricultural centre on the outskirts of the small town of Oberursel, it consisted of a ramshackle collection of brick buildings lightly guarded by barbed-wire fencing. From December 1939 onwards, Dulag Luft would become the first point of call of most Allied airmen caught in Nazi-occupied Europe.

Wings Day became the SBO at Dulag Luft once more. He rapidly formulated policies for dealing with the new situation that the captives and their captors found themselves in. It was then that he confirmed his policy to observe the correct military courtesies towards the Germans, as the Geneva Convention required. It was Wings's belief that should he ever have to demand the rights of the much-abused international treaty be observed towards his officers, then he would be on much firmer ground if he had observed them himself. Another decision he took breached British military regulations, which stated categorically that parole was not to be granted under any circumstances. Day decided that the cramped conditions of Dulag Luft did justify giving parole in certain circumstances. His men would be driven mad unless they were allowed to leave their quarters occasionally.

Day could be excused his flagrant breach of orders. When the RAF men arrived at Dulag Luft in late 1939 and early 1940 the war didn't seem quite so real. There was an air of a charade about the whole thing. The war at that stage was, after all, called the Phoney War. However, as the weeks turned into months the reality of war struck home. At first the officers were housed in the permanent brick buildings of what had once been the experimental farm. The living conditions were congenial. The prisoners lived in small rooms off a central corridor and were locked in at night but free to roam the buildings during the day. However, by the spring of 1940 a compound of timber barrack blocks had been constructed, and the men settled down into surroundings that would become familiar to all air force prisoner-of-war camps in Germany in the Second World War, as the conflict would become known. The compound of three barracks (East, West and Central) provided dormitories, cooking and cleaning facilities, and was surrounded by barbed-wire fencing and guardtowers. Even then, however, the regime was a comparatively lax one. There was still a faint hope that the Phoney War would not develop into a real one, and the bulk of what the RAF dropped over Germany was leaflets exhorting the population to rise up and throw Hitler out of office. All that changed with the Nazi onslaught on the Low Countries and the fall of France in the summer of 1940. In June of that year, with Britain standing alone and stubbornly defiant, the French airmen were separated from their British allies and deposited in their own camp. In July, Dulag Luft became an interrogation centre to which all British and most American airmen were sent immediately after they arrived in Germany.

Despite the seriousness of hostilities, however, Dulag Luft in the early years continued to be a home-from-home for most of its unfortunate inmates. They soon became familiar with the inedible German rations of (usually) ersatz coffee made from acorns and dry black bread of questionable provenance for breakfast, Sauerkraut soup and a portion of mouldy potatoes for lunch, followed by some sausage or a peculiar cheese made from fish by-products. It was the Germans' standard diet for a non-working civilian, but at 800 calories per day it offered far less than the optimum 1,200 calories recommended for a normal healthy adult. But supplies of Red Cross parcels were plentiful and the Luftwaffe made sure their prisoners were well fed. In fact there were so many Red Cross parcels that the Germans gave banquets of four or five courses every two weeks just to keep the surplus down. There was plenty of wine and spirits, and culinary delicacies too, looted from occupied France. The Germans were unstinting in their generosity in dispensing these supplies among the prisoners for birthdays or farewell celebrations. And instead of ten to twelve officers per room, which became the norm in later camps, the rooms at Dulag Luft housed as little as two or four men. Walks out on parole were frequent for visits to church or recreational outings. It would have seemed remarkable to prisoners of a later stage of the war, but for the first two winters some officers enjoyed skiing holidays with their German counterparts. In the summer it was not unusual for the Kommandant to give permission for berry-picking excursions into the woods.

It was not just thanks to the Germans' benevolent spirits that these comfortable conditions prevailed in the early years at Dulag Luft. The Germans hoped that they could break the prisoners' will to fight. And they believed a congenial atmosphere was more conducive to their charges letting slip confidential information that would be useful to the Nazi war effort. It emerged later that the barracks were wired with secret microphones. Unfortunately for the Germans, however, it turned out the recordings they obtained proved to be almost unintelligible. It is unlikely that the German eavesdroppers obtained any useful information from this method. And it would soon become apparent to the Germans that, despite their best efforts to do so, the imprisoned airmen's combative mood was not sapped. Some prisoners, it is true, unashamedly took up the offer to sit out the war quietly. But the majority devoted every waking moment to continuing the war from behind the wire.

This attitude was by no means disapproved of by the German Kommandant of Dulag Luft. Major Theo Rumpel was an aristocratic officer who had flown in Göring's squadron in the First World War. An engaging, courteous man, Rumpel was not by any stretch of the imagination a Nazi and didn't have the slightest sympathies for Hitler or his henchmen. But he was regarded as the best intelligence officer the Luftwaffe had, and he spoke almost perfect English. Consequently he had been persuaded to take on his present role. Rumpel was keen, as the air Reichsmarschall was, to continue the spirit of chivalry that he supposed bonded his men with those of the Allied air forces. He sometimes entertained officers to dinner at his own quarters and was always solicitous of their needs, sometimes sending them packets of fine cigarettes for special anniversaries. The British officers, in turn, returned the compliment, invariably writing Rumpel letters of gratitude for small favours he had bestowed on them.

It was soon clear that Dulag Luft was

intended to be not an ordinary prisoner-of-war camp but a transit post. Newly captured airmen would be sent there initially for interrogation before being dispatched to one of several new camps the German armed forces were building in different parts of Germany and occupied Europe. To ease the transition, Rumpel appointed a Permanent Staff of some 25 British officers at Dulag Luft. Its function would be to liaise between the new RAF arrivals and the German officers. New prisoners were first interviewed by the Germans in the old brick agricultural buildings, which were rapidly being transformed into an interrogation facility. Under the Geneva Convention prisoners of war were required only to give their name, rank and serial number. The German interviewers tried to trick more information out of their charges. But in these early days they had not developed the sophistry or duplicity in such techniques that were to be a hallmark of their efforts at Dulag Luft later. Afterwards the Allied prisoners were handed over to the Permanent Staff, which provided them with a Red Cross parcel and any clothing replacements they needed before giving them a welcoming meal. It was all very civilised. The permanent RAF staff were mostly selected from the older officers, who were presumed to have a sense of responsibility and more maturity than their hot-headed youthful comrades. Rumpel also demonstrated a marked preference for officers with blue blood in their family.

To Major Rumpel, Wings Day was the perfect embodiment of the English officer. And to his great delight the British SBO cultivated friendly relations with most of the German officers, not least the Kommandant. When Day asked Rumpel if he could have a cat for a companion, his German counterpart responded warmly by providing the British officer with a kitten. (Day promptly named it Ersatz as it was a substitute, like so much of what else the Germans provided their prisoners with.) It was not unusual for the senior German officers to take Wings out to dinner, and he was invited around to Rumpel's private quarters for dinner or drinks on many occasions. It was a comfortable relationship that was to be the source of some irritation to many other British officers who passed through Dulag Luft. Day and other members of the Permanent Staff were later openly accused of collaborating with the Germans or, at the very least, being a bit too friendly with them. What their accusers didn't realise was that the men were using their privileged position within the camp to plan and prepare what would become the first great escape from German captivity. Their apparently harmless excursions out on parole in fact provided them with valuable intelligence about the surrounding district. On one trip to a restaurant, Day managed to get hold of a radio receiver which he smuggled back into Dulag Luft.

Among the Permanent Staff members at Dulag Luft there were two pilots who had been among the first to serve in the Royal Navy's flying force, the Fleet Air Arm. Lieutenant Commander John Casson (the son of the actors Sybil Thorndike and Lewis Casson) had been shot down over Norway flying a Skua plane from HMS *Ark Royal* in an attack on the German pocket battleship *Scharnhorst* in Trondheim fjord. (His navigator was Peter Fanshawe, who would play an important role in escapes to come.) He was joined several weeks later by his Fleet Air Arm friend and comrade Lieutenant Commander Jimmy Buckley, who had served in the aircraft carrier HMS *Glorious* before the war. He was shot down over the coast of France in May 1940 while strafing German lines at Dunkirk. He had been taken prisoner along with the thousands of other British servicemen who did not make it back across the Channel. When he arrived at Dulag Luft, Wings Day appointed him his deputy as SBO. Buckley was a small man with dark hair and eyes that always seemed to twinkle with laughter. A born comedian, he would occupy much of his time in captivity writing and acting comic sketches for many of the theatrical shows that would become such a part of Kriegie life. But these innocent activities were not just a way of relieving the boredom. They disguised Buckley's far more important role as the first chairman of the Escape Committee. At Dulag Luft, the Escape Committee was little more than a nascent body that affirmed the prisoners' will and desire to escape. But it would soon grow into a formidable outfit, known as the X-Organisation, that controlled every aspect of escaping activity from behind the wire.

Jimmy Buckley turned to a remarkable young RAF officer to provide the backbone of the Escape Committee. Squadron Leader Roger Bushell was a Hurricane pilot who had also been shot down over France during the evacuation of Dunkirk. Twenty-nine years old when he fell into enemy hands, Bushell was the wealthy son of a South African mining engineer. He had moved to England to study engineering at Cambridge University, but ended up practising as a barrister. Bushell was a man of formidable build and an equally formidable personality. Thick-set and of aggressive appearance, he was a fearless skier of Olympic standard and sported a permanently drooping left eye, thanks to a skiing accident before the war. He had joined the RAF long before the war began and belonged to 601 Squadron of the Royal Auxiliary Air Force. It was dubbed 'the

Millionaires' Squadron', thanks to the wealthy former public schoolboys who mostly made up its number, and it had a reputation for louche ribaldry. In the air Bushell displayed all the characteristics that he possessed in his career on the ground, not least his outrageous daring and complete fearlessness. One of the ornaments of the officers' mess of 601 Squadron was a road signpost he had lopped off when landing his plane at a country pub for a quick drink.

When war broke out Bushell was ordered to set up 92 Squadron, a unit of Blenheim night fighters, at Tangmere on the south coast of England. He arrived there to discover the only problem was a lack of any pilots to fly the machines, although there was a sprinkling of ground staff to maintain them. By the time the war was being fought in earnest, however, 92 Squadron had been converted to the far more deadly Hawker Hurricanes, which were being churned out in their thousands by factories up and down Britain. Bushell was in his on 23 May 1940 over the beaches of northern France when a Messerschmitt 110 got the better of him in a dogfight. The British pilot managed to land his Hurricane inland intact and, presuming he was in Allied-held territory, waited by his stricken machine for assistance to come. Unfortunately, he was quickly to discover that the area had by then been occupied by the Germans. Shortly afterwards he was under German guard and on his way to Dulag Luft.

Buckley appointed Bushell the Escape Committee's chief of intelligence. He was to become probably the most persistent and indefatigable escaper of all the Allied prisoners and the man without whom the future Great Escape would never have happened. But if Roger Bushell was to play a key role in the escape organisation, the Permanent Staff was shortly to be joined by one of the most colourful personalities of the story that was about to unfold. Major Johnny Dodge was also one of the oldest Allied prisoners of war, being 46 when he fell into German hands in 1940. He was not, however, destined to be SBO for the simple reason that, being an army officer, he really shouldn't have been among air force officers at all. But that story is just one of the many peculiar twists in the life of Johnny Dodge.

A tall, big man, John Bigelow Dodge sported a peculiarly small moustache above his invariably smiling lips. Born in 1894, Dodge came from a distinguished and wealthy American family related to the US side of Winston Churchill's forebears. His maternal grandfather was a brilliant writer, newspaper editor and US diplomat. His uncle was another famous journalist who had been a close friend of Kaiser Wilhelm II. Johnny Dodge himself was something of a maverick and adventurer who did not fit into the conventional mould of any sort of careerist.

He had had a colourful and chequered military career, having managed to gain a commission, despite his American citizenship, in the British Royal Navy at the beginning of the First World War. He subsequently transferred to the British Army towards the end. His only guiding light appeared to be an overwhelming desire to be where the action was. In the Navy, in 1915, he won a Distinguished Service Cross (DSC) at Gallipoli. Later, after having transferred to the Army as a lieutenant-colonel in the Royal Sussex Regiment, he was wounded twice in France, mentioned twice in dispatches, and won the Distinguished Service Order (DSO) and the Military Cross.

Dodge's inter-war career was almost as colourful as that of his fighting years. A natural adventurer, he turned his interest in the problems of international trade into a travelling mission that encompassed most of Persia, Asia and the Antipodes, including a 1,700-mile horseback trek across Siberia. His journeys took in exotic locations as far apart as New Zealand and Mesopotamia, Mongolia and Japan. He also visited Thailand and Afghanistan. Finally arriving in Georgia on the Black Sea in 1921, he fell into the hands of the Russian secret police and was arrested on suspicion of spying. In the absence of any evidence he was released and made his way back to England.

He had become a British subject in 1915, and once back in London he worked for London County Council in an east London ward. Twice Dodge attempted to become a Conservative Member of Parliament, and twice he failed. He had more success in his commercial endeavours, joining the London Stock Exchange and becoming the director of a New York bank. His private life too was a success. He married—happily, which was a little out of character for someone so footloose and fancy-free—and fathered two sons. As soon as the war broke out, he joined up and found himself serving with the British Expeditionary Force (BEF). In the summer of 1940, like hundreds of thousands of other British and French troops, he was caught between the devil that was Hitler's Panzer divisions and the deep blue sea of the English Channel. He tried to swim away to a small boat offshore, but the boat was heading away to England faster than Dodge could swim. He was shot at and forced to return to the mainland, where he was eventually captured after further efforts to get away. By a stroke of fate he was handed over to the Luftwaffe rather than the German Army. When Major Rumpel set eyes on the distinguished new arrival to Dulag Luft, he immediately identified him as exactly the sort of officer the

British Permanent Staff required. He could not believe his luck to have a relative of the British Prime Minister—no matter how distantly removed—as his 'guest'. Discreetly, Rumpel had Dodge's papers altered to identify him as an officer in the RAF.

The nucleus of the X-Organisation was slowly being formed. In the summer of 1940 one of its most successful members was to arrive. Bertram 'Jimmy' James was the very picture of a gentle, mild-mannered Englishman. James was to be one of the most prolific and irrepressible escapers of the Second World War, rarely allowing a week to go by without indulging in some form of escape activity. His persistence would eventually incur the wrath of the German High Command, and Heinrich Himmler himself. Jimmy James was born in India, the son of an English tea-planter, and was educated at King's School, Canterbury. After his father died, James decided to see the world, took a steamer to Panama and worked his way up the length and breadth of North America before ending up in British Columbia. He worked at the local branch of a big bank, but as war approached James saw an advert for RAF personnel and applied for a short-service commission. He scored so well on his navigation tests that the RAF assigned him to a new bomber squadron, 9 Squadron of Wellingtons, based at Honington.

James was the second pilot of a Wellington when it was caught by heavy flak over the Dutch coast on 5 June 1940. The 'Wimpy', as Wellingtons were fondly known, was hit by flak as it made its way fully laden towards Germany. The bombs inside exploded at once and James recalled the stricken plane plunging to the earth 'like a fiery comet'. He baled out and as he was floating down towards the moonlit enemy territory below James decided he must have been about 25 miles south of Rotterdam and possibly the same distance from the sea. It was about 11 p.m. when his feet finally touched the ground with a thud, breaking his ankle as he did so. His sudden arrival was witnessed by a herd of friendly cows. James picked himself up and began walking in a westerly direction towards where he supposed the coast would be, hoping to find a boat and make his way across the Channel back to England. At first he made promising progress. After travelling some 15 miles before daybreak, he encountered a friendly Dutchman, who sheltered him in a farmhouse and gave him bread and cheese. The man indicated that James should rest there for the day and continue his escape the following night. But unfortunately his family proved less receptive to the idea of harbouring an English airman. After some discussion he was driven to the double gate leading to the German administrative compound (the Kommandantur) in Rotterdam. There he discovered from a Luftwaffe officer that three others of his crew had also been captured. Then the German issued the immortal phrase: 'For you the war is over.'

James's initial questioning at the hands of the Germans is instructive in how methods of interrogation were subsequently developed and perfected. He was interviewed by a colonel in the presence of some six other officers and one civilian interpreter. As the questioning progressed, however, it became obvious that the civilian was from the Gestapo. It was he who took over the proceedings. They tried to browbeat James into giving more information than his name, rank and number. At one stage they implied that if he gave them more information they might be able to help two of his injured crew who had been heard crying for help in a ditch near the downed Wimpy. James pointed out that if they knew there were injured men there, then there was little further information he could supply them with. Eventually they tired of trying to wear him down and sent him to the Luftwaffe's Dutch headquarters at the Carlton Hotel in Amsterdam. There James was subjected to a charm offensive. In his room was a table laden with glasses of beer, ice and cheroots. Presently a Luftwaffe officer entered and offered James a drink, which he gladly accepted. The German officer claimed he had been to Oxford University and lamented the fact that the two countries were at war with one another. When it became obvious that James was not going to disclose any information of value, the officer's mood changed. The beer and cheroots were removed and the following day the English airman was dispatched by car to Dulag Luft.

Once more James was subjected to a familiar litany of German tricks. He was presented with a 'Red Cross' form that asked for details of his family and service background so that, purportedly, his next-of-kin could be informed that he was a prisoner of war. Once more James refused, and gave them only his name, rank and number. Once more the Germans gave up and sent their new prisoner to the prisoners' compound. There for the first time James met Wings Day, who greeted him fondly stroking his kitten, Ersatz. In Dulag Luft James was delighted to be reunited with the American-born rear gunner of his Wimpy, who told him two more of the crew were alive and well, but the other pilot and the navigator had died. James and Wings Day would come to know one another very well indeed, finding themselves in the cells of Sachsenhausen concentration camp in the dying days of the war. But their acquaintance at Dulag Luft was short lived. After three days James was moved out with 13 other RAF officers, two Fleet Air Arm lieutenants and two French Air Force officers. Their destination was to be the newly built camp of Stalag Luft I near Barth on the bleak and cheerless coast of the Baltic, opened in the summer of 1940.

*   *   *

By that same summer in Dulag Luft, the prisoners had hatched their first escape plan. The men had used their parole walks to reconnoitre the surrounding countryside, and had obtained railway timetables. Just outside the wire fence was a dry ditch with a small bridge over it. Buckley and Bushell believed that it would be easy enough to dig a tunnel that would break through just below the bridge and give them enough time to get through several prisoners before their absence was noted. The plan was to head off in lots of different directions. Bushell was aiming for the Swiss frontier at Schaffhausen, a noted skiing area that he was intimately familiar with. It was a laughably simple break-out plan, without much of the sophistication that would characterise future endeavours, but it would teach the men valuable lessons in the art of escaping. Their first tunnel was an abject failure. It started out of the East Block's toilet facilities. But the water table proved higher than they had thought and the tunnellers found themselves clawing their way through mud. After only a few weeks they gave up some six feet short of the footbridge. They started another tunnel shortly afterwards from underneath Wings Day's bed, but that was discovered by the Germans. By then the winter had set in and what was becoming known as 'the escaping season' had come to an end. Even the most resolute escapers, including Bushell, realised that trying to survive the German winter on sparse rations and in inadequate clothing was out of the question. All the prisoners could do now was make their plans for the forthcoming spring.

As the spring of 1941 approached, the escapers discovered the tunnel from the East Block toilets was still in good condition, despite the disastrous flooding that had turned it into a channel of mud and sludge the previous year. They decided to rebuild it, and over a period of several weeks members of the Permanent Staff slogged away beneath the toilet block scraping away the soil. This time they successfully completed the tunnel all the way to the footbridge without any flooding and surprised themselves that by May they were ready to break out. The Escape Committee earmarked the first moonless night in June to make the break. In all, 19 men were to take part in the bid led by Bushell and Buckley and including Casey, Day and Dodge. They were all armed with fairly rudimentary false papers and had altered their RAF tunics to look as much like civilian clothing as possible. Most of them planned to spread out and make off in different directions in pairs or alone.

Roger Bushell was to be the exception in that he was the only one not going through the tunnel. He had decided he would go out alone, a day earlier, via a different and ingenious way out of the camp. This was because of another problem the escapers were going to encounter regularly in the future—the vagaries of weekend train travel. Bushell was going disguised as a German Army ski instructor on leave. From his pre-war life he had acquired an intimate knowledge of that part of the Swiss–German frontier around Schaffhausen. Unlike the other escapers, Bushell had managed to acquire a nicely cut civilian suit that would help him meld into the background a little bit better than the rest. Speaking German fluently, with a slight Swiss accent, he thought he stood a plausible chance of bluffing his way to the border and getting over it one way or another. His plan, though, depended upon him getting as quickly as possible to the Swiss frontier by train from Frankfurt and unfortunately the first moonless night fell on a weekend when train services were generally sparse and unreliable.

Therefore, he formulated his plan to go the night before the rest, hiding that afternoon before evening Appell in a goat shed which was a quixotic feature of the exercise yard outside the compound. All prisoners who arrived at Dulag Luft were made aware of the old goat in this shed, a playful and occasionally aggressive beast. Many of them took such a shine to the goat that it was not unusual for them to help out with cleaning his shed and giving him food. Bushell and a colleague seized the opportunity of this apparently innocent activity to excavate a hole in the floor of the shed just large enough to conceal a man. They disguised the hole with a trap sturdy enough for the poor goat not to fall through, and carried the earth away gradually during the course of several visits.

Bushell planned to slip into the shed during the Thursday evening before those using the tunnel were due to break out on the night of the following Friday or Saturday. There was only a single strand of wire that surrounded the practice ground and it presented no obstacle at all to escape. In the past it had proved so easy to falsify the count at roll-calls that he did not anticipate any problems disguising his presence and getting a good 24 hours' start on his comrades in the tunnel. The Escape Committee held a conference and the plan was passed. When somebody made the obvious quip about the problem of the smell in the shed, somebody else replied with the equally obvious: 'I'm sure the goat won't mind.'

Bushell's strategy went according to plan.

While the other prisoners staged a mock bullfight with the goat to distract the guards' attention, Bushell slipped into the shed. He was not discovered that night when the goatherd put his charge to bed, and neither he nor his host protested at one another's company. Shortly afterwards, Bushell was on an express train bound for Tuttlingen. As he had rightly predicted, nobody noticed his absence at the following morning roll-call. From Tuttlingen, Bushell took a secondary line to Bonndorf, from where he set out across country on foot. He was confident that he could sustain a casual conversation if he was stopped, but miraculously he didn't meet a soul. He arrived later that Friday on the Swiss frontier, which was now beginning to buzz with weekend skiers. It would soon be night and Bushell faced the dilemma of waiting until nightfall and trying to cross the border in the dark or making a bid for it in the daylight. He chose the latter. But entering a village on the border he was accosted by a man who emerged from a house halfway along the street. The German challenged Bushell, who, to disguise the problem of his accent, slurred his words, pretending to be happy-drunk and hoping to charm the man with his bonhomie. The villager, however, proved to be an uncharmable character and insisted that he take Bushell to the police station. At that moment, Bushell legged it and, sprinting around the corner, ran into a dead-end. For the time being, once more, Roger Bushell's war was over. 'I could have taken a girls' school across if I'd chosen a spot a few hundred yards to the west,' he later reflected morosely.

At least he had made better progress than his fellow escapers. The Friday night after Bushell had made his getaway the other 18 escapers made their way through the short tunnel. Their progress was disguised by a party held elsewhere in the compound. All managed to break out of the tunnel undetected and it was not until roll-call the following morning that the absence of much of Major Rumpel's Permanent Staff was noticed. However, all their journeys across Germany were quickly thwarted. Most were recaptured within 24 hours after being given away by their poor documentation and unlikely disguises. Others made basic mistakes—such as Johnny Dodge, who walked down the middle of the Autobahn, not realising this was against the law for pedestrians. Dodge's escape ended when he and his companion arrived at a bridge guarded by Germans. Shortly afterwards they were on their way back to Dulag Luft. The best German speaker got as far as Hanover, but he too found himself swiftly back in the hands of the Germans.

Nevertheless, the RAF had staged the first Great Escape of the Second World War. The

Germans were shocked enough by it to begin urgently revising their strategy for keeping Allied air force prisoners. Despite discovering the earlier tunnel, the Germans had been lulled into a false sense that the British officers would not betray Kommandant Rumpel's kindness to them. One of the German officers later lamented that he should have realised what was going on, considering the number of showers the prisoners were in the habit of taking at all times of the day. But now the honeymoon was over. After they were recaptured, all the escapers were made to serve the mandatory sentence of two weeks in the cooler for attempted escape. (Every prisoner-of-war camp had a cooler, slang for a solitary confinement block of single, stark cells, where they were served starvation rations.) But afterwards, the Germans decided that most of the escapers were to be transferred to Stalag Luft I, the new far-flung Luftwaffe camp near Barth to which Jimmy James had been dispatched shortly after he arrived. Roger Bushell was an exception, as he would often prove to be. He was sent to the even more miserable compound of Stalag XC at Lübeck, which rivalled Barth for squalor and was mainly occupied by British Army officers captured in the debacle of Crete.

In the future, escape would prove more difficult from Dulag Luft, and the Germans selected for the British Permanent Staff prisoners who appeared temperamentally inclined to accept captivity. In the meantime, Kommandant Rumpel bore the brunt of the blame for the escape. He was ejected from his job, not a penalty likely to have greatly perturbed him. Before he departed he made sure a case of champagne was delivered to the escapers for them to enjoy on the train to Barth. Accompanying it was a note with his compliments.

CHAPTER TWO

SCHOOL FOR SCOUNDRELS

Stalag Luft I was a misleading designation. 'Stalag' is a contraction of the word 'Stammlager', which interpreted literally means a prison for 'common stock', or servicemen below officer rank. It would have been far more appropriate to label it an Oflag. But for whatever reason, the Luftwaffe insisted on calling all its air force camps Stalags. This particular Stalag was a miserable, dreary and dispiriting place, usually known simply, as 'Barth', after the small town it was nearest to. It was situated 16 miles north-west of the port of Stralsund on a narrow, unprotected isthmus on the Baltic coast, a landscape of flat dunes, creeks and bleak pine forests. It was the first permanent camp for air force prisoners. Jimmy James had arrived there shortly after it had opened after an odyssey that had taken him via a dreary camp at Limburg. From there he was moved to Berlin, where the group of prisoners of war were marched through the capital followed by crowds of curious onlookers, and then to a German Army barracks 50 miles north of Berlin that was being used to house Polish POWs. Along the way James met Paul Royle, an Australian Air Force flight lieutenant of 53 Squadron who had been brought down in his Blenheim on his first operational mission over France. When James met him, Royle was clinging to a dog-eared copy of *Cold Comfort Farm* that he had somehow managed to find. Royle would go on to be one of the greatest of great escapers.

James was among the initial party of 20 prisoners at Barth who arrived on 5 July 1940 and were joined shortly afterwards by a further 60-odd prisoners sent from Spangenberg. The prisoners were housed in two wooden barrack blocks in a cramped and dusty compound some 125 by 70 yards. It was a dreary enclosure surrounded by a double row of barbed-wire fence and continually overlooked by guards in watchtowers with searchlights and machine guns. Sentries and dogs patrolled the perimeter at all times. (By now the guards were almost universally referred to as 'goons' and the watchtowers had become 'goon boxes'.) There was one gate that led to the Vorlager, which housed the punishment block—consisting of the solitary confinement cells that were universally known as the coolers—the sick bay, and administrative buildings. Adjoining it was the NCOs' compound with six barrack blocks. A recreation field was immediately south of the main officers' compound. The camp stood on the western side of a tiny peninsula projecting northwards into the bay. Barth was just about visible to the south, but a long dark row of pine trees obscured the prisoners' vision to the north and the Baltic Sea beyond. The Baltic province of Pomerania, in which Barth was situated, is a desolate place that might have something to recommend it in the summertime, but in the winter the landscape is one of freezing desolation.

When Jimmy James arrived, there were even greater reasons to view life with gloom. The news was full of details of Hitler's victorious armies bulldozing their way across Europe, and James and his companions knew that Britain was the next trophy in the Führer's sights. France had fallen and the British Army had escaped to England only by the skin of its teeth; Churchill had just made his promise of nothing but 'blood, toil, tears and sweat'; two of the most common phrases RAF prisoners heard from their German captors were 'England in sechs Wochen' (England in six weeks) and 'England kaputt', which requires no translation.

'As we surveyed this bleak, grey prison it seemed that we had reached the nadir of misfortune,' James recalled in his memoir, *Moonless Night*, a classic account of his time in captivity during the war. 'This could be our home for the duration which, at that time, could have been for a very long time, with an uncertain end.'

In the circumstances it is hardly surprising that the prisoners' thoughts quickly turned to escape. As at Dulag Luft, a group of persistent escape artists began to form at Barth and a young Fleet Air Arm officer would take the leading role.

Lieutenant Commander Peter Fanshawe had been the navigator of the *Ark Royal* Skua plane that had been piloted by John Casson in the famous attack on the German battleship *Scharnhorst*. He had entered Dartmouth Naval College in 1925 when he was 13 years old. Born with the sea in his blood, he had the punctilious manner of the quarterdeck that contrasted sharply with the louche ribaldry of the RAF's officers' mess. The RAF officers immediately awarded Fanshawe the affectionate sobriquet 'Hornblower'. In August 1940 Fanshawe presided over the first serious escape conference.

Another important escape artist to arrive in Barth at that time was RAF Flight Lieutenant 'Wally' Valenta, a Czech, who had been the navigator of a Wellington bomber of 311 Squadron (the RAF's 'Czech' squadron). Like many patriots in occupied Europe, Arnost Valenta, who had grown up in one of the 'German' regions of Czechoslovakia, had been put in an awkward situation by the advance of Nazism. He elected to support the Czech cause and became embroiled in the underground intelligence game between the partisans and the ascending German forces. He eventually fled Czechoslovakia. In July 1940 he found himself in England in 311 Squadron. In February 1941 his aircraft crash-landed in bad weather, and shortly afterwards he found himself in Barth.

*   *   *

It was at Barth that the RAF officers would first meet the German security staff, some of whom would become sworn enemies, some useful 'tame goons' and some almost friends. Hauptmann Hans Pieber had been an engineer in civilian life and became adept at sniffing out the prisoners' many tunnelling operations. A mild-mannered and conscientious Austrian, he boasted that he held the Nazi Party's 49th membership card and had been awarded the Nazi Blood Medal (or Blutorden, the honour awarded to those few who had taken part in the notorious 1923 Beer Hall Putsch). Pieber, however, had refused to wear it after the Anschluss, which had aroused his indignation. Pieber was generally liked by the prisoners, not least because of his habit of trimming his sails to the wind when the need arose. They were to discover that as the chill winds of war changed to Germany's disadvantage, Pieber would become a good friend indeed.

Feldwebel Hermann Glemnitz had worked

in Yorkshire before the war and not only spoke English well as a result but also understood the British mentality, which was perhaps a more valuable asset. He too had been an engineer, and would over the forthcoming years earn the respect of the prisoners for his ability to find their tunnels. A shrewd and clever man, the Kriegies awarded him the ironic nickname of 'Dimwits'.

Captain Gustav Simoleit, the head of the Lagerführung (the compound 'control' office of four intelligence officers whose job it was to monitor prisoner escape activity), was formerly a professor of history, geography and ethnology, and also spoke English well. He was at first apprehensive at being taken off his anti-aircraft battery and being made a jailer, but after a while he began to enjoy the company of the 'reasonable and well-educated' men in his care. He later said that 'the POW camp in Barth was one of the few places in the world where, during a merciless war, soldiers of both fighting armies could meet and establish personal contacts'.

Corporal Karl Griese did not come to have such a comfortable rapport with the prisoners. Griese would become the head of the ferrets, the team of guards specially created at Barth to sniff out escape attempts. (As their role evolved they would be equipped with long iron rods to probe the ground, and sniffer dogs. Unlike the regular guards, the ferrets wore boiler suits so that they could scramble under the huts and into roof attics and keep their uniforms clean.) Griese was nicknamed 'Rubberneck' because of his extraordinarily long neck that seemed to be able to poke its way around any corner. Rubberneck went about his duties with a psychopathic passion. He despised the Allied fliers and in turn was disliked by prisoners and German staff alike. There was another ferret known simply as 'Keen Type', for self-explanatory reasons, and one called 'Adolf' because of his uncanny resemblance to the Führer.

The German staff, on the whole, behaved very well towards their charges. One of the Luftwaffe officers taught a German-language class for the prisoners. Undoubtedly part of the intention was to discover which prisoners were fluent in the language, but it was a friendly gesture nonetheless, which non-German speakers like Jimmy James eagerly took advantage of. (James would also begin learning Russian.) In the hot summer, the Germans took prisoners who promised to sign a parole register down to the local creek for a swim and there were also walks outside the camp (again for those prepared to give their parole) once a week. Relations improved further when the Germans introduced camp money (Lagergeld), which was deducted from their pay and which could be used to buy cigarettes or a crude wine the inmates dubbed

'Red Biddy'. Nevertheless, the prisoners still called the German guards 'goons' and 'goon baiting' was too much of a temptation for some of the younger and, perhaps, less-mature RAF officers as a way of killing the boredom of captivity.

At this early stage, too, the distinction between the Luftwaffe and the Nazi higher authorities was beginning to emerge. After one Kommandant sent over several crates of beer to the RAF compound one night with his best wishes, he was promptly relieved of his command. The Nazis were not to blame for all the ill-feeling, however. Relations suffered when two prisoners escaped from the camp having included themselves among a group that had signed the parole register for a swim in the creek. The two men were caught three days later and nobody particularly blamed the Germans when the privileges were subsequently curtailed.

Barth had several features that greatly assisted the prisoners in escaping and several that militated against them. First, the Germans' security and surveillance techniques were at that stage very primitive. Detection of escape was left to the casual observation of two camp interpreters. There was no system of passes for Germans entering or leaving the compounds. The barrack blocks were all clad in timber that went all the way down to the ground, hiding any tunnelling activity that went on beneath the buildings. The compound had also been built in a very cramped area and as a result there was only a comparatively short distance to tunnel before reaching the outside of the wire.

On the minus side, the water table was rarely less than six feet beneath the surface. Consequently, tunnels had to be at shallow depths and were vulnerable to detection (though ground microphones were not introduced until the summer of 1941). Also, despite the many opportunities presented for escape, the prisoners had no organised escape committee. As a result there were very many half-hearted and ill-thought-out escape attempts that ended in failure.

Despite these difficulties, the RAF prisoners at Barth were able to boast prolific tunnelling operations. No less than 43 tunnels were constructed from the officer and NCO compound in less than two years after Barth opened. One prisoner managed to make it home after escaping through a tunnel. But there were also a great deal of other escape attempts, some comical in their simplicity, others audacious in their daring. One other prisoner (as we shall see later) managed to get back to England using a method other than tunnelling. This success rate might not seem encouraging. But few escapers seriously thought they would make it home.

Escape fulfilled several functions. It

diverted the resources of the enemy, who had to spend precious hours and manpower securing the prison camps and searching for escapees. It diverted the attention of the prisoners themselves, who might otherwise have gone mad in their miserable confinement. And, to a lesser extent, escape was a form of intelligence activity. The information gathered by escapers about enemy emplacements, civilian morale and so forth, was useful to the military authorities back in Whitehall, relayed there via the underground resistance movement. It was a primitive form of intelligence gathering, especially at the beginning. But, as we shall see, the Allied officers soon turned their escape activities into a formidable intelligence-gathering exercise that was very useful indeed to the governments in London and Washington. It was at Barth that these activities first attracted the attention of the Gestapo, and where the worrying accusation of 'espionage' was first seriously levelled at an officer. Technically, of course, it was espionage, and everybody knew it.

When Jimmy James arrived at Barth he was to find a tunnel already being built from his barracks, which was the most westerly of the two blocks and was then called the West Block. The diggers had sunk an entry shaft six feet deep and the tunnel aimed to travel 150 yards underneath the wire to the north. At first the men tunnelled in the dark, which was an intimidating experience in itself. But a Rhodesian officer came up with the ingenious idea of melting butter out of the tin cans the prisoners got from their Red Cross parcels and using pyjama cord as a wick. The resultant 'fat-burning lamps' would become a mainstay of tunnel building, even when the diggers were lucky enough to acquire electric cable to tap into the camp's power supply.

While this tunnel was being dug, the Germans were constructing a third barrack block to the west of the West Block (which consequently meant that it became the West Block and Jimmy James's barracks became the Central Block). Frustratingly for James, he could not take part in this escape bid because he arrived as the plans were well advanced. He was put in the highly unusual position (for him) of having to sit and watch helplessly.

As the summer turned into autumn, many of the new prisoners who were admitted to Stalag Luft I had been shot down over France pursuing German bombers and fighters that had been involved in raids on Britain. The inmates thus learnt of what Churchill would later call the 'Battle of Britain', although at the time the participants in the fight merely thought of it as a prolonged and almost ceaseless aerial tussle. There was some revival of the prisoners' spirits when a parcel of clothing arrived wrapped in a copy of the *Daily Express* dated 15 September 1940. The headline read: '184 German Aircraft Shot Down'.

Among the new arrivals that summer was Lawrence Reavell-Carter, who had been shot down in a Hampden bomber that had been on a mine-laying mission. Reavell-Carter was a distinguished Olympian. Shortly afterwards, 'Dick' Churchill arrived at Barth. Flight Lieutenant Sidney Albion Churchill (no relation to the British prime minister) was only 20 years old when his Hampden bomber of 144 Squadron was brought down over Ludwigshafen in September 1940. He lost no time in joining the nucleus of persistent escapers.

Sadly, in November the first tunnel (from what was now the Central Block) was discovered by the Germans after it had just gone under the wire. The prisoners were punished by being confined for three weeks to the cramped conditions of the Vorlager, from which they were only allowed out for an hour a day. When they were allowed back into the compound they discovered the Germans had implemented changes that would become familiar in all POW camps. The side-boards that covered the underneath of the barrack blocks had been removed and a new type of guard had been introduced. With their dark-blue boiler suits adorned with a single leather belt, and Luftwaffe Field Service caps, these guards looked more like caretakers than soldiers. They were not armed but carried long metal rods that they used to poke the ground as they looked for tunnels. These new camp personnel soon became ubiquitous, crawling under the barrack blocks and into the rafters through the trap-doors, looking for excavated sand. The prisoners immediately dubbed them 'ferrets'. A requirement of the job was perfect English and the prisoners soon became used to stumbling upon a ferret eavesdropping on their conversations. The ferrets were entitled to enter any barrack whenever they wished, and they would barge in without a moment's notice.

That Christmas was a dispiriting one, made worse by the malevolent Baltic weather. The Germans' efforts to bring some festive cheer to the prisoners in the form of a gooey substance they called 'Christmas pudding' was appreciated but failed to raise morale perceptibly. Nevertheless, things were becoming a little bit more comfortable in the camp. The prisoners were issued with wallpaper to cheer up their cheerless barracks. And the Germans provided board games, ping-pong tables and a well-stocked library. There were occasional performances of plays and concerts in the NCOs' compound. As the winter had approached, the Germans obtained some warm winter coats and distributed them among the prisoners. The officers constructed an ice-hockey rink between two of the barrack blocks, and soon Red Cross parcels were coming at the rate of one per man, per week. It was a welcome development and Jimmy James recalled the reaction to the first arrival of these precious treats.

> We ate solidly for some hours, it seemed, as goodies from various tins appeared: cheese, corned beef, stew, biscuits (hard tack), prunes, even cocoa, but best of all delectable tea. We were careful to eat slowly; a man in another camp died after bolting the entire contents of his first Red Cross parcel too quickly.

By now, what was to become another familiar pastime of POW life was being taken up. Regular theatrical shows were held in the dining-room and, just as a hard-core of persistent escapers was beginning to form, so there would develop a group of thespians who sought to dull the pain of captivity in this harmless and sometimes enlightening form of escapism.

Some prisoners were overcoming the problem of boredom by producing their own 'hooch' under the auspices of one of the prisoners who was a former employee of the Johnnie Walker whisky distillery. Initially the prisoners resorted to potato peelings but found them unsatisfactory. It was only when

Red Cross parcels began arriving that they learnt to use dried prunes mixed with yeast provided by a friendly guard and heated to 98 degrees to produce a concoction that was genuinely alcoholic and quite tasty. Different groups of prisoners produced their own 'labels' and competed with one another to see who could produce the best.

In early 1941 there were four new significant arrivals at Barth, two of them from Jimmy James's 9 Squadron. Flight Lieutenant Johnny Marshall was a Spitfire pilot with No. 3 Photo-Reconnaissance Unit (PRU) brought down over France in January. He had already tried to escape out of the train that brought him to Barth from Dulag Luft, managing to stay on the loose for two days before falling exhausted into the hands of the police. When he was returned to captivity he discovered that Tim Newman, a New Zealand RAF officer, had also managed to escape from the same train along with an Australian comrade. They too had been recaptured after being on the loose for a day or so.

After Newman and Marshall arrived in Barth came John Shore and Cookie Long of 9 Squadron. They had fallen into enemy hands after baling out when their Wellington developed engine trouble after a raid on Cologne. Long had been known by his real name of James in Honington but would soon acquire the soubriquet 'Cookie', thanks to his legendary abilities cooking up illicit alcohol. By the same token John Shore became better known as 'Death' Shore, so called because the other prisoners thought his enthusiasm for all sorts of hair-raising escape schemes would inevitably lead to his death one way or another.

Shortly after the failure of the first tunnel, work began on another in early 1941. This one was from East Block. This time Jimmy James took part in the tunnelling. The problem was finding somewhere to disperse the soil. The prisoners dug trenches beneath the blocks. These were quickly discovered by the Germans and the tunnel had to be closed. Shortly afterwards, Jimmy James got himself transferred to the new West Block and began to work on yet another tunnel from there. This tunnel was a precursor of the tunnels to come. It would be 100 feet long, emerging 30 feet on the other side of the wire. There was a ventilation pump and a rudimentary airline made out of wallpaper. No shoring was necessary and they dispersed the sand underneath the East Block to distract attention from the West.

In the meantime, Flight Lieutenant Harry Burton came up with a simpler and more novel form of escape. Burton was a dour Scotsman who had been an instructor at Jimmy James's Operational Training Unit (OTU), and the two ended up as roommates in Barth. Burton was spending a spell in the cooler for some minor misdemeanour when he spotted a chance for the escape. In May 1941, he managed to get himself thrown back inside, this time smuggling in a small hacksaw. Over the next five nights he managed to saw through the bars across his cell window. On the fifth night, at 11 p.m., he removed the bars and climbed through the window. In the darkness he crawled to the Kommandantur. Once there he tried to scrape a hollow under the gate with a piece of metal he had picked up on the way. His efforts were interrupted by the changing of the guard and by the arrival of another German who simply wanted to have a cigarette and a chat with the sentry. Burton bided his time in the shadows of the cooler during these unnerving moments. A further unsettling hazard was an Alsatian guard dog that was allowed to roam freely on the other side of the perimeter fence. Eventually Burton managed to burrow under the gates, dart silently past the German administrative buildings and clamber over the perimeter fence, which was patrolled but not lit. It was 2.30 a.m. and he was a free man.

He was dressed in service trousers, which he had dyed black, and had with him a blanket, shaving tackle and towel, and two bars of chocolate. Equipped with these sparse provisions, Burton set off walking in the direction of Stralsund, travelling by night along railway lines and through woods wherever possible, and hiding by day. He got to Stralsund in the early morning of 28 May and there was confronted with a quarter-mile bridge that crossed to the large island of Rügen. No sooner had he begun walking over the bridge than he realised that it was guarded by five sentries at equal intervals along its route. Realising it was too late to turn back he nonchalantly sauntered past them, as he did so greeting each with 'Guten Morgen!'

Burton continued walking for some 50 miles across the island until he reached Sassnitz from where ferries ran to Trelleborg in Sweden. It was 3 a.m. on the morning of 30 May. Burton saw a ferry flying the Swedish flag and discovered it was due to depart for Sweden the following afternoon at 4.30 p.m. That night he rested. But the following day, when Burton arrived at the embarkation point, he saw that every conceivable boarding point of the ship was ringed by barbed wire and watched over by sentries. Either he tried to bluff his way on as a passenger or he somehow got on through the entrance reserved for lorries. Burton had no papers, and no choice. He found a suitable truck and hid underneath it, suspending himself from the axle. It was loaded onto the deck at 4.15 p.m. and Burton waited underneath it until the ferry disembarked. When the vessel arrived at Trelleborg he repeated the procedure and once safely on dry land handed himself over to the Swedish police. It was the early evening of 31 May and Burton was on neutral soil. Shortly thereafter he was sent to the British Legation and repatriated to Great Britain. It was the first successful RAF 'home run' of the war, and when news of Burton's success reached Barth, it raised spirits considerably.

*   *   *

At the same time an ingenious plot was hatched to dig a tunnel beneath a compact structure in the south of the compound. This was known as the 'incinerator' but though rubbish was dumped there, nobody had ever seen it incinerated. Its most useful function to date had been to provide a makeshift grandstand for prisoners watching football matches in the adjoining recreation field. However, one bright spark suggested to the Escape Committee that if a tunnel could be dug from beneath the incinerator, it would only have to be about 25 feet long to get into the recreation field. From there it would be much easier to escape because, as at Dulag Luft, the field was surrounded by only one low wire. Two officers did begin a tunnel, but shortly afterwards the concept was abandoned as too dangerous.

When a Scottish Hampden pilot called Ian 'Muckle' Muir arrived in Barth, Jimmy James found a kindred spirit. Flight Lieutenant Muir had a wonderful 'P/O Prune' (a popular cartoon character in RAF training literature) moustache and an irrepressible spirit to match. The two of them formed a tunnel-digging partnership and began sinking a shaft from the East Block. Sadly, this was soon discovered by the ferrets and the men joined the others tunnelling from West Block instead. This tunnel proved to be ready to break out in the late summer of 1941. In all 30 escapers were planning to get out. They had altered their uniforms to look as much like civilian clothes as possible, but none were equipped with false papers. Jimmy James was number 13, which was to prove an inauspicious number. The air was buzzing with excitement on the night of 20 August, the first moonless night available. The 30 men squeezed themselves uncomfortably into the tunnel and lay toe-to-head waiting for the order to begin. Shortly after it came, the men beneath ground were concerned to hear the muffled report of rifle shots from above. The first three men out of the exit shaft had been spotted by goons as they emerged into the night. One, comically, had had his trousers pulled off in the squeeze to get through. He was spotted legging it across the compound half naked, carrying his trousers in his hands and chased by German guards and dogs. The three men did get out of the immediate surroundings of Barth but they were all caught some days later.

This escape attempt encouraged the Germans, once more, to reappraise their security apparatus. One of the innovations of the West Block tunnel had been the use of Klim processed milk cans from Red Cross parcels to form a ventilation shaft. The cans had each end removed and they were stuck together and laid in a line down the length of the tunnel, allowing air to reach the farthest reaches. The prisoners had not yet developed anything more than an elementary method for pumping air into the cans. But the ventilation they afforded was a welcome supplement to the practice of pushing up air holes through the tunnel roof. However, having discovered the ingenious uses to which the prisoners put Klim cans, the Germans now resolved to supervise the disposal of all the cans as soon as they had been used. A large bin was placed in the compound and the guards collected every Klim can they could find and threw them in the bin. Little did they realise that some RAF officers had sawn an escape hatch in the bottom of the bin, and one of them lay underneath the growing pile of cans. After the bin was removed from the camp, he made his getaway. It gave everybody a good laugh and the escape was executed in the spirit of a schoolboy prank. But, sadly, the escaper was caught shortly afterwards, and the experience encouraged Peter Fanshawe to start thinking that it was time their escape operations took on a slightly more professional air.

*   *   *

During that summer a new party of officers arrived from Dulag Luft—the group of the 'first' Great Escapers led by Wings Day and Johnny Dodge who had been sent there after being caught. It was the first time Jimmy James had seen Day since his brief introduction at the transit camp the previous year and he was delighted to see him. Day and his comrades were surprised and a little annoyed to be given a hostile reception from some of the other officers when they arrived in Barth. As they were marched into the compound they were greeted by catcalls and boos. Many of the onlookers shouted insults; others simply stared at the new arrivals with ill-disguised hostility. Day was initially angered by the reception they received, but when he learnt the reason he sympathised with the Barth men. Most of them had passed through Dulag Luft and subsequently contrasted the civilised surroundings of the Frankfurt transit camp with the dire conditions they had had to endure. Unflattering stories spread throughout the POW system of the Dulag prisoners enjoying regular walks in the woods, and visits to Frankfurt even, not to mention convivial dinners with German officers and plentiful supplies of wine and tobacco. However, when the Barth men learnt why their Frankfurt counterparts had suddenly been sent there, all hostility towards them ceased.

Roger Bushell was not among them. The Germans, perhaps, had already identified him as a potentially dangerous troublemaker. Bushell had been sent to the even less congenial surroundings of a camp in the far north, near Lübeck. It would be many months before Wings and Bushell would be reunited at the yet-to-be-built camp of Stalag Luft III and by then both men had learnt vital lessons in the art of escaping. In Stalag Luft I Wings Day once more found he was the SBO among the British officers.

The arrival of the Dulag Luft party saw the beginning of a properly organised and controlled escape organisation. Until then everything had been conducted in a spirit of enthusiasm. But after ordering an inquiry into the escape system, Day instituted a system moulded on the Dulag Luft model and on which the organisation of all future escapes in RAF camps was to be based. Jimmy Buckley was ordered to make the organisation of escape his full-time job and set up an Escape Committee.

It was after the arrival of the Dulag Luft escapers in Barth that another key figure would arrive. Flight Lieutenant Sydney Dowse was another PRU pilot shot down off the

French coast in his Spitfire on 20 August 1941. He had been photographing the *Gneisenau* and *Scharnhorst*, the two mighty German battle cruisers that had wrought such havoc on the Allies' Atlantic convoys and Arctic supply routes. After being brought down he tried to link up with the Resistance, but was soon caught. Thanks to a bad leg wound, however, he was sent first to a prison camp near Leipzig from which he was able to escape. He was caught again, though, and sent to Barth.

*   *   *

The potential of the 'incinerator' as a base for an escape attempt had already been mooted. Indeed a small five-foot tunnel had been begun but work was postponed as officers feared the risk of discovery was too great. The incinerator was a small box of a building in the compound that was used to dispose of garbage near the perimeter wire. If a tunnel could be sunk from the incinerator the diggers would only have to progress 25 feet or so to get out. The incinerator had a roof that sloped slightly towards the recreation ground on the other side of the wire, and thus made it an ideal 'grandstand' for spectators of the two daily football matches. On the wire side was a small entry-hole through which the rubbish was thrown. Inside, it was a gloomy structure some three feet high, divided into two parts, each

71

about six square feet. The one on the side of the barrack blocks had a door from which the rubbish was removed and was a rather dusty receptacle for rubbish piled in there. The other room, from which it was divided by a low wall, had escaped use. It was beneath this that the prisoners had built a short tunnel entrance concealed by a trap-door.

The work had been completed months beforehand and the idea had been abandoned. But now Death Shore suggested to his old 9 Squadron comrade Jimmy James that they revive the possibility. At a loss for anything else to do, James agreed. The plan was for the two men to be smuggled into the incinerator during the morning football match under cover of the crowd of spectators swarming around and over the little building. Dick Churchill, Lawrence Reavell-Carter and Paul Royle were among the spectators. Shore and James would dig all day long. And during the afternoon football match their dirty and dishevelled forms would be borne back to the barrack block huddled in among the crowd of spectators once more. The escapers made good progress. They found there was no need to shore up the tunnel so long as its roof was a sturdy arch. They progressed at the rate of almost a foot an hour. The excavated sand was disguised amongst the garbage in the incinerator. They had about seven hours' tunnelling a day. After four days they had travelled the required 25 feet underground, and the tunnel exit hatch was within six inches of the surface.

The men's plan was to repeat the successful journey of Burton, walking to Sassnitz, crossing to Rügen and boarding a ferry to Sweden. Four other prisoners, including Muckle Muir and Tim Newman, had asked if they could follow them. Shore and James agreed but demanded the others give them at least a four-hour start. The plot almost came to a disastrous end when one day the men noticed a German guard emptying the rubbish from the incinerator onto a horse and cart. Thankfully, the German didn't seem to notice that much of his load was excavated sand.

On this occasion, the escapers eschewed the usual idea of waiting for the first moonless night and decided to take their opportunity at the first sign of an air raid. Whenever an air raid began, Barth was plunged into darkness as the power was turned off and the attention of goons tended to be elsewhere. The only problem was that it was not possible to predict when the next air raid would be, so all six escapers had to be prepared at a moment's notice. For several nights therefore they went to their beds with their escape outfits and disguises on, ready for the first inkling of the siren.

On 19 October it finally came and the perimeter lights suddenly went out. Shore and

James quickly grabbed together their escape gear of haversacks and emergency rations. The plan was to slip from underneath their barrack block through a trap and dart across the darkened compound to the incinerator. But as the two men emerged from underneath their blocks suddenly the compound was alive with the hazy shapes of German guards and dogs. James hesitated, undecided what to do for several crucial seconds that he was later to regret. Rather than continue running he decided to hit the deck. But he was alarmed shortly thereafter to see one of the guards coming directly towards him, flashlight in hand. James stood no chance of making it to the incinerator undetected now and began wriggling his way across the ground, back towards the barrack block. Unfortunately, once there he couldn't find the trap-door and was left with no alternative but to lie there silently and hope his presence had not been noticed. In fact the goons had not spotted him but the dogs were soon sniffing him out. The game was up. After a few uncomfortable moments James decided to emerge from his hiding place rather than wait for the hounds to sink their teeth into him. He was led out into the compound, which by now was flooded in dazzling light. The only source of consolation was that the Germans could not possibly know where he had been planning to escape from.

The capture of James greatly assisted Death

Shore because the goons had been distracted by the emergence of the cowering RAF officer. In the maelstrom Shore had emerged from the tunnel and crossed the recreation field, where he waited for some anxious minutes at the appointed rendezvous point. When there was no sign of his companion he set off for Barth, and from there to Stralsund. Shore did, more or less, repeat Harry Burton's epic journey. There were a few variations of modes of transport, and the escape route was not exactly the same. There was one particularly hair-raising encounter with the Gestapo. But eventually, Shore found himself steaming across the Baltic in a ferry bound for Sweden and sitting in the offices of the British Legation shortly afterwards with a contented look on his face. He arrived back in Britain on 29 October and was subsequently awarded the Military Cross. For the remainder of the war Jimmy James had to live with the frustrating thought that but for his initial hesitation he might very well have been one of the few people to have escaped from Germany. Instead, he was to endure a further four years in captivity.

But remarkably, he remained undeterred and once he emerged from the cooler began digging yet another tunnel from underneath his barrack block. Sadly, that too was quickly discovered. 'Herr James', as the goons referred to him affectionately, was beginning to get something of a reputation as one of the most persistent of escapers. Once more he was dispatched to the cooler. He was serving his time there when in November 1941 another pilot of his 9 Squadron arrived at Barth. It was just two days before Lester 'Johnny' Bull's 24th birthday when the Wellington he was flying developed engine trouble over France. The Wimpy had left Honington on an intelligence-gathering mission over the German radar network that stretched along the western French coast. The crew all baled out and all were eventually caught. It was a dismal way for Bull to celebrate his birthday but his reluctance to let his spirits be dimmed is evident in the fact that within days of arriving he was digging a tunnel out with one of his Wimpy crewmates, Jack Grisman, a postman's son who had once served as driver to the British Ambassador in Baghdad. The two men resolutely dug their way through rock-hard soil throughout the winter.

Christmas 1941 was an even more depressing one than the last for the rest of the inmates in Barth. The Russians were crumbling under the onslaught of Hitler's Operation Barbarossa, and the *Prince of Wales* and the *Repulse*, two of the Royal Navy's proudest vessels, had been sunk. Nevertheless, in the spirit of the festive season, the prisoners put on a pantomime for the men and invited the senior German staff to attend. The title of the play was *Alice and Her Candle* and Wings began cringing with embarrassment the minute the curtains went up. 'The first four lines of dialogue dispelled all hope of innocent fun,' he later recalled, noting that with every line it became more vulgar and lewd. Whether or not the Germans grasped the peculiar form of theatre that was the English pantomime is impossible to tell—they sat stony faced throughout. But at the end the Kommandant congratulated Wings on 'the fine standard of Shakespearean English'.

There were two significant new arrivals to Barth that Christmas. Squadron Leader Tom Kirby-Green grew up in Nyasaland (now Malawi), the son of a colonial governor, with parents who epitomised the sort of eccentric English aristocracy that the Dark Continent tended to breed. Kirby-Green was educated in England and had his dream of becoming an RAF pilot fulfilled in 1937 before being transferred to Jimmy James's 9 Squadron at Honington. He went on to serve as a flight instructor for 311 Squadron of Czech RAF pilots, and ended up in 40 Squadron when he was shot down in a Wellington over Germany in October 1941. At Barth he became a popular figure with his brightly striped kaftans, bedroom slippers and gramophone records of Latin music and exotic food packages from home. He had a pair of bongo drums with which he entertained his block mates. One of

77

them who fell under his thrall was Flight
Lieutenant Roy Langlois, a youthful native of
the Channel Islands, whose Wellington crash-
landed after a raid on Aachen. The two new
prisoners had at least something to keep their
spirits up in the form of the United States'
declaration of war on Japan and Germany.

Throughout the winter months various
tunnelling attempts continued apace and other
prisoners adopted other escape tactics. Some
tried to leave the camp dressed as their
German guards. One escaper, who bore a
startling resemblance to one of the German
ferrets, Karl Pfelz (whom the prisoners called
'Charlie'), almost made it. Jimmy James had
the novel idea of waiting for an air raid to
cause the lights to go out and marching up
to the guards in a German uniform demanding
to be let through. He was on the verge of
succeeding when the lights were turned on at
the last minute and he beat a hasty retreat
back to his barracks. None of the escape
attempts came to anything and one ended in
tragedy when an NCO was shot dead by the
guards.

In fact the prisoners did have something to
look forward to, as they were shortly to find
out. Throughout the last few months of 1941
the Germans had been building a bigger and
more complex camp in the depths of Silesia. It
was built on Hermann Göring's direct orders
and to such a specification that it would be

'escape proof'. Most of the Barth prisoners would be transferred there as soon as possible. But, as the Germans were soon to discover, there was no such phrase as 'escape proof' in the English lexicon.

CHAPTER THREE

GÖRING'S ESCAPE-PROOF CAMP

Stalag Luft III was built on Göring's orders specifically to house the growing number of airmen being shot down over German-occupied territory. With the entry now of the United States into the war the numbers were escalating daily, and the difficulties in keeping them secure were expanding. Stalag Luft III was the largest of six main camps built by the Germans. The new facility was intended to be the perfect camp—one impossible to escape from, but also comfortable enough to persuade most inmates, perhaps, that escape was not worthwhile.

'We had clean sheets practically every week and orderlies to come in and change them,' Bub Clark once recalled, a little flippantly, but the point he wanted to make was that their daily existence was nowhere near as hard as that of many other prisoners of war. 'The living conditions, the sanitary conditions and the food rations were good. We were probably the best-treated POWs anywhere in the world at the time.'

The camp was built near the historic town of Sagan, about 102 miles south-east of Berlin and halfway between the German capital and

Breslau. At first it was just two compounds of six barracks each: one for officers—the East Compound; the other, the Centre Compound, for NCOs. But it would quickly grow to be a much larger and sprawling complex, expanding all the time as more and more Allied airmen were shot out of the sky. The countryside surrounding Sagan was a featureless landscape of endless flat fields broken only by long lines of gloomy pine forest. Just south of the town was a forest some 25 miles deep. It was on the northern edge of this gigantic clump of timber and pine that Göring ordered his model camp to be built. With Switzerland some 500 miles to the south and the Baltic 200 miles to the north, Sagan was about as far away as it was possible to be from those twin glimmers of salvation to the imprisoned airmen.

The camp itself was a huge expanse of soft sandy ground covered by a thin layer of topsoil, the only features being the ugly severed trunks of the trees that had been cleared to make way for the camp, and row after row of identical barrack blocks. There was not a blade of grass to be seen. The dirty grey soil crumbled to dust in the summer and in the winter mixed with the underlying yellow sand (which itself was to be one of the obstacles to escape), to become a mire of sludge. In the summer the heat could be unbearable. In the winter the camp was battered by icy Silesian winds of up to

30 degrees below freezing. For all that, though, Sagan was an improvement on Barth to most men. In Sagan's wide-open compounds there was not the same sense of claustrophobia or the strange sense of hellish desolation that Stalag Luft I had imparted.

All the barrack blocks were of a uniform design, clad in prefabricated timber panels and topped by tarred felt for roofs. Each measured 160 feet long by 40 feet wide. Those intended for officers were divided into rooms housing between four and eight men, extending along the side of a long central corridor. Those for NCOs were divided in half. Each block contained a small kitchen with a stove and a primitive night urinal. By the time Stalag Luft III was opened in April 1942 the Germans had learnt their lessons and the camp incorporated dozens of the new security measures that the Luftwaffe confidently predicted would make it 'escape proof'. To start with, each barrack block was built on stilts and the only 'hidden' parts that descended into the earth were the concrete piles that supported the small area of the kitchens and washrooms above. The ferrets and their dogs would have a clear view of what was going on underneath the buildings, and if the prisoners planned to tunnel out, they would have to go through the concrete. And inside the barrack blocks all of the ceilings and the floors were lined with trap-doors that facilitated quick inspection and detection of clandestine activity. It would not be easy for the prisoners to hide all that bright yellow sand in these rafters.

Each barrack block was a considerable distance from its neighbour, reducing the prospect of dark shadows at night disguising furtive movements around the camp. And the compound could be flooded with light from the watchtowers that ringed each compound 15 feet above ground and at 100-yard intervals. At Sagan, even the nearest barracks were at least 100 feet from the wire and some 200 feet from the forest line, which had been cut back purposely to leave a great swathe of open land surrounding the compounds. Any tunnel would have to be at least 300 feet if it was to emerge in the shelter of the woods, and deep enough to evade the new seismographs that ringed the compound, ever alert for underground noises.

The compounds themselves were surrounded by a formidable double fence ten feet high and topped with razor wire. The space in between each fence, about seven feet apart, was layered with huge coils of more razor wire. At regular intervals along the outer perimeter wire were the goon boxes, permanently manned by guards with machine guns and powerful spotlights. Dogs patrolled the outside perimeter fence. And there was a low (18 inches high) 'trip wire' 30 feet inside the fence that prisoners were forbidden to cross without permission.

Besides these new physical security measures, the Germans had by now perfected their systems of security. The ferrets now knew what they were doing and were properly equipped. Pairs of them were likely to emerge at any second to take the prisoners by surprise. Other ferrets patrolled in the dark shadows of the woods, surreptitiously watching the prisoners' activities through binoculars hidden behind 'ferret fences'. Stalag Luft III was as escape proof as 'escape proof' could be. But it did not have the daunting effect on the new inmates that the Germans had hoped. As that indomitable escaper Jimmy James once reflected: no prison camp is truly escape proof. So much depends upon human ingenuity—and human shortcomings—and less on the overcoming of physical obstacles, the challenges of which have formed mankind's evolution. And the Germans had not got everything right. One serious security anomaly of Stalag Luft III was that it was located a little more than half a mile away from the town of Sagan, one of the busiest railway junctions in Germany. Almost within a stone's throw of the perimeter wire was a constant traffic of passenger and freight trains whistling past to all corners of the Reich—and beyond.

Sagan was a pleasant enough but nondescript sort of town. It was an area steeped in history, having been the seat of the

Duke of Courland in the days when Courland was a Russian province. The plains around Sagan had witnessed the historic defeat of Frederick the Great at Russian hands. During Napoleon's time, Sagan fell into French hands and the Duc de Sagan reigned in splendour from an impressive chateau built in the style of the French eighteenth century. The chateau was still there in 1942, though by then the Germans had requisitioned the property for the duration of the war.

Sagan, however, boasted another stately pile of some note. Jeschkendorf Manor was not quite so grand, but had a parochial charm of its own. The house, built in the vernacular style, was the proud home of Colonel Friedrich von Lindeiner, one-time member of Hermann Göring's personal Luftwaffe staff, and now the newly-appointed Kommandant of Stalag Luft III.

Friedrich-Wilhelm von Lindeiner-Wildau was not the ineffectual and somewhat bumbling character (ludicrously named 'von Luger') portrayed in the Hollywood movie, *The Great Escape*. A decorated (and thrice-wounded) veteran of the First World War with two Iron Cross awards, he was a brave man—and his bravery would be put to the test by both the Nazis and the Allies as the war reached its bloody climax. Von Lindeiner was not unlike Dulag Luft's Major Theo Rumpel in temperament, background and outlook. He

85

too believed in the natural chivalry between the officer classes, and the natural affinity between the upper classes. It was a snobbish viewpoint, perhaps, and might seem dated in our more democratic age. But if the story of the men of Stalag Luft III and their eventual Great Escape proves anything, it is that there is a very clear distinction between those who are noble and those who are not. The men of the Great Escape, who came from remarkably diverse backgrounds, though, proved that nobility has nothing to do with where you were born or to whom you were born. It has everything to do with the moral choices you make in life.

Von Lindeiner was himself of minor aristocratic stock and before the war had married a Dutch baroness. They had settled on her estate in Holland, where they had extensive land-holdings, only returning to Germany after the Nazis came to power. They were both shocked by the dramatic changes the coarse new regime had wrought on the country in a comparatively short period of time. For his part, von Lindeiner did everything he could to avoid becoming embroiled with it. Like many of his class he found himself walking a tightrope between his own traditional values and the harsher realities of the new government. But in any totalitarian country it is not always possible to completely evade the demands of the all-powerful state.

He and the baroness owned an apartment in Berlin, but they preferred to spend their time in what they thought would be the isolation of their Jeschkendorf estate. There they led the life of to the manor born and treated the growing Nazi diktats of local officials with a lofty disdain. As war loomed, the colonel joined Hermann Göring's staff in the Luftwaffe (although Göring never knew him personally), the least Nazi of all the German armed forces. It was perhaps natural that the Luftwaffe saw him as the perfect candidate to run Stalag Luft III when it opened. When the colonel took over command of the camp he was already 61 years old. Von Lindeiner, like Major Rumpel, approached his new duties as a 'common jailer' with some reluctance, but resolved to perform them in the spirit of gallantry that he felt the difficult situation demanded.

'Most of us had a great deal of respect for the Colonel,' says General Albert 'Bub' Clark. 'He had an extremely difficult job. He always tried to be fair. He tried to follow the Geneva Convention. He gave us the equipment to play hockey and basketball. There were excellent orchestras and bands. The libraries were well stocked. His theory was that if he was nice to us and let us have all the sports and recreational equipment we needed it would lessen our desire to escape. He couldn't have been more wrong.'

*   *   *

The new prisoners started arriving between March and April from camps all over Germany. Canadian flier Tommy Thompson came from Spangenberg along with compatriot George McGill, who had been an observer with 103 Squadron, shot down in January. From Oflag VIB at Warburg came Wing Commander Douglas Bader, the legless fighter ace, and Stanislaw 'Danny' Krol, a tough little Pole. Danny Krol was a championship swordsman who at Warburg had a penchant for washing himself in the nude in the snow. He joined the Polish Air Force before the war, but had to look on helplessly as the Nazi Blitzkrieg overran his country because his squadron's planes had been put out of action within the first few hours. He made his way to France, where the Polish General Sikorski was regrouping his country's air force. But after the fall of France, Krol was evacuated to England. There he joined 74 Squadron of Spitfires and it was on an operation over France that he was shot down. His unit's loss was Stalag Luft III's gain. Krol was to be one of the most effective contributors to the X-Organisation.

But it was from Barth that the majority of new inmates came, among them Wings Day and Johnny Dodge, Jimmy Buckley and Mike

Casey, Peter Fanshawe and Cookie Long, Jimmy James, Johnny Marshall and Muckle Muir—all veteran escape artists who would prove to be the core of Stalag Luft III's escape organisation.

Jimmy James's first impressions of the new camp were not dissimilar to many others'. 'The Silesian pine forest marched darkly around the barbed wire defences . . . bare sandy compounds . . . austere wooden barrack huts,' he wrote in *Moonless Night*. But Sagan did not fill him with as much gloom as Barth.

> I did not have the same sense of finality as when I entered Stalag Luft I nearly two years before. Although German armies were thundering across the Russian steppes towards Stalingrad, Rommel was rolling our army back in the Western Desert and the Japanese were thrusting up through Burma, there was a feeling, now that the Americans were in the war, the Germans and Japs would be stopped in their tank tracks before long and that this could be the beginning of the end.

A key new arrival around about that time was Wally Floody, a Canadian fighter pilot who had been a mining engineer in civilian life.

Stalag Luft III was specifically intended to

house all air force prisoners. Unfortunately, the numbers of Allied airmen being shot out of the sky always exceeded the numbers the German High Command had counted on. (Eventually, some 90,000 Allied airmen were shot down over Europe, about half of them surviving to become prisoners of war. Bomber Command lost 58,000 men.) Consequently, other air force camps had to be built—or reopened, as would be the case with Barth. Nevertheless, Stalag Luft III would remain the main camp for British and American Air Force officers until the end of the war. It originally began with two compounds for some 2,500 officers and NCOs, but rapidly expanded to six compounds, housing more than 10,000 officers and their orderlies. So overcrowded did Stalag Luft III become that the NCOs were eventually evacuated to their own camp. At its largest, the perimeter fence of Stalag Luft III was more than five miles long. It was not the intimate little camp implied by the movie, but a sprawling, bustling community of many different nationalities, although it is true that the first new arrivals were confined to the relatively small East Compound with eight barrack buildings, a separate cookhouse, latrine and bathhouse.

Wings Day settled down into his familiar role as Senior British Officer in the offices provided by the Germans for him and his staff. But if von Lindeiner thought that Day would use his clean and rather well-equipped new facilities simply to preside over the efficient administration of the British prisoners, he was wrong. Within hours of arriving Day had put Jimmy Buckley in charge of the X-Organisation.

The move to Sagan coincided with a period of reflection on Wings's part, during which he formulated a new approach for escape. Up until then he had approached escape like most of the other men, almost as a game, with the International Red Cross as a referee. Now, however, he told his men that the time had come 'to change into higher gear'. Prisoners of war should no longer regard themselves as semi-neutrals merely because they had had a brush with death and fallen into enemy hands, he explained. They were to be an extension of the Allied war effort. Their battlefront was the razor-wired fences that surrounded them on all four sides. Before arriving at Sagan, Wings thought of escape as a way to maintain the prisoners' pride and boost their flagging morale, but now escape was to be pursued mainly to impede the German war effort and there would be less concern for the effect on the men's morale. The concept of bringing the battlefront to Sagan was to have profound consequences for his men and Wings did not arrive at his decision lightly. Beforehand it had been his policy to counsel caution to men like Death Shore, who suggested escape attempts that were transparently suicidal. But on the battlefield, operational decisions were not calculated on the basis of whether they would end in death or not, or whether they would cause discomfiture to the combatants. Indeed, it was generally accepted that they would invariably end in death. All that mattered was to deliver an effective blow to the enemy. From then on that was how decisions would be made on the battlefield of Sagan.

Escapes were going to be more carefully planned. Buckley divided the Escape Committee into three operational sections to oversee three types of escape: under (tunnels), over (wire jobs) and through (gate escapes). All three would be attempted with varying degrees of success, but tunnelling remained the most popular form of escape. Escape from a tunnel usually ensured a head start of at least eight hours and caused the Germans the most trouble. There had been 100 tunnels built at Barth and there would be an equal number built at Sagan before the most famous one of all would put an end to tunnelling.

Buckley went about recruiting the other veterans of the escaping fraternity, mostly from the veteran escape artists and general trouble-makers from Barth. But the steady stream of new recruits who were arriving from other camps was very much to the Escape Committee's advantage as they brought their own different experiences of escape and contributed their own unique skills. If the Germans had learnt by their mistakes, the prisoners had also learnt by theirs. Many of them were now adept in the arts of forging, map-making and tailoring. Many of them were to put their ingenuity to the test in creating all sorts of devices, mechanical and otherwise, that would aid escape. And no longer would this escape material be produced at a whim, or willy-nilly. The X-Organisation, regrouping in Stalag Luft III, was to oversee the advent of mass production on an industrial scale.

Not everyone wanted to escape, recalls Bub Clark. 'About a third of the men wanted to sit out the war and finish their education. They worked very hard on their studies and some of them even got degrees. About a third wanted to do nothing but read, push iron, exercise, or just sit around bitching. The final third were dedicated to escaping. But practically everybody in the camp would help anybody who wanted to escape in some form or another. I'd say about 60 to 70 per cent of the camp were involved in some way or another in the escape effort.'

The Escape Committee was immediately inundated with tunnel proposals but early on ruled that only a small number should be authorised. It was felt that if resources were concentrated on three deep tunnels (to avoid detection by the seismographs) from three barracks, the men were more likely to succeed in the more onerous circumstances they faced. However, it soon became difficult to enforce this stricture. New prisoners arriving in Stalag Luft III felt they were being excluded from a chance to get out. When one of the three deep tunnels was discovered, the policy was dramatically reversed. It was reasoned the more tunnels there were, the more likely at least one would succeed. Remarkably, during the summer of 1942 alone some 30 to 40 tunnels were begun from the barracks of the East Compound. Sadly, all but one failed.

Veteran tunnellers Peter Fanshawe and Johnny Marshall were joined by boisterous Scotsman Bob 'Crump' Ker-Ramsay and Wally Floody, the Canadian fighter pilot and former mining engineer, who were put in charge of tunnelling. In Canada, Wally Floody had worked for Harry Oakes, the rags-to-riches mining mogul who was to die in mysterious circumstances in the Bahamas during the war. Floody joined 401 Squadron of the Royal Canadian Air Force and was posted to Biggin Hill, the legendary RAF fighter base in Kent. He was in one of three squadrons of thirty Spitfires over St-Omer in France when they were attacked by more than 200 Messerschmitt 109s. Before Floody had a chance to react, his machine had been blown out of the sky and he was baling out over rural France. He landed on the doorstep, literally, of a farmhouse and was being offered a stiff glass of Cognac by its mistress when a squad of German soldiers arrived to take him prisoner. Shortly afterwards he was being interrogated at Dulag Luft.

*   *   *

One of the immediate problems that the tunnellers anticipated was that the grey soil upon which the camp was built disguised a distinctive yellow sandy soil not far beneath the surface. It would be difficult to disperse and, they were to discover, even more difficult to work with. On the other hand, Sagan had its advantages. The most notable was that the water table was some 350 feet beneath the surface, making the environs ideal for tunnelling.

Jimmy James was one of the first to start digging. His roommate was Charles Bonnington (father of the future mountaineer, Chris), a parachute captain shot down in the Western Desert. It was Bonnington's idea to dig a tunnel from a barrack block near the wash house about 300 feet underneath the sports field. James agreed to undertake the tunnelling side of operations. The tunnel was going smoothly when one day James was flattened by a cave-in. He was alone down the tunnel and unable to move his limbs. Fortunately, he could move his head and was able to call for help. Somebody dragged him out. The men had stumbled upon one of the biggest obstacles to tunnellers in Sagan.

'At first we thought the sand would make it easy to tunnel and we could, perhaps, progress at up to six feet a day,' he says. 'Well, it did make it easy. But the problem with soft sand is that it's always falling on you.' The men were beginning to realise that any successful tunnel out of Sagan was going to have to be very thoroughly shored up.

But there were literally dozens of other tunnels built in those spring and summer months. Most of them were shallow and virtually all of them collapsing of their own accord or being discovered by the ferrets. No sooner was Bub Clark in the camp than he had volunteered for digging duty and found himself in one of the shallow tunnels with Wally Floody. Sometimes the men would be sealed in overnight, digging while their comrades above slept.

'It was not for everybody,' he concedes. 'We had no lights unless we used the little fat lamps, but they usually went out by four o'clock in the morning, which gives you some idea of how foul the air was down there. However, other than having a foul headache by the end of the night we could all survive longer than the fat lamps, which surprised me.'

The Germans, of course, knew what was going on and spent a great deal of time driving a heavy fire truck around the compound and on one occasion flooded the camp with water. The problems were obvious. Besides the sand being unstable it was difficult to hide. The prisoners hid much of it in the barrack block roofs, but when one roof collapsed the game was up. Most of the tunnels depended on air holes for ventilation, but these could easily be detected by the ferrets. The distances the tunnels needed to travel were just too intimidating. Many of the diggers were buried in falls, but surprisingly, despite scores of cave-ins, no tunnellers were ever killed in Stalag Luft III.

Muckle Muir came up with one of the most brilliant ideas for a tunnel, which the Escape Committee agreed might succeed where all the others appeared to be failing. It would consist of a shallow tunnel just a few feet down, followed by a much deeper tunnel. The first shaft would go down eight feet and continue horizontally for some 40 feet, where it would appear to reach a dead-end. If the Germans discovered this tunnel, as they had stumbled on all the others, they would presume it had been abandoned. But beneath a cleverly hidden trap would be a shaft going down 20 feet and leading to a deeper tunnel. Wings Day thought it was a capital idea and ordered that it be given top priority.

Peter Fanshawe was put in charge of sand dispersal and Wally Floody managed the tunnellers. There were two teams of 17

tunnellers, under Harry Marshall and Bob
Ker-Ramsay, who would work in continuous
shifts. They chose to start the tunnel from
barrack block 66 because, at more than 400
feet from the wire, the Germans would not
suspect anyone would be stupid enough to
build a tunnel from it. The tunnel advanced to
the cookhouse block, which was near the wire
and then extended backwards towards block
67. This tunnel would prove to be the
blueprint for all future tunnelling attempts and
provide the Escape Committee with the first
inklings of problems digging at such a depth.
There was the problem of safety. If you were
caught in a cave-in at four feet down you were
likely to be able to pull yourself out. If you
were caught in a collapse under 20 or 30 feet
of sand, the consequences could be fatal. The
men also discovered that air was a problem at
such a depth. Oxygen was so scarce that they
could hardly breathe. The fat lamps they took
down rarely lasted more than a few minutes.
To cope with this they designed far more
elaborate ventilation pipes with their Klim
cans than they had used in the past. With little
bits of cable stolen from the Germans, they
sometimes managed to tap into the camp's
power supply for lighting. And Muckle Muir's
tunnel saw the beginnings of the underground
railway trolleys that were to be indispensable
in sand dispersal and transporting diggers to
'the coal face'.

It took them three months to reach the concrete foundations of the kitchen block. By the time they got that far the amount of sand they were excavating was causing severe dispersal problems for Fanshawe. They literally had nowhere else left to put the stuff. The roofs in some huts were sagging under the weight of sand in the rafters. It was then that Ker-Ramsay came up with another unique idea. Block 68 had side panels going right down to the ground. Why not dig a short spur of the tunnel under Block 68 and hide the sand there? There would be no need for prisoners dispersing the sand in other parts of the compound to make the journey above ground and alert the suspicions of the Germans. The plan was agreed upon and the tunnellers began building another tunnel.

As Muckle Muir's ingenious tunnel progressed, there were more important arrivals in the camp. That summer Wings Day was supplanted as SBO when Group Captain Herbert Massey arrived at Stalag Luft III. Massey was the possessor of a DSO and Military Cross and had been in the Royal Flying Corps in the First World War. He was just about to be promoted to Air Commodore when he was shot down in a Lancaster in which he was a passenger. But Massey became the SBO in name only, ordering Wings Day to continue in the job that he had been doing so well. The two were old friends, having served together in Egypt. Massey was slightly handicapped by an ankle injury that made him walk with a limp and, besides, he recognised that Day had far more experience of prisoners' affairs than he did. Another arrival was Des Plunkett, shot down on 20 June 1942 over Holland. Again, it was another case of the RAF's loss being Stalag Luft III's gain: Plunkett would prove indispensible to the X-Organisation.

In July 1942 there were two other new arrivals at Stalag Luft III. RAF Flight Lieutenant Bob van der Stok would play a prominent role in future escape activity from Stalag Luft III and would earn himself an important role in the history of the Great Escape. Van der Stok was born on 30 October 1915 in Dutch Sumatra. He was one of the four children—three boys and a girl—of a Shell engineer, whose job would take the family all over the world. They spent their childhood in Borneo before moving to Curaçao in the Dutch West Indies. They were all educated in Rotterdam. Bob went on to the prestigious Lyceum Alpinum in Switzerland, and from there entered Leiden University to study medicine. However, his fondness for sport—mainly rowing and playing ice hockey—hindered his studies and he was not to graduate. He seriously discussed the possibility of becoming a professional ice-hockey player in Canada, but at his father's suggestion joined the Dutch Royal Air Force on a short-service commission. He trained as a fighter pilot and developed a love of stunt flying, one time finding himself on charges for flying a plane under a bridge. Eventually, van der Stok left the Air Force and returned to his medical studies, this time at Utrecht University, now determined to complete them.

The war put paid to those ambitions. With hostilities looming, van der Stok rejoined the Air Force and found himself flying Fokkers against the Germans when they invaded on 10 May 1940. He claimed at least one 'kill' of the enemy's superior Messerschmitt machines, but Holland collapsed in a matter of days and hostilities were brought to an abrupt end. On 15 May, like every other Dutch serviceman, he was ordered by the occupying authorities to resume his life as a civilian. He did for a while, but would soon be embarking on the role that would occupy him for much of the remainder of the war: that of a great escaper.

When two Dutch Air Force fliers escaped to Britain in a stolen aircraft, the Germans began rounding up all their grounded comrades. Van der Stok quickly went underground and began his own efforts to flee to freedom. It took him three attempts and almost a year before he swam out to a neutral ship in Rotterdam harbour and hid on board. After the ship left port it was stopped by a British Royal Navy vessel and van der Stok, along with several other escapees, emerged from hiding to volunteer to join the Allied cause. For much of the next two years van der Stok flew Spitfires in the Royal Air Force for 91 Squadron in a defensive role over the south coast. Later he was assigned to 41 Squadron and was flying sweeps in Spitfires over France. On 14 July 1942, in a skirmish with a prowling pack of Messerschmitts, his machine took a lethal hit and he baled out over enemy-held territory. In his career with the RAF he had been credited with six more kills. But now van der Stok was a prisoner of the Germans once more.

When he arrived in Stalag Luft III Bob van der Stok started as he intended to go on and was given a job in the hospital, thanks to his medical training. But he was to become a persistent escaper. His first two attempts were both a little slapdash and amateurish. On the first he and a fellow officer planned to simply dig a quick hole under the wire at night and run off. They were thwarted when a commotion in a different part of the camp raised the alarm and they had to beat a hasty retreat to their barrack block. On another occasion he and his companion managed to hide in the shower block with a pair of shovels planning to emerge at night and again dig a quick hole under the wire. They were caught when the guards noticed their absence at roll-call.

The second important arrival that summer

was Roger Bushell, at last reunited with his old comrades, who had not seen him since he disappeared on the Dulag Luft 'Great Escape'. Bushell arrived at Stalag Luft III in the company of two Gestapo officers. After his attempted escape from the Frankfurt transit camp, Bushell had been separated from the rest and sent to Stalag XC at Lübeck. Subsequently he had been among a contingent of prisoners sent to Oflag VIB at Warburg. On the train journey there Bushell, with several other officers, managed to cut a hole in the floorboards and drop down onto the tracks from the train. Bushell took off with a Czech officer, Jack Zafouk, and they made their way to Prague, where the resistance movement found them a safe house. They waited there while an escape route was prepared for them, but on 27 May 1942 fate intervened when the SS Obergruppenführer Reinhard Heydrich, Deputy Reich Protector of Bohemia and Moravia, was assassinated in an ambush in Prague by Czech partisans parachuted into Czechoslovakia by the British.

The attack produced an immediate and ruthless retaliation from the Germans, who rounded up more than a thousand members of the resistance movement and anybody remotely connected to it. (They also razed to the ground an entire village, murdering the men and sending the women and children to concentration camps.) It was the misfortune of

Bushell and Zafouk to be betrayed in this frenzy of barbarous retaliation, and they ended up being badly beaten by the Gestapo. Zafouk was sent to Colditz Castle in Saxony, that other 'escape-proof' camp that proved to be anything but escape proof.

Somehow or other Bushell ended up being sent to Sagan—why, has always been a mystery. Paul Brickhill, the author of the book *The Great Escape*, was also a prisoner in Stalag Luft III. He suggested that it was thanks to the intervention of Stalag Luft III's camp censor, Corporal Hasse, who knew and liked Bushell. Others have suggested it was Colonel von Lindeiner who intervened. What is certain is that when Bushell was delivered back into Luftwaffe hands it was with the explicit warning that if he attempted to escape again he would be shot. Bushell himself was always reticent about his time in Gestapo captivity, but it clearly radically altered his perception of the Germans. Beforehand he had harboured a tremendous amount of goodwill for the German nation as a whole—hardly surprising given that he had spent so much time skiing with Germans before the war. His attitude to the Nazis was ambivalent, but he did not like the impact they were having on a country he regarded as one of the most civilised in the world. After he arrived back in Stalag Luft III, however, he appeared to loathe every last German with a passion, and his desire to escape took on an almost messianic form.

* * *

In the middle of the steaming heat of one typical Silesian summer day, some RAF prisoners dreamt up an ingenious—but fatally flawed—ruse to inflict damage on German morale. Stalag Luft III had its own herd of pigs, which fed off the camp's rubbish tip. The British officers thought that if they threw their used razors into the garbage, the pigs would choke on them, thereby reducing, to a modest extent, Germany's supplies of bacon and ham. (The officers don't seem to have taken account of the fact that the pigs could still have been butchered for bacon if they died.) And unfortunately, the ruse did not work quite as conceived. The pigs carried on gorging on the rubbish, regardless of the razor blades. However, the German guards couldn't help but notice the blades as several of them cut their hands handling the rubbish—to their intense irritation. They decided to take revenge and from then onwards refused to remove the garbage. The result was a stinking heap of rubbish that spawned a constant cloud of flies and caused several outbreaks of dysentery. It became so insufferable that the British eventually gave in. Wings Day ordered that no more razor blades were to be thrown on the rubbish tip and the Germans agreed to

105

clear up the mess, but by that time the swarm of flies had become a persistent presence, made worse by the already-malfunctioning latrines, which had been badly designed. At this stage the residents of East Compound were grateful for the arrival of a young American officer, who had just been shot down in his Spitfire over France.

Lieutenant Colonel 'Bub' Clark's father had been a State Health Inspector in Colorado and as a youth in the Depression, Clark had accompanied him on trips to Civilian Conservation Corps camps in Colorado. As a result, Clark was well versed in the construction of pit latrines. With the SBO's approval he secured the tools and materials needed from the Germans to improve the latrine facilities by draping them with mosquito screens and installing ventilation traps. In fact, he improved them so much that the Germans adopted his design in other camps. Wings Day also appointed Clark 'Big S'—head of security in the X-Organisation.

Albert Patton Clark was better known as 'Bub' because of his youthful appearance, or sometimes 'Red' because of his red hair. A gangling 6 ft 2 in., he bore a physical resemblance to the Hollywood film idol James Stewart and had something of the actor's transparent good nature. But Clark's boyish innocence disguised a shrewd brain, as was to be discovered by many Allied prisoners who would come into contact with him over the forthcoming years. Despite his youth, he was second-in-command of one of the first American fighter squadrons to arrive in Britain. In order to familiarise him and other American airmen with British planes and tactics, Clark was assigned to the 31st Fighter Group, based at Tangmere on the southern coast of England. The fighter base directly faced the enemy on the other side of the Channel and 31st Group flew those planes so cherished by young American fliers, the Spitfire. His honoured position as the only American in the group mainly made up of former Battle of Britain pilots may have been the unintended cause of his downfall. While his RAF comrades shared quarters on the airfield, Clark was being fêted at a local hotel where the fare was finer than the base mess and the conditions considerably more comfortable. But it meant that by the time his driver had delivered him to the airfield on the morning of Sunday, 26 July 1942, he had missed the briefing session and was confronted with the sight of his comrades rushing headlong across the airfield to jump in their machines. Clark had no alternative but to follow suit. He was still wearing his light-coloured slacks and leather jacket. There was no time to change into proper flying gear and all he could do was grab a flying helmet as he strapped himself into the Spitfire, with no idea what the mission was. 'I was probably the most uninformed airman in the skies that day,' he later reflected with a wry smile.

In fact the group had been ordered into a sweep over Abbeville, one of the main Luftwaffe bases along the northern coast of France that were home to some 1,000 German fighter aircraft. The Spitfire squadrons' job was to surprise and destroy as many of the enemy as possible. Without the benefit of this knowledge, Clark simply attached himself to the pack, pointed his Spitfire's nose in the same direction as everyone else and took off over the English Channel. Clark was part of Yellow Flight. The flight commander, Yellow One, was a Canadian called Freddie Green. Clark was Yellow Two. They crossed the Channel at zero altitude and began climbing once on the other side. Soon Clark was to experience the thrill of seeing tiny little Focke-Wulfs and Messerschmitts taxiing on a runway thousands of feet below. Yellow One peeled off to attack. Clark, as Yellow Two, followed. Yellow Three and Four were so taken by surprise by this sudden movement that they lost touch with their leading officers. Clark and his Canadian leader would soon find themselves perilously alone among the pack of German Focke-Wulf 190s.

The two aircraft swept low over the enemy as the Germans began to take off. One was hit, but when Yellow One realised the size of the force they were up against, he pulled the throttle back on his machine and headed away as quickly as the emergency power booster in the Spitfire would allow. Unfortunately, Clark's machine did not appear to have been quite so finely tuned. He watched in alarm as his leader disappeared into the distance, the Focke-Wulfs steadily gaining air space on him. He was heading for the sea only 50 feet above the ground at top speed when one of the German aircraft shot up his left wing. None of his companions were in sight and Clark began a fight for his life, twisting and looping with the Focke-Wulfs in hot pursuit. At one stage he performed a 180-degree turn to confront two of them head on, their guns blasting at one another as they whisked passed. Eventually he found no less than four of them on his tail roaring across the Channel only feet above the water. Clark performed another 180-degree turn and blasted his guns into the pursuing aircraft, which, caught suddenly by surprise, broke away and headed for home.

Relieved, and a little surprised at his own combat skills, Clark did the same, skirting just above the waves. Shortly afterwards, however, with his engine failing, he spotted what he took to be the coast of England and, clearing the cliffs, performed a rough crash-landing. His trials had left him hopelessly disorientated. He was not in England but France. Soon after clambering out of the cockpit, bruised and shaken, he was greeted by German soldiers from a nearby gun emplacement. Clark would spend the rest of his war in captivity.

That evening Clark was taken for a convivial supper at the Luftwaffe Officers' Club in St-Omer. He was interviewed by several fighter pilots who had been involved in the skirmish earlier in the day. Clark concluded they were mainly interested in finding out which one of them had shot him down. (To this day, Clark has not discovered the answer, though he was amused in the late 1990s to be provided with photographs of his downed aircraft that he had never seen before.) Thereafter, via a circuitous route across France and Belgium, he arrived at Dulag Luft. The authorities at Dulag Luft were puzzled as to why an American colonel had been flying an RAF Spitfire. They kept him there for a month before sending him to the new Luftwaffe prisoner facility at Sagan: Stalag Luft III.

Clark's first impressions of Stalag Luft III were typical. 'Barbed wire, grey huts, single-storey prefabricated huts and guardtowers. And everything was grey, even the dust that hung over the camp. We could hear the busy sounds of the train station, and the marshalling yards, but otherwise you were left feeling very isolated.'

Clark's arrival, as the first American inmate

of Stalag Luft III, was also to produce signs of a slight but significant rift between the way the British and Americans approached captivity. Many of the early British POWs came from public schools and some had quite distinguished aristocratic pedigrees— with attitudes to match. There was a great deal of senseless 'goon baiting'.

'You saw a great deal of courage among the British officers in the way they faced up to the Germans,' says Clark. 'But sometimes it was more trouble than it was worth. Some officers that came into the camp were shocked, literally shocked, to see any relationship at all, let alone a friendly one, between the officers and the Germans. But you couldn't run a camp without people bringing in food and taking away the garbage. We needed the Germans' goodwill. One day Wing Commander Bader gave a speech at roll-call to say there was to be no more fraternising with the enemy. Well, the Germans just threw him out into a punishment camp and we never saw him again.'

Wing Commander Douglas Bader, of course, was famously legless, having lost both his limbs in a foolish flying stunt that went wrong. Since then he had flown with a pair of artificial legs and when his plane was hit over enemy territory he discovered the legs were jammed in the cockpit. So he simply unstrapped them and baled out. He was soon in captivity. The Germans had, in their view generously, allowed an RAF plane safe passage to drop a new pair of legs for Bader. Yet despite this, the RAF man had been a continual thorn in the side of his captors. One day von Lindeiner had told Bader he was forcibly removing him to Lamsdorf Medical Compound, where he would get better medical care and attention. Equally forcibly, Bader refused to go and threatened to throw himself in the fire pool. The Kommandant sent a troop of heavily armed guards into the compound to remove him. A baying crowd gathered around. In the end the Wing Commander was escorted out of the camp by two columns of armed guards. Shortly afterwards, Bader escaped from Lamsdorf only to be recaptured and dispatched to Colditz.

This marked difference in attitudes to the Germans continued. Generally, the Americans presented themselves for Appell in an orderly fashion. The British on the other hand made virtually every roll-call a nightmare for the goons, messing one another around in conspicuous displays of horseplay, and moving around, making it impossible for the Germans to count. It meant that the men had to stand out for twice as long as the Americans, or sometimes more, and only achieved anything when they needed to disguise the absence of an escaper—but their behaviour gave the game away anyway. It is hard not to agree with

Clark's prognosis that much of the British officers' 'goon baiting' was little more than juvenile public-school delinquency. Their defenders might claim that many of them were, actually, only just out of school. But the same applied to the American fliers, most of whom seemed to display a more mature and sympathetic approach to their enemies.

*   *   *

Later, in that autumn, Paul Royle began a tunnel identical in design to Muckle Muir's, pushing out towards the wire from barrack block 68, almost parallel to the other effort. And at about the same time there was a daring escape attempt that was to earn the commendation of Colonel von Lindeiner. Two officers had noticed a 'blind spot' in the perimeter fences created by the positioning of the watchtowers. Ken Toft and William 'Red' Nichols realised that the razor wire in between was so dense that they could probably cut their way through it without being seen. The Escape Committee agreed, provided the men with false papers, and organised a boxing match to act as a distraction while the two men set about their task. In fact they were seen by one of the guards—but only as they ran towards the fir trees in the distance. For whatever reason the guard failed to shoot to stop them and Toft and Nichols were free, for the moment at least. Sadly for them they were later caught when an official questioned their papers. They were returned to Stalag Luft III where Toft, an Irishman, and Nichols, an American serving in one of the RAF Eagle squadrons, were surprised to be presented by the Kommandant with a bottle of whisky in recognition of their daring.

Many of the escapers were not convinced that it would be possible to build a successful tunnel out of one of the barrack blocks. And with that in mind some of them revived an idea that was first mooted at Barth. This was to find a patch of land close to the wire from where it would be possible to dig a tunnel, the digging and the trap-door somehow or other hidden from view.

During that first summer at Sagan, the first of several of these 'mole' attempts were made, but by far the most successful was proposed by two crewmates, Bill Goldfinch and Henry Lamond, a New Zealander. With a third member of the team, Jack Best, they put the idea up to the Escape Committee. The biggest obstacle was finding a place close enough to the wire. The prisoners' solution was to deliberately flood the wash hut and complain to the Germans that the drainage system was not adequate. The Germans knew the problem had to be resolved quickly because pools of stagnant water were fertile breeding grounds for typhus. When the officers confronted

Pieber with the problem he was perplexed and concerned, but not prepared to release his own men from guard duty to dig drainage ditches. Instead, he agreed to Wings Day's request to give the prisoners the tools to do the job themselves, warning them, before they began, that he had carefully counted the number of shovels issued. The prisoners set about digging a deep ditch to soak away the water.

The digging went on for some days in a casual sort of fashion intended to convince the Germans of the prisoners' innocent motivations. Finally, Best, Goldfinch and Lamond began digging a narrow tunnel from the end of the ditch, about two feet beneath the surface, and aiming to go under the wire equidistant between two seismograph microphones. It took several days of clandestine activity before the tunnel had stretched 50 feet and was close enough to the wire for the mole attempt to begin. On the night of 21 June, after Appell, the three officers were sealed into the tunnel by their comrades and the drainage ditch was filled with water. All they had to breathe through were three narrow airholes. After the camp was closed at 10 p.m. they began moling their way towards the fence. Goldfinch was the front man who scraped away the sand with a coal shovel, passing it back to Lamond, who scooped it behind him to Best, who packed the sand as tightly as he could behind him. In this fashion they crept forward painfully slowly. They managed to tunnel 25 feet that night before stopping for fear of being heard. It was an uncomfortable night for men completely entombed in darkness.

The following day the men managed to survive beneath the surface for the remainder of the day without alerting the guards to their presence, tunnelling a further 75 feet. By nightfall they calculated they were now comfortably beyond the wire, and decided to break through to the surface in the early morning. Their comrades watching from the barrack blocks were anxious to note that their position beneath the ground was betrayed by three columns of steam, which could clearly be seen rising from the airholes. In the middle of the night they broke through the surface and made good their escape. Goldfinch and company were at large for five days and finally reached the Oder, where they stole a boat and planned to sail towards the Baltic. They were only recaptured when the boat's irate owner tracked them down and reported them to the police. Thus ended one of the most audacious and courageous escape attempts of the war. Goldfinch and Best were promptly sent to Colditz. Lamond was returned to Sagan.

Their success led to many similar 'mole' attempts, some more successful than others. The Germans became so alarmed at this outbreak of digging activity that the senior

Abwehr officer, Major Peschel, decreed a 'moat' should be dug around the entire compound to deter such attempts. The moat would be deep enough to prevent moling efforts. For two weeks of the scorching-hot summer, his men dug the moat eight feet deep and three feet wide. But the moat, which became known as 'Peschel's Folly', only encouraged more moling attempts. Because it was so deep, the sentries in the goon boxes had no way of seeing if anyone was hidden at the bottom of the moat. In one instance, several prisoners therefore hid there before the camp closed and dug their way under the wire after nightfall. The attempt failed, but towards the end of the summer the Germans realised their folly. The moat was refilled with sand.

A new arrival at Stalag Luft III that late summer was a Norwegian RAF officer, Per Bergsland, who went under the assumed name of Peter Rockland. Bergsland had seen the horrors of Nazism first hand. As a student in Germany in 1938 he protested at the burning of synagogues and the treatment of Jews. For his pains he was expelled from his college and returned to Oslo. At the outbreak of war with Germany he joined the Norwegian Army and after the brief campaign escaped across the North Sea to Scotland. He transferred to the RAF and was sent for training at Little Norway in Toronto, Canada, returning to England in 1942, where he was posted to

332 Spitfire Squadron. He was enrolled as 'Peter Rockland' to protect his family in Oslo should he ever be taken prisoner—a fate that was to befall him all too quickly. He was shot down by an FW 190 over Dieppe in August 1942. Under interrogation at Dulag Luft, Bergsland stuck to his story that he was an English flier called Peter Rockland, and that his family had been killed in the Blitz in London. Shortly thereafter he was sent to Stalag Luft III. There he met Jens Einar Muller, another Norwegian flier, who was shot down on 19 June 1942, flying with the RAF's 331 Squadron. He had arrived at Sagan in June. The two men were to become important contributors to the X-Organisation and with Bob van der Stok would earn themselves a unique part in the history of the Great Escape.

A week after Peschel's Folly was destroyed, his men were tearing the side panels of Block 68 to discover the piles of sand from Muckle Muir's tunnel. It didn't take the Germans long to work their way back along the tunnel and discover the deeper one. By that stage the prisoners had completed an astonishing 300 feet of tunnelling. The Germans were amazed at the size and complexity of the operation, simply not believing such a sophisticated tunnel was possible. After they found it they collapsed the tunnel by flooding it with water from the fire hoses, but only after they had photographed it for their records. One

118

fortunate aspect of the whole debacle was that the Germans had not discovered the other tunnel being dug from under Block 68 and started by Paul Royle, which was making good progress towards the wire. Nevertheless the Escape Committee was forced to consider other alternatives as well. It became obvious that the entrances to tunnels needed to be concealed more ingeniously. And the possibility of starting a tunnel in the open needed to be explored.

*   *   *

That October arrived one of the most important future members of the X-Organisation. George Harsh was another remarkable American who was to play a key role in the true story of the Great Escape. Harsh was another young man from a wealthy and well-connected American family. His father had left him $500,000 in the late 1920s—an enormous fortune in those times. But in 1929 Harsh had shot and killed a young grocery store attendant in his home town of Atlanta. Harsh would be the first to admit that he was a spoilt, bored young man. He had planned with a group of four other wealthy friends to hold up the store for the sheer thrill of it. They wondered if it was possible to commit the perfect crime. Harsh had not intended to use the heavy Colt .45 that he was brandishing in his hand when he entered the store shouting, 'This is a stick-up: open the till!', but he didn't count on his victim also being armed. What happened next is open to dispute. Harsh always insisted that the attendant fired first, diving behind the counter as he did so. Harsh was hit in the groin and said he instinctively shot back. Whether this was the correct sequence of events or not is academic in a sense because Harsh was eventually to go on to pay for his crime and redeem himself morally. The immediate effect, however, was that he was injured and his victim would shortly be dead from his wounds.

Harsh did not hand himself over to the authorities and would have got away with the murder had not the maid at his friend's house discovered his discarded bloodstained clothes with a bullet hole in them. Harsh and his main co-conspirator, the son of a well-known newspaper proprietor, were sent to trial. 'Two Atlanta Students Confess They Entered Crime for Thrills', screeched the newspaper headlines. It took the jury 15 minutes to sentence them both to death—with no recommendation for mercy on their youthful souls. It was only after both families spent the equivalent of millions in today's terms on a legal challenge that the sentences were both adjusted to life imprisonment. Harsh soon found himself on a chain gang with, amongst others for companions, a Cherokee Indian and a defrocked Jesuit priest.

There, Harsh's life may very well have come to an ignominious end had it not been for two episodes on his road to redemption. In the first, two prisoners overcame the chain-gang boss, killed him in cold blood, and escaped. Harsh and his companions did not join them. When it came to giving an account of what had happened, his description of the horrors of chain-gang life encouraged the authorities (under scrutiny of the national media) to transfer Harsh to a conventional prison. There he became an orderly in the prison hospital. One day, a 60-year-old black prisoner was admitted with stomach pains. Harsh realised the man's appendix was about to rupture, but there was no doctor present, and a violent storm had rendered communications with the outside world impossible. The man would die within two hours if nothing was done. Harsh gulped down a glass of illegal brew and performed the operation himself. Had it failed, the patient would undoubtedly have died. As it was, the man lived. Soon after the Governor pardoned George Harsh.

Harsh had been incarcerated for 12 years. The Governor pronounced: 'This man has served 12 years in prison for taking a human life. By his recent actions he has restored a human life. To my mind the scales have been balanced.' Perhaps to his mind, but maybe not

Harsh's. The death of that young store assistant still weighed heavily upon his shoulders. It was approaching the winter of 1940. Harsh now took the next step on his road to redemption. The United States was not yet at war with Germany, but many Americans were travelling north of the border to Canada to volunteer to fight Hitler in one of the branches of the Commonwealth armed forces. At the RAF recruiting office in Montreal a young British officer asked Harsh what branch of the aircrew he would like to serve in. 'Air gunner,' he replied, knowing that the role of rear air gunner was the most dangerous position in a bomber aircraft. It was also the answer that would get him to England most quickly. After three months of training at the Royal Canadian Air Force Aerial Gunnery School in Ontario, Harsh passed out with flying colours. By joining the RCAF he had to forfeit his United States citizenship. When he was finally commissioned the hairs on the back of his neck must have bristled slightly when he made his declaration of allegiance to George VI: the King of England, Ireland, Scotland; the Dominions beyond the Seas, and Defender of the Faith. Shortly thereafter Harsh was in England, squadron gunnery officer of 102 Squadron, 4 Group.

George Harsh wrote his own account of his remarkable odyssey from a spoilt kid murderer to one of the leading lights in the Great

Escape. *Lonesome Road* contains some of the best passages of any book describing aerial warfare, and particularly the perilous role of a rear gunner—or Tail-End Charlie as they were known. How Harsh survived almost two years of operational flying is a small miracle. His luck finally ran out on the night of 5 October 1942 when the Halifax bomber he was in was shot down over Cologne. Harsh baled out, not in the most graceful of jumps, and felt as if his rib cage had collapsed in the process. As it was, he landed with a thump, on the ground, only to be bemused to be greeted by cheerful German captors who seemed to find his ordeal unaccountably hilarious. He was offered Cognac by a Wehrmacht major who said that the best consequence of invading France was that the brandy got better. Shortly afterwards Harsh was sent to a hospital in Cologne run by Roman Catholic Sisters of Mercy. His time there was almost as hazardous as it had been in the air. The German officer in charge of the hospital refused to allow him to shelter in the basement during air raids. In compassion, one of the Catholic nuns gallantly stayed holding his hands by his bedside as the bombs crashed down in the city. He survived, though not without being given a taste of the fear Allied bombing raids were bringing to cities all over Germany. When he was deemed fit, Harsh found himself on his way to Dulag Luft.

Harsh's own account of his journey across

Germany illustrates the strange ambiguities that war can create. His guard was a young Luftwaffe soldier called Adolf. Their route was by rail. In a crowded railway station Adolf was suddenly overcome by an attack of diarrhoea. The platform and waiting room was heaving with Wehrmacht and SS. In a blind panic Adolf ran for the toilet and in the process, inexplicably, took off his holster and Luger pistol, which he handed to Harsh. The surrounding German soldiers looked balefully at the man in the RAF uniform as he stood among them cradling the lethal weapon with a vaguely embarrassed look on his face. But nobody said, or did, a thing. After Adolf returned, with a look of relief etched across his features, Harsh handed him back his weapon and the two continued on their journey to Frankfurt. They found themselves in a compartment with soldiers on leave from the Russian front. They felt nothing but sympathy for the injured Allied officer and shared their schnapps with him. In gratitude and genuine friendship, Harsh joined in as they burst into several boisterous renditions of the Nazi 'Horst Wessel' song. Eventually, Harsh arrived at Dulag Luft. His stay was brief, and he would shortly become one of the first prisoners to occupy Stalag Luft III.

*   *   *

With the Allied officers' appetite for escape clearly undiminished, the Luftwaffe quickly began to realise that putting all the rotten eggs in one basket might not have been such a bright idea after all. In response it decided to send some of the prisoners to a different camp. In November 1942 a consignment of officers was sent to Oflag XXI B, an army camp at Szubin in north-east Poland. Among the men selected to go were some of the most persistent escapers: Jimmy Buckley, Dick Churchill, Peter Fanshawe. Jimmy James was also one of them and accepted the decree with his usual equanimity, reflecting that a change of scenery was as good as a rest. Wings Day wasn't on the list but asked if he could go because so many of the men were his friends. Johnny Dodge also found himself on the train heading east, from which he chose a quiet moment to alight illicitly. He was soon afterwards being escorted back to his companions. 'No harm in trying,' he said as the German guards bundled him back onto the train.

As James had hoped, Oflag XXI B offered a change from the ubiquitous wooden barrack buildings of Sagan and Barth. Situated on the gentle slopes over Szubin, it consisted of brick-built barracks, a large white house that was a former girls' school and a chapel and other buildings interspersed with small gardens and allotments. At Szubin the RAF prisoners found themselves in the company of many British Army officers from the camp at Warburg, including the future author and broadcaster Robert Kee, and the future British Chancellor of the Exchequer Anthony Barber. The army officers had their own distinctive ways of going about the business of escaping. One method they adopted was to employ four teams of ten escapers, each equipped with scaling ladders. The men blew the electricity supply, plunging the camp into darkness. They then hastily stormed the wire with military precision. The idea was that they would climb over and run for it. This had proved a successful tactic at Warburg, from where a couple of dozen officers had escaped, two making it all the way back to Britain. But unfortunately, when it was attempted at Szubin, the Germans quickly turned on their emergency electricity supply. The officers hastily beat a retreat.

Shortly afterwards some American aircrew arrived under the command of the Senior American Officer (SAO), Colonel Charles 'Roho' Goodrich, a West Point graduate. Goodrich was a stocky young man of medium build with wiry red hair. At 35 he was actually senior to Wings Day, but was happy to allow the British officer to remain as camp leader because he recognised that the British were far more experienced in camp administration and clandestine activities. The two became close confidants and Wings was to let Roho in on every aspect of British escape activity.

*   *   *

In the absence of much of the X-Organisation the prisoners of Stalag Luft III had not embarked on any ambitious plans, but individual escape attempts continued unfettered. Two prisoners, Des Plunkett and Ivo Tonder, tried to get out by burying themselves under a heap of garbage that was taken out of the camp in a dustcart. Bob Ker-Ramsay had helped bury them under an enormous heap—and it proved to be an insurmountable heap of garbage indeed. The two men couldn't budge inside without causing a cascade of tins and cans to come crashing down around them. Deciding to give themselves up they threw caution to the wind and pushed and punched their way out, causing a disturbance that they thought would wake the whole camp. They were astonished to discover that nobody seemed to have heard and decided to try the stunt one more time, asking Ker-Ramsay to cover them with slightly less rubbish this time. This he did, all too successfully, because when a couple of guards came along and threw a load of hot ash over the garbage it didn't take long for the two figures of Tonder and Plunkett to emerge, desperately patting the smoke off their clothes.

Oddly, once more none of the German guards seemed to notice.

A young South American officer attempted a more successful reprise of Toft and Nichols's 'blind spot' escape. The goons had attempted to reconfigure the positions of their towers to eliminate the blind spots, but in closing down some they merely created more. Buenos Aires-born Flying Officer John Stower had only just arrived in Stalag Luft III in November, but volunteered immediately to try and break out. He managed to get through the perimeter fence, but when a guard spotted him he stumbled and hit the ground, probably saving his life in the event. Sydney Dowse and Danny Krol teamed up for a wire bid that ended almost as soon as it began and were promptly sent off to the cooler. It was not the most auspicious way to begin the festive season.

*   *   *

That Christmas the airmen at Szubin were delighted to find themselves recipients of season's greetings from Buckingham Palace in the form of a card from the King and Queen with photographs of them and the young princesses. Although this raised their morale a little and impressed the Germans, the airmen were disconcerted to find themselves under the command of a Wehrmacht colonel who did not share the Luftwaffe's chivalrous sentiments towards his charges. On one occasion Wings Day was made to stand to attention while addressing him, even though he reminded him that they were of comparable rank. So irritated was he by the officious nature of the new regime that Wings made an uncharacteristically harsh address to his men that New Year.

> You are aware that it is everybody's duty to escape if possible. I have been accustomed to polite and correct treatment by Luftwaffe Kommandants. Here I have not received that courtesy, in fact this Wehrmacht Kommandant has been damned rude to me. He hopes to retire as a General. He won't. I intend to get people out in large numbers. So get busy. Happy escaping and Happy New Year.

They had the tacit endorsement of Feldwebel Glemnitz who had accompanied them from Sagan. He too had been treated less than respectfully by the German Army personnel. Glemnitz told the airmen: 'These Army Dummköpfe—they know nothing, so I tell you escape!'

Shortly afterwards one officer was shot in cold blood as he attempted to climb the fence. Flight Lieutenant Edwards had had enough.

He made his attempt in full view of the guard, who shouted at him to stop. He continued regardless and was the recipient of an entirely unnecessary and fatal burst of machine-gun fire. The brutality shocked the men and hardened their attitude towards their German Army captors. It was at Szubin, also, that the RAF men first began to get some inkling of what was happening to Europe's Jewish population under Nazi tyranny. Jimmy James recalled seeing a party of Polish Jews press-ganged into working for the Germans. They were treated pitilessly, he noted, the women forced to urinate in full view of the guards. Little did James realise then that before the war's end he himself would be incarcerated with the wretched victims of Himmler's death camps and witness the barbarity of the Nazi regime first hand.

Jimmy James and Charles Bonnington were among some of the first to have staked their claim to a tunnel in Szubin. It departed from the uncongenial surroundings of the latrines, and their digging was not a pleasant business. There were several other tunnels being built at the same time. Jimmy James's tunnel eventually had to be abandoned. Instead, it was another tunnel from another latrine that bore fruit. The entrance was through one of the lavatory seats (which the prisoners reasoned, rightly as it proved, the Germans would hesitate to inspect) that led to a trap in a brick wall. Beyond was one of the most sophisticated tunnels yet constructed, with boarding, ventilation and a workshop. It took most of the winter to complete and was eventually some 150 feet long. It reached a depth of 17 feet to avoid seismographs.

In February 1943 the prisoners heard a rumour that the Air Force contingent was going to be transferred back to Sagan. Not wanting to see their efforts go to waste, they decided to break out on the next moonless period, which was in March. On the afternoon of the break, the escapers descended into the tunnel, where they would have to wait for four hours between Appell at 5 p.m. and lock-up at 9 p.m. It was estimated that 33 could be kept down the tunnel for such a length of time without suffocating, but it was a horrendous experience for those who were chosen for the task. For several hours they had to breathe in one another's air, the only ventilation coming from an air pump that sucked air from the latrines above. Among them were Jimmy Buckley, Wings Day, Anthony Barber, Robert Kee and Danny Krol. Soon after 9 p.m. the tunnel broke through and, one by one, the men quietly edged their way out. Remarkably, it was not discovered the next day as they had expected it would be. In all, 34 men got out, after a South African, not with the original 33, decided to take a chance when he realised the Germans still had not found the tunnel.

The security staff at Szubin were mortified. More than 300,000 Germans were tied up looking for the escapers over the next two weeks. One by one they were returned, except Buckley, who disappeared without trace. He had been with a Danish naval officer who had attempted to escape from Copenhagen to Sweden in a small boat. The Dane's body was recovered off Copenhagen but not Buckley's. It was speculated that he had been run over by a larger vessel.

This escape attempt was enormously embarrassing to the Germans and would prove a forerunner to the Great Escape. It was the first that attracted the protracted attention of the Sicherheitsdienst (SD), the intelligence section of the Gestapo. Many of the Wehrmacht officers were court-martialled. The Germans decided that it was time to bring the prisoners' Polish interlude to an end. In April 1943, all 800 air force prisoners of Oflag XXI B were evacuated to Stalag Luft III.

As a footnote to the Polish interlude, it should be recorded that the only escape that had been successful from Szubin was by an NCO. Sergeant P.T. Wareing slipped away from his guards on an outing to collect bread from Szubin railway station. He walked and cycled his way to Danzig and smuggled himself on a coal ship to Halmstad, Sweden, arriving Christmas 1942.

When they arrived back in Stalag Luft III the POWs were amazed at how much the camp had expanded in such a short period of time. While they had been away scores more prisoners had arrived at Sagan, many of them Americans. The returning Kriegies discovered that rooms were accommodating twice as many prisoners as they had been designed for. The Germans were busy at work building another compound to accommodate them. The new compound was on the other side of the Kommandantur. In March 1943 the North Compound, as it was called, was finally completed. It was larger than the East and Centre Compounds put together, being almost a mile in circumference. It was also considerably more comfortable. The barrack blocks contained not only kitchens, but washrooms and lavatories that flushed.

The Germans gave the Allied prisoners the opportunity to work on the construction of the new compound. The prisoners took the opportunity to thoroughly chart the dimensions of their future home—the drainage systems and so forth. They also used the opportunity to acquire clandestine materials. In April 1943, 850 prisoners were transferred from the East Compound to the new North Compound.

Among the new American arrivals was

David Jones, who joined the United States Air Force shortly after graduating from the University of Texas. He was assigned to a bomber-attack group and spent the months before the war practising manoeuvres over the desert. After Pearl Harbor, Jones volunteered for a highly secretive and dangerous mission, in which his commanding officer would be Colonel Jimmy Doolittle. The plan was to deliver a psychologically wounding blow to the Japanese that would equal the effect of their unprovoked attack on the American Pacific Fleet based at Hawaii. Four squadrons of B-25 bombers, 16 planes in all, would be taken across the Pacific on board the aircraft carrier *Hornet*. Some 650 miles from the Japanese coast they would take off and head for Tokyo, where they were to deliver their devastating surprise to the capital city below. There was only one problem: after completing their mission there was no way aircraft the size of B-25s could land back on the deck of an aircraft carrier. Instead they would just have to find somewhere to land in China—in uncharted territory, in the dark.

The *Hornet* set sail on 1 April 1942, accompanied by two other carriers and eight destroyers. The plan was to attack Tokyo late on 18 April, but very early in the morning of that day the carrier was spotted and engaged by a Japanese ship. Doolittle gave the order for the B-25s to take off straightaway. They were more than 800 miles from the Japanese mainland and consequently hadn't a chance of getting to China after their mission. Jones managed to find Tokyo and drop his B-25's load. By a stroke of fortune the aircraft picked up a strong tail-wind on the way back and reached the coastline of China. However, in the dying light it was only possible to discern mountains below so Jones gave the order for his crew to bale out. Thus began an adventure amid the exotic charms of the Chinese backwoods that ended in Jones and one of his crew being welcomed as heroes by the mayor of a small town. The local citizenry had heard of the Doolittle raid on the radio. More than 5,000 people turned out to cheer Jones and his comrades, who were soon on their way back to the States.

Jones was promoted from captain to major and dispatched to continue his war in England. In November 1942 he arrived in Tunisia to support the invasion of North Africa. Shortly afterwards, while making a low-level attack on German positions, Jones was brought down. He was delivered to the Luftwaffe desert base, where his host was a dashing young commander sporting an Iron Cross. The other German pilots were soon engaging him in friendly banter before Jones found himself being taken to the Nazi heartland itself. He arrived in Stalag Luft III in January 1943. He was greeted by Bub Clark, then still the SAO

(Clark was replaced a couple of months later, however, when Roho Goodrich arrived from Barth). David Jones would become one of the hardest and most persistent diggers in Stalag Luft III. But it was at a time when the business of escaping was becoming a much more perilous affair.

In April 1943, the High Command issued an order that stated:

> Each POW has to be informed that by escaping in civilian clothing or German uniform he is not only liable to disciplinary punishment but runs the risk of being court-martialled and committed for trial on suspicion of espionage and partisanship, in the affirmative he may even be sentenced to death.

Later that year, von Lindeiner felt compelled to write to the senior officers of all the compounds, clarifying the grounds on which a POW might be court-martialled by the German authorities. They included wearing civilian clothes or a German uniform. (Although, despite a common misconception, the Geneva Convention did not forbid officers escaping disguised in the enemy's uniform.) But von Lindeiner wrote that even the theft of bed boards for tunnel making would be regarded as damaging to the German war effort and therefore liable to court-martial. Indeed, so all-encompassing was the order that virtually everybody engaged in any form of escape activity, no matter how far removed, could have been, theoretically, dragged before a German court martial.

CHAPTER FOUR

TOM, DICK AND HARRY

By now the Luftwaffe had decided that Stalag Luft III would be an officer-only prison camp. As a result, that spring the NCOs were moved out to their own camp. Colonel von Lindeiner believed that if he made the new North Compound as comfortable as possible, the prisoners would be quite content to sit out the war in peace. Consequently, he indulged them in a manner that his superiors in Berlin found irritating but many of the Allies appreciated. Indeed, the opening of the North Compound was later referred to by some as the beginning of 'the Golden Era' of Stalag Luft III's history. There was more space, more food, more recreational and athletic activity than ever before. Against the advice of his security staff, von Lindeiner allowed some trees to remain in the space separating the compound and the Kommandantur and he gave the prisoners permission to build their own theatre—which they did, using excess timber donated by the Germans and old Red Cross boxes. Over the forthcoming year the theatre was to stage everything from *Hamlet* and *A Midsummer Night's Dream* to *The Importance of Being Earnest* and *The Man Who Came to Dinner*.

Besides von Lindeiner's natural decency, one reason for his generosity was that he had been lulled into a feeling that the prisoners were giving up on their attempts to escape. This was in part due to Roger Bushell taking Wings Day's advice and toning down escape activity for the last few months of 1942 and early 1943. So convinced of the prisoners' goodwill was the Kommandant that he allowed them to go over to the nascent compound in the months before it was built. The result was that the prisoners had plenty of time to make sure their various escape materials could be transferred to the new compound. They had time to plan and execute the dismantling of the radio which they had constructed out of stolen valves, wire and batteries. And they had time to plan the next new escape. Prisoners began trickling over to the new compound in late March. Von Lindeiner may not have realised that he chose an ominous date for the main move of the prisoners into the North Compound: 1 April.

Even before they moved in, the prisoners were hatching plans for a mass break-out of the North Compound. Before Jimmy Buckley had been transferred to Szubin, and Wings Day with him, the then SBO appointed Roger Bushell 'Big X', the chairman of the Escape Committee. It was not entirely true, as some have claimed, that Roger Bushell was entirely indifferent to the Gestapo's threats. 'He

139

thought very carefully about it,' recalls Bub Clark, who messed with Bushell for a while. 'It was only after a great deal of consideration that he agreed to take on escape duties once more.' But it is true to say that Bushell was hellbent on causing the Germans as much aggravation as possible. 'He had some very radical ideas about escape. His dream was a massive escape. Whether they all got home or not, he didn't care. The idea was to cause as much disruption to the German war effort as possible.'

Bushell's appointment marked a new beginning for the X-Organisation. Gone would be the amateurish attempts of the past and the foolish risks of the gentleman escapers; from now on the business of escape would be treated as a professional undertaking that evaluated every plan carefully and executed each one with meticulous attention to detail. From now on the Escape Committee would be dominated by 'the big four' overseeing the key aspects of escaping. Bushell was in overall command of planning and strategy. Peter Fanshawe was responsible for the onerous task of dispersing hundreds of tons of sand. Wally Floody was in charge of tunnelling. And Bub Clark was 'Big S'—responsible for creating a watertight security operation that would keep all these activities a secret from the goons.

Under Bushell's leadership, the Escape Committee quickly came to three important decisions that were to govern future break-outs. First, every escape would be conducted under the auspices of the committee. In the past the committee had merely approved and authorised various escape plans, making sure they didn't clash with others and offering the escapers any help or advice they could. From now on there would be no more 'freelance' operations. The committee would approve, authorise and control each escape.

Second, it was decided that the main emphasis of escape activity would be on tunnels and the tunnels would be as large and sophisticated as possible. In the past there had been too many tunnels compromised by shoddy workmanship, or given away through lack of security. One barrack block had actually sunk into its foundations because there were so many tunnels running underneath it. From now on the security operation would be watertight and X-Organisation would be run with military efficiency. Sand dispersal, which in the past had so often given away tunnel activity and led to blanket searches by the goons, would now be a carefully controlled operation.

The escape organisation would start building three tunnels that would be minor feats of engineering genius. The plan was for the tunnels to be sunk 25 feet down to evade the ring of seismographs the ferrets had constructed around the compound. They would be built to the standards of industrial

141

mining shafts with ventilation pipes, air pumps, trolleys and electricity diverted from the compound supply. Bushell was not worried if one of the tunnels was to be found. The Germans would be so impressed by what they found they wouldn't believe it was possible similar structures could simultaneously exist.

Finally, the direction of each tunnel was decided in advance. In this respect the prisoners had very little choice. The Kommandantur was situated directly to the east of the North Compound (behind the thicket of trees von Lindeiner had kindly agreed to keep) and beyond that were the Centre and East compounds. It would be far too dangerous going underneath the Germans. And the distance before the tunnel reached the cover of the woods was too great. A similar problem existed to the south. The South Compound had yet to be built, but there already existed a sports field and, again, the woods were many hundreds of yards beyond that. The tunnels would have to go west and north. The Escape Committee decided on both directions. Two tunnels would go west, the most direct route out of the camp. One would start in Block 123 close to the wire. Another from Block 122 next to 123 and a little nearer the centre of the North Compound. The last tunnel would go north directly under the parcel store and cooler from Block 104. So that no mention of the word 'tunnel' would alert the Germans, each was given a name: Tom, Dick and Harry, respectively. If Colonel von Lindeiner did not realise that 1 April was April Fools' Day in Britain, it was unlikely he understood the waspish connotations of 'Tom, Dick and Harry' either.

Ironically, von Lindeiner's concern for the comfort of his charges produced the circumstances that allowed the prisoners to hide the entrances to their tunnels. The new compound was indeed luxurious compared to the old one. In the East Compound the prisoners had to walk in fair weather or foul to the communal washroom and latrine blocks. In the North Compound each block boasted its own toilets, washing and basic cooking facilities. As in the old compound, each barrack block was raised off the ground on stilts. But the new blocks had at least a small section of solid brick and concrete work beneath the new domestic facilities. The ferrets and their dogs could look under the blocks as much as they liked, but they would never be able to see what was going on inside the concrete and cement. The Germans presumably thought that it would be impossible to conceal a tunnel entrance in the smooth concrete base of the showers and beneath the stoves. They were wrong.

The trap entrances to each tunnel were ingenious. They had to be because in one respect the Germans were right: it is difficult to hide a hole in a smooth concrete surface. The task of concealing the entrances was given to a group of Polish RAF officers who were skilled engineers. They were equipped with the best tools that had been scavenged and pilfered over the previous months and they were blessed with the easy availability of cement, which was in ample supply thanks to the numerous repair and construction jobs that needed to be done almost every day. The contribution of these Polish officers to the tunnel operation cannot be underestimated. Without their skill and ingenuity it is unlikely the tunnels would ever have got beyond the drawing board.

The tunnel entrance in Tom was situated in a passageway in the Polish officers' barracks near the kitchen. It was probably the most audacious of all the entrances, because it was situated in an area that the German guards would walk over regularly. It had to be constructed with such precision that no hollow sounds or cracks betrayed its existence there in front of the eyes of anyone who cared to look. It consisted of an 18-inch square hole in the concrete floor, just wide enough for a man to descend into. The hole was disguised by a square slab of concrete in a wooden frame constructed to be the same size as the hole to within a fraction of an inch. The wooden frame allowed two wire handles to be attached either side. These handles would lie beneath the surface, but could be lifted up by the insertion of a specially designed knife into the minute crack surrounding the concrete slab. The crack was disguised by being pasted up with cement and having floor dust sprinkled around it. The Polish officers had completed their task with such precision that even they sometimes had difficulty locating the edges of the trap-door.

The tunnel entrance of Dick in Block 122 was also through a concrete base, but it was of an entirely different design to Tom's. It was constructed in the washroom, which had two washbasins on either side. The used water from these basins drained into two sides of a drainage sump in the middle of the room. The sump was eighteen inches square and about two feet deep. On its third side ran the waste-water pipe. The sump was usually half-full of waste water, offering a perfect disguise. The prisoners emptied the sump, and removed the fourth side that had no pipes attached to it. They replaced this with a concrete slab that could be moved up or down and was the entrance to the tunnel. When it was in place, a mixture of clay and cement rendered it watertight. The waste water that was thrown back in the sump rendered it virtually invisible to the enquiring eye.

The trap-door in Harry was beneath one of the stoves that was in the corner of every room. The cast-iron stoves stood on a tiled surface about four feet square. The tiles were laid on a flat cement surface that was part of a sturdy brick-and-concrete pile that descended into the sandy ground beneath Block 104. The engineers constructed the trap-door by removing the tiles one by one and replacing them on an identically sized concrete surface of their own construction. This concrete slab was designed like the one in Tom: surrounded by a sturdy wooden frame with wire handles that could be lifted out of the cracks either side with a knife and used to pull up the trap-door. It was hinged at the back and could be lifted into a vertical position. Before this could be done, of course, the heavy cast-iron stove had to be removed from the tiled surface. This was achieved using bed boards that had been crafted into lifting handles. The final precaution of the prisoners concerned the chimney pipe that led from the stove into a brick chimney on the wall. In the course of removing the stove the diggers would inevitably interrupt the flow of smoke. Hence a removable extension chimney pipe was built at an angle to the chimney so that smoke would continue to flow.

One of the biggest problems that needed to be overcome in constructing these entrances was disguising the noise of the cement being chipped away. The solution was provided in the form of Johnny Dodge, who held choir-singing practice whenever noisy work was under way (a role immortalised in the film of the Great Escape by the fictional Cavendish).

The constructions of these three trap-doors were minor feats of engineering in themselves. But what was equally impressive was the way the Polish engineers overcame the onerous conditions under which they had to build them. And while each trap was being engineered the prisoners ran the greatest risk of detection. However, once the trap-doors had been manufactured, a major obstacle had been overcome.

The next hurdle was to dig three shafts down 25 feet deep into the sandy soil beneath each block, cutting through, first, up to two feet of solid concrete and brickwork. There were three tunnelling teams. Wally Floody, as tunnel engineer in chief, was responsible for Harry; Ker-Ramsay and Harry Marshall took charge of Dick and Tom respectively.

The first priority was to create a shaft in each case that would have at its base three distinct chambers: one for a ventilation pump; one to house a workshop; and one to temporarily store the sand excavated. This last point was important because if the sand had to be taken out of the tunnels as the digging progressed, the entrances would have to be kept open, increasing the risk of detection. The diggers excavated at the rate of five feet a go. The tunnels were a uniform two feet square with on one side a cavity about six inches square that would accommodate the ventilation tube. When five feet of digging had been completed the walls were securely shored up with four wooden bunk-bedposts in each corner, attached to one another with cross pieces. Once they had been secured, the walls were lined with wooden bed boards, the last side being completed after the ventilation tube had been added. The ventilation tube was constructed by attaching used tin food cans to one another, with their tops and bottoms cut out. A ladder was also constructed on one side of each shaft. Each shaft had five of these segments, making them all 25 feet deep.

The three chambers at the base of the shafts were testimony to how serious Bushell was about these tunnels. The ventilation chamber consisted of two different-sized boxes. One of two feet square housed the pump—one of the most important innovations of Stalag Luft III. The men who designed the pumps were Bob Nelson, a Yorkshireman captured in North Africa in September 1942, and the Norwegian RAF flier Jens Muller. Their creation consisted of a simple rectangular structure made out of Red Cross boxes. Fitting snugly inside the box were the tubular bellows made from kitbags sewn together and reinforced with wire. These bellows could be pushed in and out with a large handle. Leather flaps acted as valves, drawing air in at one end and expelling it at the other. The intake pipe (made of Klim cans) snaked its way up the entry shaft through the ground above where it was camouflaged behind a ventilation brick. The exhaust pipe was attached to the ventilation ducts made of Klim cans along the tunnel. The prisoners had experimented with primitive kinds of ventilation pumps before, but Nelson and Muller's invention marked a new departure as far as reliability and capacity went. The machines were easy to use and install, and easy to repair. It meant that the diggers could now guarantee far longer working hours down the tunnel, in far more pleasant conditions.

Adjacent to the main chamber for the ventilation pump was another about four feet by four which gave the pump operator sufficient space to move backwards and forwards when he was operating the machine. The other two chambers had their sizes dictated by the dimensions of the double bunk beds on which they depended for their frames. They were both 5 ft 6 in. high, and 2 ft 9 in. wide. The storage room was a full six feet long and the workshop was three feet long. The dimensions of the storage room were enough to store the excavated sand from about 20 feet of tunnel.

*   *   *

While the digging was going on underground a much bigger operation was going on above. Construction and digging on this massive scale created all sorts of supply problems. The timber was acquired from Red Cross boxes and pilfering any supplies the prisoners could get their hands on in the compound. But the most consistent supply came from the boards underneath bunk beds. A 'levy' was raised on all the 2,000 beds in the compound, gradually increasing as the tunnelling progressed.

Peter Fanshawe quickly solved the problem of disposing of the enormous amount of sandy soil. Fanshawe devised an ingenious new system of what became known as 'penguins'. Inside their own trousers, the penguins would carry bags made out of sewn-up trouser-legs full of small amounts of sand. A string that led from their pockets to the bag pulled a pin that released the sand. The penguins simply ambled about the compound scuffing the sand into the surface.

At the same time, hundreds of prisoners were working in 'factories' all over the camp producing the myriad of escape material necessary once the men had got out. There was a tailoring department set up under Tommy Guest and Ivo Tonder, mainly manned by Czech and Polish RAF officers. The tailors produced civilian suits and German uniforms from the officers' own uniforms but also from new material acquired from tame goons, or simply stolen.

Tim Walenn was put in charge of the forgery department. Flight Lieutenant Gilbert William 'Tim' Walenn was a quiet but waggish young man who sported a bushy, ginger handlebar moustache that belied a sharp mind and uncompromising nature. He was barely 26 when he found himself in Sagan after falling into German hands when his RAF plane crashed near Rotterdam in the early hours of 10 September 1941. In civilian life Walenn had been a banker but fortunately for the escapers of Stalag Luft III he had started out as a graphic artist designing wallpapers and fabric for his uncle's design studio in London. Up until now, very few RAF escapers had embarked on their adventures with anything remotely resembling good forgeries of passbooks, railway tickets and so forth. But from now on the X-Organisation decided accurately produced forged documents were essential accoutrements to the escaper's survival kit. Walenn's graphic skills would prove to be extraordinarily useful in reproducing a panoply of forged papers that were required for passage around the Nazi heartland. They called the forgery department 'Dean & Dawson', after a well-known London travel agency. And over the following months Dean & Dawson would employ scores of prisoners producing intricately copied government passes and typewritten paperwork indistinguishable from the originals.

The task was an important one because of the Germans' obsession with documentation of all sorts. The ubiquitous Ausweise and vorläufiger Ausweise were passes and temporary passes respectively that had to be carried by every civilian, and it was almost impossible to get around Germany without one or the other. The light grey Kennkarte was another form of identity card. A carte d'identité would suffice for France. A Soldbuch was the pay book without which no German soldier could survive. A polizeiliche Bescheinigung was a police permit for foreign workers, of which there were some 6,000,000 in the Reich at the height of the war. An Urlaubsschein was also a pass for foreign workers: a temporary pass permitting leave. The Rückkehrschein was the pass a foreign worker needed to release him to return to his country, and a Dienstausweis was a brown card that granted a foreign worker permission to be on Wehrmacht property. This is just a handful of the dozens of passes and identity cards required as an everyday part of life in Hitler's Germany.

Some of these documents were complex affairs, often with intricate patterns woven into the paper and sometimes with ornate Gothic script. Others were more basic but most of them required patience and diligence to re-create and the best part of a month's work to produce for each individual item. These documents were reserved for the prisoners who had a very real chance of escaping, but Dean & Dawson also created other types of documents. Some were entirely fictitious passes, letters and forms that might nevertheless be impressive enough to convince some of the more dimwitted Reich officials. Simple, typewritten documents were little more than that. Typically, they might be letters on headed notepaper from important firms, like Siemens for instance, asking that an employee be granted passage while more permanent documentation was prepared. Or letters from girlfriends, wives or parents, intended to convince any enquiring minds that the escapers were who they said they were.

Dean & Dawson also accumulated a treasure trove of real documents on which to base their forgeries. These were acquired by theft, bribery and blackmail by prisoners in the camp and those who escaped and returned.

'There were always some German soldiers who for some American cigarettes or some honest-to-goodness soap would take considerable risks on our behalf,' recalls Bub Clark. 'We had people in the X-Organisation whose sole function was to obtain this kind of material and information. Some of them became very skilled. I often wondered what kind of jobs they went into after the war!' One officer commented that there was more extortion going on in Stalag Luft III than an entire small American town.

Sydney Dowse had a contact who worked in the censor department in the Vorlager. Corporal Hesse was a veritable fount of many authentic documents as was the Hundführer, the German in charge of the camp's guard dogs. One of the most effective Allied officers was Marcel Zillessen, nicknamed 'the scrounger', who had tamed Keen Type and was reliably thought to be able to get his hands on anything that was asked for. The raw materials with which to make the forgeries also sometimes came from friendly guards who were prepared to supply paper, card, ink, pen-nibs and other drawing implements. Bob van der Stok managed to create a waterproof black ink after acquiring from a Polish worker in the hospital some glycerine, ether and oil that he mixed with soot. But these raw materials were also foraged from the hundreds of books and Red Cross parcels that were sent to the prisoners. Book bindings could sometimes be refined into hard pass covers. If suitably thick the end papers might make adequate pages for passbooks. They could always be stained to the correct colour in the time immemorial method of soaking them in coffee or tea. The prisoners were allowed much drawing material anyway, such as paintbrushes, for what von Lindeiner presumed were legitimate artistic pursuits.

There were only a handful of forgers, partly because the job was so demanding that few could do it properly, and partly for security reasons: the forgers all needed to have access to light, which meant working by the windows and sometimes under the prying eyes of ferrets. The forgery department made use of every conceivable material available in the camp. Official stamps were crafted out of the rubber from the soles of boots. Toilet tissue and wafer-thin flyleaves from books were used as tracing paper. There was a department for duplicating maps, which used gelatine from food parcels.

Bub Clark recalls that the forgery department brought out hitherto unknown talents in people. 'My favourite story is about one of the most wonderful forgers we had in the camp. He could take a quick look at a passport and do a wonderful job imitating it. He retired as president of a bank in Blacksburg, Virginia. Very fine man!'

The manufacturing operation went far beyond Tommy Guest's tailoring department and Tim Walenn's forgers. An Australian Kriegie, Al Hake, was in charge of the compass factory. Hake, unusually, was a non-commissioned officer who had joined the Royal Australian Air Force Reserve in 1941. He was flying a Spitfire on an escort mission over France when he was shot down by a pack of Focke-Wulf 190s. Hake baled out and was sent to hospital to have minor burns treated. Because his insignia had been burnt off his uniform, the Germans had no idea of his rank but presumed he must have been an officer to be flying a Spitfire. Hake did nothing to disabuse them and shortly afterwards he found himself in Stalag Luft III. Once in the POW camp the Escape Committee was able to draw on Hake's talent, fostered at school, for technical drawing and metalwork. As a boy he had always enjoyed making gadgets and to make the compasses Hake had acquired a large magnet from one of his German contacts and collected as many of the prisoners' razor blades as they would allow him to lay his hands on. A team of prisoners then went about magnetising the blades by painstakingly stroking the razors over the magnet in the same direction. The process took the best part of a day but by the end of it the result was a perfectly magnetised razor blade.

The blade was then secured in a vice—in fact a hinge from the shutters that barred the barrack-block windows—and snapped into narrow slithers producing several perfect magnetic needles. The compass case was made from the melted Bakelite plastic of phonographic records moulded into a case. The compass card was made from thin discs of cardboard. Hake made a thin paintbrush out of his own hair and meticulously painted the compass points on the cardboard in white paint. The luminous compass points were made from the hands of the Kommandant's alarm clock, which had been stolen from his office. The razor blade was balanced on a needle made from the phonograph needle. At the end of the process, Hake stamped every compass with the inscription: Made in Stalag Luft III. Patent Pending. By March 1944 more than 500 of these compasses had been made.

It was Bub Clark's job to keep all this activity away from the prying eyes of the goons. To do so, Clark developed a security system that depended upon an elaborate system of watchers (called stooges), a complex semaphore system, security officers in charge of each barrack called 'Little Ss' and, finally, officers responsible for controlling each tunnel trap (jokingly dubbed 'Trapführers'). (Each barrack also had its own 'Little X', whose job mirrored that of Big X, Roger Bushell, on a lower level.) The compound was divided down the middle from north to south. The eastern section of this division was known as the safe, or 'S', zone because it was the furthest away from the tunnels. The western section was the danger, or 'D', zone. The rule was that digging and other covert activity could continue as long as there were no ferrets in the 'D' zone, but the moment a ferret walked over the line, everything was closed down.

Keeping an eye on the ferrets were scores of prisoners positioned all over the compound.

The stooges would all be engaged in innocent activity—reading books, jogging, sunbathing or digging vegetable patches—but their eyes would be following every movement of the ferrets both inside the compound and outside. And at the gate of the compound a stooge, called a 'duty pilot', was on guard. It was the duty pilot's job to count the ferrets and guards who went in and out of the compound, keeping a tab of how many, and which, German staff were inside the compound at any one time.

It was the job of the Little Ss to make sure that their individual barracks were always empty of ferrets—either hiding in the lofts or underneath the block. Finally, the duty pilot, stooges, Little Ss and Trapführers, all communicated with one another, either by word, or by a semaphore system developed by Clark's deputies, George Harsh and George McGill. The system depended sometimes on standard semaphore hand signals but also on surreptitious signals—such as a man reading a book. If he closed it or opened it and how he did so could send a variety of different messages.

The system was by no means perfect. Given his prominent position, it was not always possible for the duty pilot to remain inconspicuous. Glemnitz and Rubberneck often took great delight in reminding Allied officers to put their names down in the book

158

when entering or leaving the compound. Nor were the Germans quite so foolish as to think their movements were not being watched. The stooges often missed a trick and the goons often managed to evade them. Sometimes the goons would break into a run, catching the stooges by surprise. Often the only response the prisoners could muster was to 'accidentally' stumble into them, or stage a mock fight that blocked their way. It was a game of cat and mouse and there were plenty of incidents when a goon nearly walked right into one or other of the tunnelling, forging or tailoring operations.

Much of X-Organisation's escape material was obtained from the Germans by bribery or coercion. With their Red Cross parcels the prisoners were in possession of a valuable commodity to their hapless guards. After years of surviving on the ubiquitous ersatz creations of the German catering corps, real chocolate, cigarettes and coffee were tempting luxuries. Some of them even developed a taste for tinned British bully-beef. Some of the bribery, though, came in the form of cash and it did not take a great deal to persuade the Germans to part with valuable goods such as wire cutters, pliers or magnifying glasses; equally valuable was information in the form of railway timetables and so on.

It was a ruthless business. The officers were well aware of the fact that they were using their 'privileged' position to manipulate ordinary German soldiers who were labouring under a brutal regime and faced terrible penalties if they were caught, but many members of the German staff of Stalag Luft III were far from reluctant to help the prisoners, regardless of the risks, especially as the tide of the war began to turn. Some helped in ways that went far beyond casual assistance. They tipped off Kriegies when barrack blocks were to be searched. They provided the airmen with copies of the signatures that appeared on various documents. Hauptmann Pieber lent the prisoners his Leica camera and developed and printed their photographs for them. Ostensibly they were to send to their relatives back home; in reality they were being used on fake passes—as Pieber well knew. One of the Germans was actually given an all-expenses-paid trip to Paris by the Escape Committee, and in return provided it with details of documents escapers would require in the French capital and methods of contacting the resistance movement. This sort of illicit trade is almost impossible to prevent between captives and captors in any situation. In Germany, as the war turned against the Germans, it expanded exponentially.

The prisoners were reluctant to bribe the goons with cash because they were building up a stash for themselves, to be used when the break-out came. But some of the cash that was used to bribe the Germans came from a communal 'escape fund' that was managed by some of the Canadian officers in the camp. The fund was built from profits from a system called 'Foodacco' brought in by the RAF officers from Warburg. It was a form of *Exchange and Mart*, whereby food and tobacco were exchanged on a system of points, the unit of which was the cigarette. All the profits, which turned out to be considerable over the months, went to the escape fund.

Last but not least was the Escape Committee's intelligence section, which came under the auspices of Wally Valenta. The value of this section was incalculable in devising escape routes for the escapers to follow and providing all the various manufacturing plants—Tim Walenn's forgery department, Des Plunkett's maps department, Tommy Guest's tailors—with the correct information they needed to produce suitably convincing bogus material. The intelligence department was divided into different zones. Wally was the expert on Czechoslovakia, of course; van der Stok was in charge of accumulating intelligence on the Low Countries; Bushell on Germany; and Tom Kirby-Green on Spain. Arnold Christensen and Halldor Espelid covered Scandinavia. René Marcinkus, a Lithuanian member of the RAF, was a general authority on occupied territory, but had particular responsibility for the Baltic ports, which would be vital to many of the escapers' plans.

The intelligence-gathering side of the X-Organisation touches upon a thorny issue regarding the prisoners of war because, despite their later denials to the contrary, there is no doubt they were involved in espionage activity, in direct contravention of the Geneva Convention. The intelligence sections did not just accumulate information that would be helpful to their escape plans, they also gathered anything that could be remotely useful to their governments in London and Washington DC. The sort of information they were able to provide ranged from descriptions of Luftwaffe flight movements that they could see from the ground, to details of military movements and emplacements that they could observe outside the camp either on parole walks or whenever a prisoner escaped. General knowledge about German morale picked up from tame goons was useful enough, but the prisoners also discovered secret military information from their contacts, like Sydney Dowse's Corporal Hesse, who passed it on, sometimes wittingly, sometimes otherwise.

The men communicated this information home via a variety of clandestine ways. One method was through their letters home deploying a simple code that a British bomber pilot had created to communicate with his wife in the event of being shot down. It proved such an easy code that it was adopted by the intelligence sections. Groups of officers were given the responsibility of sending intelligence home in their letters to their families; they in turn passed this information on to the intelligence services. But contact could also be made verbally by the prisoners' links with the underground movement, either facilitated via tame goons or whenever a prisoner escaped. The underground movement all over occupied Europe was in constant touch with Britain's MI9, the secret escape-and-evasion service that was set up at the beginning of the war to get pilots home. After the fall of France and the complete collapse of MI6's European espionage network, MI9 assumed much of its intelligence-gathering role.

It is important that the prisoners' extensive involvement in spying should be recorded, because each and every one of them was aware that what they were doing was in breach of the Geneva Convention. As spies, they could be shot.

*   *   *

After starting the initial work on the traps on 11 April, it took the best part of the following six weeks to construct the three vertical shafts. The work was not without its incidents, which often were hair-raising. On several occasions the diggers had narrowly escaped falls. Having to re-excavate the affected sections proved frustrating, but nobody was hurt. The fumes from the fat lamps were a major problem. Men were coming down all the time with respiratory illnesses and some got conjunctivitis. However, in one new arrival to the camp, the tunnellers found a tireless worker who seemed to be immune to any sort of illness. Porokoru Patapu Pohe was a Maori of the RNZAF who was better known as 'Johnny'. Pohe was flying a Halifax bomber of 51 Squadron when it was hit by flak over Germany in September 1943. Pohe, a very skilled pilot, almost managed to get the machine back to Britain but in the end he had to perform the lesser feat of crash-landing it in the Channel. The three crew that were left were floating in a dinghy for two days before the Germans picked them up. After Dulag Luft, Pohe was sent first to Stalag Luft VI before arriving at Sagan. Born in Wanganui, New Zealand, Pohe grew up in a big family on his father's farm. At school he was more interested in sport than academic work, mainly rugby, tennis, cricket and golf. Before joining the Royal New Zealand Air Force, he served for two years in the Manawatu Mounted Rifles. When Pohe, then aged 26, embarked for England via Canada, a prominent thought in his mind was his sisters and baby brother Kawana, almost 20 years his junior. He wrote back to his family that the thought of little Kawana often brought tears to his eyes at night. From England he carried out 22 operational flights over enemy territory as part of 51 Squadron, including dropping paratroopers in the legendary Bruneval commando raid attacking the German radar facility. It was on a bombing raid over Hanover that Pohe was finally brought down. However, the Germans may have thought his war was over, but to Pohe it never ended and he brought his cheerful and indomitable personality to the tunnellers of Sagan.

By the end of May all three shafts and their base chambers were finished and much of both Tom and Dick's horizontal tunnel was under way. The excavation teams began to move forward at a steady pace, shoring up the roof as they went along and adding a railway line every 20 feet they progressed. The railway, or trolley, line was one of the innovations that made each tunnel such a work of engineering genius. Each tunnel was only two feet square and as a result it was a physically exhausting and often painful business for the digger to crawl along. The addition of the trolleys meant that men as well as about 200 pounds of sand could be transported back and forth from the digging face. The trolleys, which were two and a half feet long and a foot wide, were made from stools and benches from the barrack blocks. Their wheels were made to normal railway design with hard wood rimmed by tin plating. The axles were made from the guard rails from the cooking stoves in every officers' room. They supported a removable box on top that was used to transport the sand.

Digging was not quite the dangerous business that might be imagined. The risks of a collapse were real, but so long as the shored-up sections were sound, the diggers were only in danger in the sections that they were actively excavating. Since these were rarely longer than four or five feet, even if the worst came to the worst, it would only be a matter of seconds before they would be dragged out. A frightening experience no doubt, but nobody lost their lives in the tunnels. It was, however, a gruelling business. The men usually dug naked. Those that were a little prudish wore long johns. But any sort of clothing merely increased the amount of washing to be done afterwards. The fabric also dragged along the sand. The process was laborious. The digger at the face lay with a trowel and scraped the sand past his body to a second man, who loaded the sand onto the trolley. Once the trolley was full, that man gave a tug on the rope and the man behind him at the haulage point would drag the trolley back. The sand would be stored in the storage chamber and the trolley sent back loaded with further supplies of shoring panels, milk cans for the ventilation pipe and so on. At the end of the day, the sand was painstakingly poured into large metal water jugs and pulled up to the top of the shaft where it became the responsibility of Fanshawe's penguins.

*   *   *

In the meantime, other escape activity was not neglected. In early June the prisoners were to stage their first mass escape attempt. It would be Bob van der Stok's third effort and it came tantalisingly close to success. It was a far more sophisticated and risky ploy than he had attempted in the past. A regular feature of camp life was delousing parties. The Germans feared any outbreak of lice, quite rightly, because the creatures could spark a typhus epidemic. The prisoners rather looked forward to an outbreak, especially if the weather was good, because it meant a few precious moments of freedom on the brief walk outside the wire to visit the delousing block in the hospital compound. The routine was for groups of prisoners to be escorted out of the North Compound under watchful guard. Once they were out of the gates, they turned right and marched along the road for a few hundred yards to the East Compound, where the hospital block was situated. The wire was on their right. On their left was the opening before the tree-line and beyond that beckoned at least the possibility of freedom in the form of the railway tracks and eventually Sagan station.

When an outbreak of lice was discovered in early June 1943 the Germans ordered parties of prisoners to be taken to the East Compound Vorlager for delousing. The Escape Committee had already forged a plan to take advantage of such a situation. They would send a bogus party to follow the real delousing parties. This would consist of 24 prisoners guarded by two fake German Unteroffiziere (junior non-commissioned officers) guards. The 'guards' were actually Belgian officers who spoke fluent German and were dressed in passable imitations of German uniforms created by Tommy Guest. Bob van der Stok had blackmailed a guard by stuffing his pockets with Red Cross food and threatening to report him as a thief unless he cooperated. The guard supplied van der Stok with Luftwaffe buttons, a field cap and some embroidered shoulder patches. The other badges and belt buckles were crafted by Jens Muller, who made the eagles for the lapels out of melted silver foil, using soap moulds to gain an impression. The guns were fashioned out of blocks of wood by another Belgian officer, Henri Picard, who took painstaking measurements of the goons' carbines. Muller and another officer also spent a week making fake rifles, the most difficult prop to create. One of the 'guards' carried a real gate pass supplied by Sydney Dowse's contact Hesse.

(Tim Walenn used it to create several imitation passes.)

The idea was that after a genuine delousing party had gone through the gates at 12.30 p.m., the Allied officers would reach a verbal agreement with the German adjutants that no other parties would go through until 2.30 p.m. By making the agreement verbal, it was hoped no written note as such would be left at the guardroom. The guard changed at 2 p.m. The Escape Committee planned to send the bogus delousing party out shortly afterwards. They would have civilian disguises beneath their uniforms, and carried with them maps, Reichsmarks and packets of concentrated food. As many as possible would be provided with passes and travel documents provided by the forgery department. Once out of the gate they would march a respectable distance before running across the road and melting into the woods.

There was one additional element to the plan. If the bogus party was to have any chance of getting away without being seen, the watchtower and perimeter guards needed to be distracted. Hence Bushell arranged a further bogus party to follow the first. This would consist of six senior officers including the Americans Bub Clark and Colonel Goodrich; and Wing Commander Bob Tuck, guarded by a bogus goon, in this instance Bob van der Stok. Again, van der Stok had the full

169

disguise and papers of a German corporal. The party would argue with the gate guard that they had an emergency meeting with the camp Kommandant, von Lindeiner. This would soon be proved not to be true. But it was calculated that during the hiatus that would ensue, the guards' attention would be diverted long enough for the escapers to abscond.

The escapers' plans were thrown into confusion when it emerged that the German guards who escorted prisoners out of camp were no longer issued with rifles. Instead they carried holster pistols. It took some time for Tommy Guest's department to come up with some passable leather imitations. Other than that the plan went remarkably well. The first delousing party with the genuine pass was waved through both gates without difficulty. The party reeled right and began its march outside the wire towards the East Compound. In the meantime all eyes were on the following party of senior Allied officers. The guard at the first gate inspected van der Stok's fake pass and waved him through. But then they came to the guards at the second gate. This time the guard scrutinised the documentation a little more closely. Bushell was watching the scene unfold from inside the compound. He could tell all was not well—the goon had smelled a rat. The party was held up while the guard telephoned the officers' mess to check whether this party of senior Allied officers really was expected. When Bushell saw van der Stok raise his hands in surrender, he knew the game was up, but by then 26 prisoners of the first party were running as fast as they could through the woods. How many of them would catch their trains before the Germans realised what had happened?

In fact, it had not yet dawned upon the Germans what had happened. For a few minutes there was some good-humoured banter between the would-be escapers held up at the gate and the Germans, who felt reassured that their security precautions had proved impregnable.

Major Broili, the Security Officer, was delighted. 'You cannot fool our guards, you know?' he joshed. Only after a guard called the East Compound and discovered that the first party had not yet arrived did the full horror of what had happened occur to Broili. Immediately the alert was sounded. Goons were dispatched into the woods, whistles blowing and dogs barking fiercely. Sagan railway station was warned to keep a look out for the escapers. That afternoon the prisoners were stood on parade for hours as the Germans conducted a photographic identity count.

Unsurprisingly, none of the escapers made it home. Most were caught within a few hours, either at the station or in the woods. A few managed to stay at large for a couple of days. Two were British officers who found a nearby aerodrome and attempted to crank up a small trainer aircraft with the intention of flying it to Sweden. No doubt their audacious attempt was inspiration for the episode in *The Great Escape,* where two officers do actually succeed in such a bid, only to crash-land when the gas runs out. In real life they didn't even get it off the ground—they were arrested by the Luftwaffe and sent to Colditz Castle. One of the escapers, Ian McIntosh, actually made it to Switzerland after two weeks' hiking across land and making contact with the Czech underground movement. His only misfortune was that he didn't realise he had crossed the Swiss frontier, which was marked by a dry river bed. McIntosh walked directly across a loop in the river and back into enemy territory. It was not long before he walked right into the path of a German border patrol.

*   *   *

There were many attempts to escape by impersonating German staff. Offizier Karl Pfelz, known as 'Charlie' to the prisoners, was one of the ferrets with a distinctive tall bearing. One RAF officer had observed him carefully, altered his RAF uniform and set off to walk out of the camp. His audacious escape attempt failed only when he had the misfortune to walk straight into Charlie on his way to the gate. A similar stunt almost succeeded when a prisoner imitating an officer called Hohendole, and also carrying a bogus identity card, managed to get out past the guard on the gate. His ruse was only discovered when the real Offizier Hohendole arrived at the gate a few minutes later. The escapee was captured shortly afterwards. These attempts prompted von Lindeiner to warn that Allied officers who made future escape attempts disguised as German officers faced execution. In any case, von Lindeiner's stricture did not discourage Per Bergsland. In 1943 he walked out of the gates having altered his RAF uniform to look like a Luftwaffe one. His fake identification didn't even have a photograph. But fortunately, of course, he spoke perfect German and he was able to convince the guard that he was awaiting a photograph. His escape was only foiled a few minutes later when he walked past Glemnitz, who recognised him.

CHAPTER FIVE

THE WOODEN HORSE

By early 1943 there had been as many as 30 tunnel attempts from the camp. None had succeeded. More depressing still, most had been detected long before they had reached anywhere near the wire. The stamina, both physical and mental, required to sustain building a tunnel 300 feet long was beyond most of the prisoners and many were beginning to be depressed by seeing their efforts go to waste. It was after the failure of yet another tunnel attempt that Lieutenant Michael Codner and Flight Lieutenant Eric Williams were walking around the East Compound reflecting morosely on their plight. Codner was in the Royal Artillery, but had been working with the Air Force when he was captured. He had met Williams at Szubin. Williams, 31, had been the captain of a Stirling of 75 Squadron, based at Newmarket. He had been shot down on a mission to bomb a car-works south-east of Berlin on the night of 17 December 1942. Before the war he had been an amateur artist and his life had been a halcyon existence devoted to music and painting that now, amid the austere isolation of the pine trees of Silesia, seemed like a world away. Williams was one of the prisoners who had chosen to dull the boredom of captivity by becoming one of the most enthusiastic theatre players and was becoming a mainstay of many of the productions. But Codner felt the torment of imprisonment more, and the desire to escape overwhelmed him. He often told Williams that he felt a greater shame at being a prisoner since his capture had involved the conscious surrender of arms, whereas Williams had been involuntarily shot out of the sky.

As Williams and Codner walked around the perimeter track, it seemed to them that the chances of escape from Stalag Luft III really were too remote to be worth thinking about. It was then that Codner posed the question that had been asked many times before: was it really necessary to start the tunnel inside one of the barrack blocks? Why couldn't the shaft be sunk as near to the trip wire as possible, Codner wondered? Williams stated the obvious: every square foot of ground was visible from at least three goon boxes and by now the ferrets were wise to every conceivable type of 'moling' operation. But then Codner recalled a botched escape attempt that he had heard about from another POW camp some time ago. Every day a crowd of prisoners settled down near the wire ostensibly to listen to one of them playing an accordion. While he played, they sat around in a circle and sang. But a group of them in the middle quietly dug a hole in the ground. After they had excavated as much sand as they could conceal in their pockets, they placed some bed boards across the hole, and replaced the surface sand. Unfortunately, the ruse was discovered almost as soon as it had been started. A sentry walked over the trap and stumbled down the hole the very first night.

The experience seemed to confirm the impossibility of beginning a tunnel from anywhere except from the comfort and security of inside one of the barrack blocks. But to Williams and Codner the idea offered at least a ray of hope. The accordion attempt had been a slapdash and amateur affair, and presumably every camp Kommandant in Germany would now keep a wary eye on anyone playing an accordion. But supposing a different, cleverer ruse could be thought up? It was while mulling over the idea that Codner suddenly remembered the story of the wooden horse of Troy. Why didn't they build their own wooden horse? An hour later Williams and Codner were presenting the idea to the Escape Committee.

The men would construct a vaulting horse like the ones that were used in schools—strong oblong structures with a padded top and solid wooden sides. There was plenty of good quality timber in the theatre in the North Compound that the prisoners had squirrelled away under the floorboards when they built the place. The Germans loved athletics and von Lindeiner, who was always looking for ways to keep the prisoners distracted and out of trouble, would surely approve of this harmless activity. The wooden horse would be kept in the cookhouse, which was the barrack block closest to the wire. It would be taken to exactly the same spot as near to the wire as possible every day. The exact location would be worked out by elementary trigonometry. Also, the footfalls of the vaulters would leave two convenient markers. The tunnel would only need to be 100 feet long. A group of prisoners would exercise and while they vaulted one of the escapers would be inside the horse, digging the tunnel.

This time the tunnel would be a professional affair. The trap-door would be at least a foot beneath the surface, while the ground above was constantly being churned up by the prisoners exercising, so there would be no problem disguising the area above the trap-door. The excavated sand would be returned in sacks inside the horse at the end of the exercise period.

The Escape Committee was sceptical. The plan was not entirely watertight. What sort of wood would the horse be constructed from? If it was anything like a real school vaulting horse it would be very heavy indeed. How much soil could be contained within the horse in any one exercise session? And given this limitation, how far would the diggers be able to tunnel each day? On their feeble rations, would the other prisoners be capable of exercising long enough? Would they be strong enough to carry the horse laden with sand back to the cookhouse? And last, but not least, would the goons really be so dimwitted not to notice anything over the many months it was likely to take? Nevertheless, Williams and Codner had 'patented' the idea as their own and the committee told them that if they could build a vaulting horse they would receive its full backing. That June, Williams wrote to his mother telling her about a play the prisoners had just staged with costumes hired from a shop in Berlin. He added, a little mischievously perhaps, 'Now doing a melodrama which is going to be very funny indeed.'

*   *   *

That July there was a happy interlude over in the North Compound. There were now some 500 Americans in the camp and they had decided to celebrate Independence Day as they would at home. On 4 July the other sleepy inmates of the North Compound awoke to the sound of banging drums and blowing bugles as a party of 'Red Indians' and 'Colonialists' marched around the camp. They were quickly joined by the British and other RAF officers and soon the whole camp was heaving with thousands of noisy prisoners sharing tin cups of an illicit and fiery alcoholic concoction, especially brewed by the Americans to celebrate the occasion. The prisoners became increasingly inebriated as the day progressed, and at one stage Johnny Dodge and Wings Day found themselves being unceremoniously thrown into the fire-pool by the American 'rebels'. The Germans looked on, at first bewildered but soon amused. Pieber could not resist a good-natured chuckle at evening Appell as the prisoners tried to stand up straight for the count. The day ended in good spirits all around.

By then in the East Compound, Williams and Codner's escape plans were taking shape. The vaulting horse had been built by a team of carpenters under a Wing Commander Waw and more than lived up to expectations. Using the theatre wood smuggled over from North Compound, and three-ply Canadian Red Cross packing cases, they constructed a light but strong horse, with a pad on top made of sacking stuffed with wood shavings. Inside the structure up to three men could be accommodated. Cross-sections were installed to help them wedge themselves in while the horse was being carried. Hooks ran along the roof of the inside for the bags of excavated sand to be hung from. Wooden boards for shoring up the tunnel had also to be carried out. There were two holes on either side of the box through which two long poles could be pushed for four men to carry it.

The Escape Committee was finally satisfied that the wooden horse project represented a viable escape plan and approval was given to begin the tunnel attempt. Before they went ahead, however, the prisoners had to submit the horse to von Lindeiner's security officers for inspection. It was a tense few moments while the Germans peered into every crevice of the wooden horse, but they could find nothing suspicious about it and agreed that it would be an excellent way for the prisoners to exercise. It was with a great deal of relief that the horse was finally taken over to the cookhouse block, which would be its home for the duration of the escape attempt. On 8 July 1943, the wooden horse emerged from the block for the first time, its four carriers taking it to a prearranged spot five yards from the trip wire, just inside the perimeter track. One of the most audacious escape attempts was about to begin.

To construct a tunnel in such circumstances was a startling achievement, but the role of the four daily carriers should not be forgotten either. Because the Germans had inspected the horse they knew it was a comparatively light structure, so it was essential that the men make light work of their task. But that was no easy achievement. The horse always contained two grown men and occasionally three. On the return trip the additional burden of up to 12 heavy sacks of sand was added. (The sacks were made from trouser-legs cut off beneath the knees and stitched up.) The carriers had to first negotiate the three steps leading down from the cookhouse block in full view of the watchtowers and the ferrets they knew were spying on them from the forest beyond. It was necessary to keep the horse as close to the ground as possible so that nobody caught a glimpse of what was inside. Annoyingly, the ferrets were occasionally actually sitting on the steps of the cookhouse as the horse was taken past them. Remarkably, while weighed down by their burden, the carriers would often use only one hand to hold the pole to keep up the pretence of lightness. It was a feat of extraordinary physical and mental stamina that would be repeated almost every day of the following four months.

Once in position the prisoners would perform their exercises for two or more hours under the supervision of a 24-year-old South African airman. John Stevens grew up in Cape Town and joined the South African Air Force at the onset of the war. He was flying a light bomber in the Western Desert when he was shot down and seriously wounded. After making a remarkably quick recovery, the Germans sent him first to Barth and then Sagan, where he would become one of the most persistent escapers. He was also one of the most athletic of the prisoners, leading an exercise group every morning before Appell.

Early on, in a ruse to put the Germans off the scent, Stevens had decided the vaulters should deliberately knock over the horse, toppling it over in full view of the goon towers to show the Germans that nothing was going on inside. The ruse proved to be successful. From then onwards, when something very definitely was going on inside the horse, an instructor always stood by the side of it and a system of tapping signals was devised so that the diggers inside could communicate with him, and vice versa. They could tell him when their shift was complete and he could warn them if a guard was approaching. Often the Germans did come to watch the men jumping over the horse and would shout words of encouragement. One day Charlie Pfelz caused a momentary pang of panic when he walked up to within six feet of the horse while digging was going on inside. Observing the vaulters for a few minutes, he came up with the helpful suggestion to Stevens that they would find it a whole lot easier if they used a springboard. Stevens agreed that the idea had merit and said he would look into it. The ferrets, it seemed, really did think the wooden horse was nothing more than a little harmless exercise to while away the days of boredom.

Underneath the horse, Codner and

Williams began their formidable task. The vaulting movements above were helpful in camouflaging their activity from the seismographs. They began by digging a shaft just three feet deep, before turning at a right angle and starting the tunnel towards the wire. In order to minimise the amount of soil they would have to excavate and thus carry back to the canteen, they made the tunnel as small as possible. It was just 18 inches square and the task of crawling along it was a horribly claustrophobic one. Williams and Codner took turns to mole their way along its length. At first only one man at a time worked on the tunnel. He would carefully excavate the soil, place it in a sack, and attach the sack to a hook. As they progressed towards the wire, the atmosphere became oppressively stifling and humid. A decision was made early on not to poke any air holes through to the surface inside the perimeter track. The risk of them prompting a collapse, either from below or if a guard stood on them, was just too great. The tunnel had to be shored up with wooden boards all the way to the perimeter track. After that the men only shored it up where the soil showed signs of collapsing.

It was a long and laborious job. They had to fill 12 bags each day. There was no light at all in the tunnel and the air became fouler and fouler the further along the tunnel they progressed. They worked naked, and 'side stroked' the sand behind their backs towards the tunnel entrance. At the end of every shift, they placed a trap-door made of three boards about two feet beneath the surface. The original soil that had covered it was replaced, and Williams and Codner tapped on the side of the box to indicate that they had done their day's work. The four carriers would make a great display of cheerfulness as they lifted their staggering burden, while Stevens's men would shuffle their feet in the sand to disguise the disturbance.

But not all the men were happy. It was hard work vaulting every day, on rations that weren't even adequate to keep an inactive adult healthy. Some of the men complained that it was they who were doing the hard work while Codner's and Williams' task beneath the ground might be uncomfortable but hardly physically draining. There was a minor revolt in their barrack block and the result was a slight altering of the mess arrangements. In the meantime, the two tunnellers decided they would need a third member of the team for the escape and they recruited Flight Lieutenant Oliver Philpot. At first, though, Philpot did not take part in the tunnelling. Instead he organised the sand dispersal operation, getting rid of most of the stuff beneath the barber shop and in the cookhouse roof.

In the North Compound digging continued apace into the summer of 1943 with Tom and Dick (heading westerly out of blocks 123 and 122 respectively) getting priority over Harry because they were nearer to the wire. The by-now familiar camp distractions continued as well. The prisoners cultivated vegetable plots outside their barrack blocks (an activity that also helped disperse the soil). Theatre groups had developed a slightly more sophisticated repertoire of plays and musicals than *Alice and Her Candle* that had so exasperated Wings Day in Barth. Many of the men exercised on a regular basis to keep their spirits up and took part in competitive games. Others signed up to language, art and drawing classes.

Johnny Dodge had established an international debating society that was becoming one of the camp's greatest attractions. Dodge had briefly flirted with socialism but subsequently never wavered from his view that capitalism within a democratic framework was the only viable form of society. Others had more radical views. The inmates established a mock parliament, which complimented Dodge's debating group. Once Roger Bushell, casting himself in the role of deputy leader of the Labour Party, proposed a motion that after the war all industry should be nationalised. Tom Kirby-Green argued that it was time the British recognised the prevalence of the black majority in much of their Empire. In raising these questions the men were really doing nothing more than thousands of other intelligent and thoughtful men at that stage of the war. They were young, highly educated men thrown into a barbarous struggle between the Nazis' hateful ideology and the Allies' far-from-perfect societies. In Britain they would eventually return from the war and some of them would form part of one of the most remarkable Houses of Parliament ever. It is curious to wonder what the 1945 Parliament would have been like had the likes of Roger Bushell and Tom Kirby-Green managed to get elected and been given the opportunity to restate the arguments they first rehearsed in the barren wastes of Silesia.

No sooner had the men arrived in the North Compound than rumours began to spread that the Germans were going to be adding yet another compound to Stalag Luft III—directly to the south of the North Compound. When von Lindeiner's men started clearing the forest to the south it was apparent the rumours were true. The men soon discovered that the new South Compound was going to be reserved entirely for American prisoners. There was a flurry of disquiet. The Americans had worked as hard on Tom, Dick and Harry as anyone else had, but it now looked as if they would be removed from the North Compound before any of the tunnels were due to break through. Bushell held an emergency meeting of the Escape Committee.

Dick was 70 feet long by now and there was clearly no chance it would be completed before the new compound was built. Harry was far from complete. Tom was nearer to the wire. But worryingly, Block 123, the barrack from which Tom was being built with the trapdoor that was the most vulnerable, had already attracted the suspicions of the ferrets. Bushell proposed that if the Americans were to be given a fair chance of escaping, the Escape Committee should focus all its resources into one tunnel. He thought that the best chances of success lay in closing down Dick for good, postponing Harry for the time being and pouring every last resource into Tom. Dick, he suggested, could be used, ironically, for dispersing the sand from Tom. The Americans protested. As one of the most important members of the X-Organisation and one of the regular diggers, Bub Clark already had a place guaranteed in one of the tunnels. But, he argued, to hurry up the digging now would jeopardise the security of the whole operation. Clark pointed out that Block 123 was the most vulnerable of the three barrack buildings and concentrating all their efforts on it might attract more attention from the ferrets. In any case, the Americans would have plenty of opportunity to escape from their new compound. The RAF officers, however, were fond of their new American friends and they wanted them to go out with them. Bushell's view prevailed and it was agreed to work flat-out on Tom.

It was a race against time. Glemnitz and his security staff had already arrived at the conclusion that there was definitely a tunnel being built on the west side of the compound—they just didn't know which block it was emanating from. However, the ferrets were keeping a very close eye on all the blocks near the wire, and 123 in particular, around about which their seismographs indicated an unusual degree of activity. Hardly surprising, since beneath the ground the diggers were working at a furious rate, this time in relays of three teams of diggers. On some days the men progressed as much as three yards.

But Bub Clark had been proved right. In their hurry to get Tom finished, the men had become less scrupulous about security. On more than one occasion the ferrets witnessed penguins kicking yellow sand out of their trouser-legs. The Germans dug trenches and probed the ground with their poles. They could sense they were getting close. The barrack blocks along the western side of the compound were repeatedly searched, 123 being subject to a nerve-wracking five-hour inspection on one particular day. Glemnitz persuaded von Lindeiner that the trees in the compound should be cut down to improve the sight-lines of the goons, and reluctantly the Kommandant agreed.

There was further bad news for the prisoners when they were informed that a West Compound was to be built directly in the path of Tom. It meant they would have to extend the tunnel by at least 40 yards and yet again raised doubt about whether the Americans would still be with them by the time they broke through. Nevertheless, by September the tunnellers had pushed Tom to 285 feet beyond the wire, arriving a tantalising ten feet short of the shelter of the woods beyond. September, though, was to prove the cruellest month. It began with the Germans conducting a series of very thorough searches throughout the compound, at one stage very nearly stumbling on the trap-door of the now discontinued Harry. Once more the ferrets returned to 123 and took the block apart with unusual thoroughness.

Typically, though, it was purely by a stroke of luck that the ferrets actually discovered the trap-door in the passageway by the kitchen. A ferret was quietly tapping away at the concrete with a pickaxe. He didn't find the hollow sign he was looking for, but he did chip a corner of the shaft, exposing the narrow clink of a line. The first the prisoners knew was when the excited man emerged from the barracks grinning from ear to ear and shouting triumphantly for Glemnitz. The POWs held their breath, hoping against hope that the inevitable had not happened. Shortly afterwards, Glemnitz arrived from the Kommandantur and pushed his way through the gathered crowd of prisoners, who were trying to look as if they hadn't a care in the world but not always succeeding. The men watched in a mournful silence as Glemnitz stomped up the barrack block steps. A dark cloud seemed to settle over the crowd of Kriegies standing motionless and silent outside. It seemed an age before Glemnitz emerged, this time smiling broadly. He did not have to say a thing as he stalked confidently across to the Kommandantur. Tom had been discovered after four and a half months of back-breaking work. It is not difficult to imagine the frustration felt by the diggers and all the other men who had contributed to the escape plans, but the discovery of Tom at least proved that Bushell had been right about one thing. The Germans were astonished by what they found.

So astonished that dignitaries from Berlin visited Stalag Luft III to see what an incredible piece of engineering the tunnel was and Colonel von Lindeiner even seemed to take perverse pleasure in showing off the engineering masterpiece that his prisoners had so painstakingly constructed. Newspaper photographers came to take pictures of their creation. Indeed, it was such a beautiful work of engineering that the Germans had difficulty in working out how to destroy it. Eventually, a sapper was brought in from a nearby army unit and Tom disappeared under 100 pounds of explosives. A good part of Block 123 was damaged too, provoking catcalls and whistles from the watching prisoners. Odd as it may seem, von Lindeiner had established a small escape museum in one of the Kommandantur barracks. It was mainly, of course, to help his men understand the lengths to which the prisoners would go and the ingenuity they could display, but it was almost with a sense of pride that he showed guests around the small room and showed them the newspaper pictures of Tom.

There were several elements of consolation for Roger Bushell and the Escape Committee. One was that the tunnel had been discovered by a fluke. Had it not been for that infuriating piece of good fortune, the Germans would probably have dismissed the clear evidence of their seismograph system as some sort of anomaly or aberration. Moreover, in four and a half months more than 166 tons of sand had been dispersed around the compound little more than one mile in circumference. Yet, except for spotting a few prisoners kicking off yellow sand in the vegetable gardens, the

Germans had not discovered the key dispersal points. Finally, it was apparent from their reaction to Tom that the Germans clearly did not think it was possible that more than one such tunnel existed. (Indeed, one German-speaking prisoner overheard Glemnitz say as much to one of the ferrets.)

Two days after the discovery of Tom, work resumed on Dick and Harry. However, the Germans increased their security activity to such an extent that it made it virtually impossible to carry out soil dispersal operations without a high risk of detection. With the winter fast approaching, it was decided to postpone all digging activities on Dick and Harry indefinitely. It was a psychological blow to everyone. Nevertheless, they could take some comfort in the knowledge that Harry was by now some 115 feet long. The whole structure had been meticulously shored up.

Late that fall the Americans were marched out of the North Compound and into their new South Compound. (By virtue of the fact that he served with the Royal Canadian Air Force, George Harsh was one of the Americans to remain in the North Compound, along with others who served in British Commonwealth uniforms. He took over Bub Clark's role as Big S.) The move was a source of great disappointment to both the RAF officers and the Americans, not just because some of the hardest workers on the tunnels were now going to be denied a chance to break out, but because the men had become used to one another and great friendships had developed. Both groups held one another in enormous respect. The Americans would play no further role in the Great Escape but they remained in daily contact with the RAF men through a regular communication system that was set up. At its most basic this was reduced to little more than a prisoner lobbing a message contained in a tin or ball over the wire. On a more sophisticated level the prisoners could communicate with semaphore signals.

Roger Bushell, however, was quick to grasp one opportunity that the removal of the Americans presented. He put the word about that it was the American, and not the RAF officers, who had been behind much of the escape activity. Bushell hinted that Bub Clark in particular was one of the biggest troublemakers. Later, it was reported that von Lindeiner had asked Glemnitz who was the most dangerous prisoner in the camp. 'Without any doubt, sir, Colonel Clark,' replied the Feldwebel without any hesitation.

The Kommandant was taken aback. 'Not Squadron Leader Bushell?' he demanded.

Glemnitz replied: 'Once I believed it was Squadron Leader Bushell, but he has quieted down, Kommandant. More interested in the theatre these days.'

For many months after the move, the Americans were puzzled why von Lindeiner's men were subjecting the South Compound to such close scrutiny. 'They came down on us 24 hours a day for weeks on end,' recalls Clark with a smile.

One point of regret to the British was that Glemnitz was dispatched to work in the South Camp, leaving the RAF at the mercy of Rubberneck, now in charge of security. Griese adapted to his new role with ill-disguised enthusiasm and his first move was to stamp down on fraternisation between ferrets and the prisoners, throwing any German guard into the cooler on the slightest suspicion of collaboration, and actually sending one reprobate to the Eastern Front for his sins. His new regime did not deter all the Germans. Pieber continued to develop passport photographs that Valenta had taken with the Leica camera that the Luftwaffe captain had provided. And the pleasant little Hundführer was not deterred from offering the Allied officers little gifts.

*   *   *

While gloom prevailed in the North Compound, a mood of cautious optimism was developing in the East Compound, where the wooden horse escape was approaching fruition. Codner and Williams had also had their close calls. On one occasion the tunnel collapsed, leaving a slight but clearly visible indent in the topsoil above and Codner stuck underneath. A vaulter threw himself over the hole, feigning injury, desperate to hide it from the view of the goon boxes. The instructor crouched by his side while a stretcher was summoned, all the time the guards in the goon boxes watching intently. Below ground Codner furiously worked to shore up the tunnel while the other vaulters hung around the 'injured' man, pretending to be concerned while casually kicking the sand back into the hole. By the time the stretcher bore the patient away, miraculously the damage had been repaired.

The going was hard though. After Codner and Williams had reached 42 feet towards the wire, both they and the vaulters were exhausted. The Escape Committee had granted Codner and Williams extra rations in view of their exertions but, for some odd reason, not the vaulters. One of the vaulters had injured his leg but heroically carried on regardless. Petty resentments began to surface, some of the vaulters wondering why they should work so hard when they were not going to get a chance to escape. Codner and Williams decided that if they were not to jeopardise the whole project they needed to work fast.

They decided the only way they could get the tunnel done was by working in unison. From then onwards they went down the tunnel two at a time. One man would dig, the other would remain at the shaft entrance, hauling the excavated soil back in a metal washbasin 18 inches deep and 18 inches in diameter attached to a rope. The rope was made from plaited string from Red Cross parcels. In this new system they dug 36 bags at a time, storing the bags near the tunnel entrance and removing them in the following three shifts.

The tunnel was progressing at a laborious six inches a day. It was such arduous work that Williams became ill through the effort and for some weeks he was temporarily laid up, receiving treatment in the camp's sick quarters. The Luftwaffe doctor would have been furious, or perhaps mildly amused, if he had known the cause of his patient's illness. At least Williams' stay in the sick bay gave him time to reflect on the approaching problem of how, exactly, the men would escape once outside the wire. One of his fellow patients was to give him some valuable ideas. The man was an Australian who had been shot in the shoulder trying to escape, and had a sardonic sense of humour typical of his countrymen. The sick bay had a gramophone player, which had been very kindly provided by the camp padre. One day it was playing Beethoven's Second Symphony when there was a sudden

Blitz Appell (an emergency roll-call, favoured by Glemnitz when he thought he could catch the prisoners out at something) and the ferrets marched in. 'Ach, Beethoven,' said one of the ferrets upon hearing the strains of the great German composer drifting across the room, 'A good German!'

'Yes,' agreed the Australian, 'he's dead.'

The Australian officer had roughed it all the way to Danzig in a cattle train. Williams learned from him that fast trains ran the risk of identity checks so it was better to go for slow trains, with small compartments only, that didn't have corridors and thus attracted less identity checks. The Australian had a goon called 'Dopey' that he had tamed. Each day Dopey would come into the sick bay with news of the latest catastrophe the once mighty Third Reich had suffered. 'Frankfurt: kaputt!' he would bemoan. 'Duisburg: kaputt!' And so on.

Williams cultivated Dopey too and always turned the conversation around to trains. 'Hamburg, Bahnhof: kaputt?' he would enquire.

'Hamburg: kaputt!' came the reply.

Williams discovered that trains were almost always overcrowded and invariably late. Foreign workers were allowed to travel on them but they needed special passes from the police in the town that they had travelled from. Williams blackmailed Dopey to obtain two copies of these passes.

The German doctor believed that Williams was so ill he needed to be operated on, but the RAF man refused to countenance the idea. It would certainly have made his life more comfortable. But it would have ruled out any further work on the tunnel. He signed himself out of the sick quarters and soon the vaulters were back in business, some of them a little more reluctant than others. The discovery of Tom in the North Compound had left a deep cloud of depression over many prisoners, but it only served to give added impetus to Codner's and Williams' efforts. By the second week of October the tunnel was 100 feet long, and comfortably on the other side of the wire. The long Silesian summer was drawing to a close. With the winter would come rain and its attendant problems for a shallow tunnel dug in sandy ground. The men realised they had to break out now, or face the prospect of spending Christmas in captivity—and possibly finding in the New Year that their tunnel had been destroyed by nature.

Codner and Wiliams had successfully overcome great odds on the inside of the wire. Now they had to confront similar ones on the outside. The tunnel extended several feet beyond the track along which the outside guards patrolled. It was perilously close to them and well within the lights of the arc lamps that extended 30 feet either side of the wire. To avoid detection, the men would have to excavate the escape shaft as quietly as possible. When they emerged they faced a sprint across a road and open countryside into the woods beyond in full view of the watchtowers. The attempt could only be made on a moonless night—when the Germans were always extra vigilant.

The night that was finally chosen was Friday, 29 October. The plan was for Codner to be sealed in the tunnel during the day, to complete the few final feet of tunnel. It would be a lonely, dangerous and gruelling several hours for the Royal Artillery officer. Williams would join Codner after the evening roll-call along with Oliver Philpot, the third member of their team. All three men would be wearing their escape outfits of overalls and hoods—all dyed black using tea and coffee grains—to make them less conspicuous when they emerged into the dark night beyond the wire. They would take their escape disguises in duffel bags down the tunnel with them to keep them clean.

Williams and Codner were going as French draughtsmen at first. They would have documentation to show that they were travelling from Breslau to the Arado aircraft works at Anklam, north of Stettin. Once there they would have the disguises of Swedish sailors in the hope that they could get on a boat for neutral Sweden. Williams' disguise consisted of a converted marine's uniform and a trenchcoat, courtesy of Tommy Guest and Ivo Tonder's toiling tailors. He had a beret made out of an old blanket, a black roll-neck sweater and a small leather case to hold his clean gear, survival rations and false papers. Tim Walenn's forgery department had supplied him with the appropriate identity and travel papers, and a couple of bogus letters addressed to his assumed identity and purportedly from a French girlfriend. It was an impressive effort. As a final touch Williams had shaved off his distinctive 'RAF' moustache. Codner was going to accompany him and had been provided with a similar outfit made out of old Australian Navy trousers and an RAF mackintosh. He carried a canvas valise for his false papers and survival rations.

Philpot was going to travel separately from the other men, posing as a Norwegian working for the Margarine Marketing Union in Berlin. His outfit was that of a petit bourgeois businessman complete with Homburg hat. The tailors' department had made it out of a similar ensemble of old RAF and Navy uniforms and other scavenged materials. He had a suitcase, too, just big enough to squeeze in the tiny tunnel. It contained high-energy rations ingeniously disguised as the sort of 'margarine' products a businessman with the Margarine Marketing Union would be travelling with. Philpot could speak passable

German but not a word of Norwegian and so was equipped with a pipe to disguise any difficulties he might experience in that respect. (He had also shaved himself a stubby Adolf Hitler-style moustache, perhaps in a ploy to win some empathy from the German travelling companions he expected to meet along the way.)

Philpot was briefed for his escape by the Norwegian flier Halldor Espelid, who, with Arnold Christensen, ran the Scandinavian section of the X-Organisation's intelligence network. Espelid was one of the many Norwegians who had escaped to Britain by boat after the Nazis invaded in April 1940. He was flying a Spitfire with 331 Squadron when it was brought down over the Pas de Calais in August 1942. Espelid had spent a short time in Szubin before being sent to Stalag Luft III, where his reputation as one of the best intelligence officers was founded.

Williams and Codner hoped to get to Sweden via Frankfurt an der Oder and the Baltic seaport of Stettin. Philpot aimed to get to the neutral Scandinavian haven by the longer route, via Frankfurt and Danzig. All three were due to travel on the same fast train to Frankfurt, which left Sagan railway station at 7 p.m. that evening. The plan was to avoid fast trains wherever possible in favour of slow trains travelling with local workers. The Germans, Williams had discovered, were used to incompetent foreign workers—there were six million of them in Germany at that time—and it was not unusual for one of them to be unable to speak German. All the escapers had to do in any sticky situation was look helpless and declare: 'Ich bin Ausländer.'

Shortly after noon on 29 October Codner had a substantial meal of bully-beef, potatoes, Canadian biscuits and cheese. At 1 p.m. the wooden horse was taken out as usual, with Williams and Codner inside. This time, though, Codner had all of their luggage and descended with it into the tunnel. Williams stayed in the wooden horse and by 2 p.m. he had replaced the trap-door and topsoil. While he was doing that, Codner below ground had pushed two air holes upwards to breathe. In the meantime, the horse was taken back to the cookhouse. Codner's absence from the afternoon roll-call at 3.45 p.m. was successfully disguised.

It was now Williams' and Philpot's turn to bid their comrades farewell, and they too were treated to a hearty meal. By now all friction between the vaulters and the escapers had disappeared and everybody wished the two men 'good luck'. At 4.15 p.m. the horse was taken outside once more, this time with the two men and another officer inside. Williams descended into the tunnel first and as he made his way along, it came as a relief to him to hear the familiar voice of Codner greet him in the dark distance. The tunnel was very hot and stank with the foul stench of sweat. Williams found Codner was filthy but surprisingly cheerful, given that he had been incarcerated underground for half the afternoon. Behind them Philpot was putting the last few bags of sand into the horse and after he finished said goodbye to the officer who remained in the horse to close the trap-door.

The officer sealed the tunnel at 4.50 p.m. and the horse was returned to the cookhouse with the news that all was well with the three men in the tunnel. It must have been an enormous relief to the four carriers when they placed the horse on the ground for the last time. Perhaps, on this one occasion, their smiles were not affected. It is hard to overestimate the excitement of the three men in the tunnel. They were going to break through the surface of the soil outside in just over an hour's time, at 6 p.m., when it would be dark but by no means pitch black. However, it was essential for them to go then if they were to have enough time to get to the railway station and catch the 7 p.m. train.

At 6.05 p.m. Codner pushed through the final few inches of the tunnel, which, he was to discover, had exited some 15 to 18 feet on the other side of the wire. But to Codner's alarm he also found that it had broken through part of the pathway that the German guards patrolled on the outside of the wire, not, as had been planned, a foot further into the darkness. This potentially grievous error was only ameliorated by the fact that the outside patrol had not appeared due to some oversight or possibly sheer laziness on the part of the goons. Codner leapt out of the tunnel followed by Williams and they ran across the road to the dank bank of trees looming in the darkness. Each experienced that peculiar sense of exhilaration mixed with fear as they sped across the open expanse of ground. Their hearts pounded as they half expected a shout of alarm from the goon box followed by the crack of a rifle shot. To their relief the shot did not come. They raced into the enveloping embrace of the dark forest, hardly able to contain their excitement as they threw their black overalls and hoods off and put on their civilian disguises. The men cleaned the muck off one another's faces. Still there was not a hint of sound from the camp to indicate anything was amiss. Just minutes later Philpot shot across the road to the woods. As he left the tunnel behind he wondered just how soon it would be discovered. Codner and Williams now helped Philpot clean himself up, leaving the forest as quickly as possible. Philpot let the other two have a head start of a few minutes.

Williams and Codner arrived at Sagan station within 20 minutes and made their way to the booking hall. Williams got the fright of his life when he walked straight into the

German doctor who had been treating him only two days earlier. His alarm turned to relief when he realised the doctor did not register a flicker of recognition at the sight of his English patient now bereft of his moustache and wearing the disguise of a French foreign worker. The English officers stood in the queue for the Frankfurt an der Oder train. Philpot arrived a few minutes later and could see the other two just ahead of him. Both parties studiously ignored one another.

Fortunately, the train to Frankfurt an der Oder arrived shortly afterwards and the journey contained no more unwelcome surprises. The compartment was crowded and dark, as they had hoped it would be. In the gloom most of the passengers sought to ignore one another's glances and get the uncomfortable ordeal over and done with. Once the train left Sagan, Philpot's path did not cross with Williams and Codner's on their flight from Germany. The train steamed into Frankfurt shortly before 9 p.m. The three men disembarked, intent on their separate routes and still unsure as to whether their absence had been discovered at Sagan. There were no further connections that night, and so the men had to find somewhere they could stay overnight in the city without arousing suspicion or being detected. Philpot walked as casually as he could through the dark streets before finding a quiet patch to settle down in by the Oder. It would be a terribly uncomfortable night in the cold, but it was one that Philpot would not exchange for the comparative warmth of his camp bed. He was a free man once more, and intended to continue to be so.

Williams and Codner had a similarly depressing night. They tried to find rooms in several hotels only to discover every one of them seemed to be booked up for some inexplicable reason. In despair, they edged their way to the outskirts of the city and, like Philpot, found a quiet place in a dry drain ditch where they could spend the night undisturbed. They were both wearing warm woollen underclothes but they were by no means warm enough. It was to be a long night.

The following dawn and Philpot was back at Frankfurt railway station at around 6 a.m. He had time to wash and shave in the station's facilities before catching the 6.56 a.m. slow train to Kustrin (now the Polish town of Kostrzyn), 18 miles from Frankfurt an der Oder and 51 miles north-east of Berlin. Philpot had deliberately chosen this opaque route out of Germany because it was the least likely and he hoped not to encounter any police specifically looking for an escaped RAF officer. (Although at that stage he had no way of knowing whether the tunnel and the men's absence had been discovered.) On the train Philpot fell into amiable conversation with an old man. He was greatly comforted by the fact that his disguise appeared not to arouse any suspicion (even though, he reflected, his German companion was practically senile). The train had arrived at Frankfurt late and arrived in Kustrin late. Philpot bade a friendly farewell to the German and boarded the express to Königsberg (now Kaliningrad), a train so crowded that he had to spend the first leg of the journey to Dirschau (now Tczew, in Poland) in the passageway of the third-class coach with many other passengers including many soldiers. Tiredness overcame him and Philpot fell asleep on his suitcase. Suddenly, he slipped off the case and awoke with a jerk, blurting out: 'Damn.' Realising his mistake he was momentarily alarmed, only to find his fellow passengers smiling benignly at him, even the soldiers. He could be excused for thinking that this escaping lark wasn't so difficult after all.

If he did, then he thought too soon. Shortly afterwards, a member of the criminal police began edging his way down the passageway, asking everyone for their identity papers. When it came to Philpot's turn he tried to appear calm as he handed over his identity card, hoping that the policeman would not notice that the photograph was of someone else altogether. (The forgery department had no photograph of Philpot and so had inserted a picture of the closest match they had.) There was a slight moment of apprehension when the German demanded to know where his Norwegian passport was. Philpot explained that the Dresden police had confiscated it and had told him his identity card would suffice. It would, replied the policeman, if they had stamped the photograph—but they hadn't. Philpot began to think his time was up. His heart started racing wildly as now the policeman began to scrutinise the photograph. Philpot held his breath for what seemed a lifetime, before the policeman airily handed the imperfect document back to him. The papers were sufficiently in order, he concluded brusquely, before moving on. Philpot inwardly sighed with relief.

Williams and Codner had also left their hiding places as soon as they could before dawn. They discovered that the Germans were early risers and Frankfurt was full of people on the way to their offices, factories and shops. The two men had a coffee at the station, casually looking around to see if they could spot Philpot. In fact he had already gone and they took a later slow train (or Personenzug) to Kustrin. Williams and Codner were relieved to find that there appeared to be no identity checks on this train and there was no sense that anyone was on the look-out for them. The first carriage was full of Russian prisoners of war and when they tried to enter it the German guard angrily ordered them to get out. They arrived at their destination just before 10 a.m. and spent the day in Kustrin idling their time away, first in a park, where they cleaned themselves up and ate some of their rations.

Later they risked venturing into a café and subsequently hit on the bright idea of whiling away the rest of the day inside the black anonymity of a cinema. Williams and Codner were also gambling on the fact that they were dawdling their way to freedom. If the alert had been raised at Sagan and anybody was looking for them, they would surely have checked the fast trains. In the late afternoon they took the slow train to Stettin, arriving at 8 p.m. Once more they were to discover all the hotels were full, but this time their evening was not going to be quite as uncomfortable as the one the day before. Wandering out into the suburbs they discovered a row of houses each with its own air-raid shelter. Inspecting them one at a time, they chose the one that appeared to be most comfortable. Settling down for another night's sleep, they prayed that for once, hopefully, the RAF would not be paying Stettin a visit on that particular night.

That afternoon Philpot had arrived at Dirschau and boarded the express to Danzig, arriving at 5 p.m., just under 24 hours after he had emerged from the tunnel at Sagan. After his hair-raising encounter with the German policeman, he could be forgiven for relaxing over a glass of beer at the railway station café before setting off for the docks on a tramcar. He had hoped to have a look around but by the time the tram arrived darkness had descended and he couldn't see the lay of the land. Philpot returned to the station and sought a room in a hotel nearby. The clerk was churlish about his identity card, but eventually gave him a spare bed in a room, sharing with another man. Acutely conscious that given a whole night of sleeping he could very well repeat his dreadful faux pas on the train, Philpot rushed to have a bath and be asleep before his room companion arrived. When the man arrived late that night Philpot feigned deep slumber. He repeated the ploy in the morning, hoping his roommate didn't think there was anything odd about someone who appeared to sleep for so long. It was an agonising wait while the man washed and shaved, but after the man had left, Philpot paid his bill and headed for the docks once more. Taking a ferry that made a round trip of the harbour, he was pleased to see a Swedish ship being loaded with coal. It would be the ship, he decided, that would take him on the final leg of his flight to freedom.

His fellow escapees spent the Sunday evening in the Hotel Schobel, finally and joyfully getting their first taste of real comfort since they left Sagan. They had left the air-raid shelter before dawn and checked into the hotel

210

at 9.30 a.m. They too had to go through the ordeal of explaining their less-than-perfect documentation to the hotel clerk. They, like Philpot, had discovered it was not such an ordeal after all. The Germans did not have the meticulous approach to documentation they were commonly supposed to have. They produced their Ausweise and filled in a form stating that they were French draughtsmen on their way to Anklam to work in the Arado Flugzeugwerke, the aircraft works. The clerk accepted their cover story and checked them in. The two men were to spend the following days of their escape checking into a variety of hotels because they were under the impression that a stay of longer than two days had to be reported to the police. Once, in the Hotel Gust, they found themselves sharing a breakfast table with three senior officers of the German Army. When it came to coffee, the British officers felt bold enough to dig into their pockets to get their American Air Force ration biscuits which they cheekily munched in front of the Germans. Their breakfast companions seemed not to notice.

The two men spent their mornings reconnoitring the docks at Freihaven and checked out the coaling station some three miles further on at Reiherwerder. But their search for a suitable Swedish vessel was to prove fruitless and depression began to set in. They spent every afternoon in the cinema, eventually seeing the same film four times and never understanding a word of it. In the evenings they made the rounds of cafés, where they hoped to meet someone who would be prepared to help them escape, and ended up consuming vast quantities of German beer, which, they concluded, appeared to contain no alcohol whatever. Neither of them could speak a word of Swedish so it wasn't possible to approach any Swedish sailors they might find. Instead they inveigled themselves among French itinerant workers in the hope that they might find one sympathetic to a couple of escaped POWs.

* * *

In the meantime, Philpot had had a remarkably smooth escape. He had been challenged only twice during his odyssey across Germany and on both occasions any inadequacies in his forged documentation had been disregarded without a great deal of concern. But now, as Philpot returned to the Swedish ship in Danzig harbour that evening, he realised that the next stage of his journey was not going to be quite without hazard. He found the whole dock was bathed in light. There were lights in every conceivable part of the dock and a huge searchlight followed the progress of the crane as it loaded coal onto the vessel. Sentries guarded every gate. Philpot was beginning to think his task was all but impossible.

However, by climbing down to water level, he found it was surprisingly easy to get around the barbed-wire fences that jutted out either side of the dock. Doing so, he walked along the dock before encountering a vertical ladder leading to the higher dock. Above him Philpot could see the gangway to the ship, guarded by a single sentry who could not possibly miss an intruder.

Philpot, though, didn't have his eye on the gangway. What attracted his attention were the mooring cables that secured the ship to the dock. There were several of them and all led directly through portholes and onto the deck of the vessel. He wondered, could he shin up them without being spotted from the shore? Philpot headed for the vertical steel ladder leading to the upper dock. It was when he started climbing it that Philpot heard a boat approaching. He scrambled to the top quickly and the movement attracted the interest of a sentry, who approached with his torch flashing. Alarmed, Philpot dived for cover behind a large obstacle. Fortunately, the sentry walked on the opposite side. Philpot overheard him exchanging words with the people in the boat, possibly harbour officials or police. Soon afterwards, calm returned. There was no further sign of the boat or the sentry. It had been a salutary lesson.

Philpot lay in wait. After a while he began climbing up one of the mooring cables. It proved a mistake. The cable was wrapped tightly around the stern of the ship and afforded no handhold for him to make his way around. Remarkably, nobody had spotted him. He returned to the dock and chose another cable. This time it led directly through a large hole in the side of the hull and on to the deck. As he made his way up he half expected a shout from the dock, but none came and he was soon safely ensconced in the Swedish ship. He looked around to see the deck was deserted, but at the same time it offered no opportunity of a hiding place, so he made his way around before finding a flight of steep stairs down to a galley. It too was deserted and to his gratification there was a warm chocolate drink on the stove. Unsurprisingly, he drank it without the slightest hesitation.

Eventually Philpot found his way to a hold that contained coal, and from there discovered the engine room and a hiding place where he settled down and soon fell into a deep slumber. He was gratified a few hours later to wake to the sound of growling engines and the gentle movement of the ship rolling through the sea. Smiling to himself, he stayed in his hiding place until he was confident the ship was well out of German waters. When that moment arose he pulled himself up, straightened out his crumpled outfit and introduced himself to a startled Swedish seaman in the engine-room. It was 2 November. The crewman took him up to the captain's quarters. There he was royally entertained before the ship docked at Södertälje at midnight on 3 November. He spent the night in a police cell, but Philpot was a free man, and the following day he was escorted to the British Legation in Stockholm. Shortly afterwards Philpot was sent back to Britain.

*　　　*　　　*

Although Williams and Codner had set out earlier and had the shorter journey, they were to spend much more time on occupied soil. Their nightly encounters with the café society of Stettin's itinerant French community were to provide mixed blessings. On one occasion they thought they had found a helper—the man seemed to enjoy his role as their co-conspirator, so much so that his efforts to help them were so theatrically histrionic that he proved more of a hazard than a help. They quickly dropped him and found themselves immersed in the capricious and potentially murderous world of the underground movement. They met two Frenchmen who were also trying to escape, but the Frenchmen were convinced that the two Englishmen were Gestapo agents and wanted to keep their distance from them. Through them, however, Codner and Williams met another French escaper by the name of André Daix, who had hatched a plan to get to Denmark by a ship but didn't think he could take the British pair with him. It was all very unnerving for Codner and Williams, who were unused to living such a cloak-and-dagger existence where nobody's word could be taken for granted—despite their experience of being incarcerated in Stalag Luft III.

Nevertheless, through Daix, Williams and Codner were introduced to two Danish sailors, Captain E. Ostrup Olsen and his bo'sun Pedersen, who appeared to be willing to help. (They did not know it at the time, but the Danes were working for British and American intelligence respectively. They had been equipped with a high-quality camera, which they used to record the comings and goings of German ships in the coastal waters that stretched from Scandinavia to France. On board their small ship, the SS *J.C. Jacobsen*, they had a quantity of incriminating photographs waiting to be delivered to London. Neither man ever let on about their secret role to the British escapers and it was only long after the war that they would find out.)

Pedersen was eventually convinced of their story and agreed to take both the British and Frenchman to Sweden. It would be a risky

Roger Bushell—the man without whom there would never have been the Great Escape. With his mother and his doting sister. (Courtesy of Liz Carter)

Jimmy James, who staged no less than 12 break out attempts, including one from Sachsenhausen. (Courtesy of Jimmy James)

Sydney Dowse—after the Great Escape he escaped with Jimmy James from Sachsenhausen. 'I was determined to get out and cause the Germans as much trouble as possible.' (Courtesy of Sydney Dowse)

Tony Bethell—RAF Mustang pilot and one of the 7 surviving of the 76 escapers. (Courtesy of Express Newspapers)

Desmond Plunkett—the avid and indomitable 'escape artist' who never let the Nazis get him down. (Courtesy of Express Newspapers)

Bob van der Stok—Dutch RAF flier and one of the three who got away. Van der Stok ended up working for NASA. (Courtesy of Ian Le Sueur)

Bernard Scheidhauer of the Free French Air Force and Raymond van Wymeersch in Stalag Luft III. (Courtesy of Ian Le Sueur)

Per Bergsland in the cockpit of his plane. (Courtesy of Charlotte Bergsland)

Per Bergsland—one of the two Norwegian RAF fliers who made the 'home run' (to England) in the Great Escape. (Courtesy of Charlotte Bergsland)

Albert Patton Clark —one of the first Americans to be taken prisoner in the Second World War. (Courtesy of A.P. Clark/United States Air Force Academy)

'For you the war is over.' 'Bub' Clark heard the familiar refrain after crash landing his damaged Spitfire in northern France. (Courtesy of A.P. Clark/United States Air Force Academy)

'Bub' (centre) in captivity explaining how he met his fate? (Courtesy A.P. Clark/United States Air Force Academy)

An early newspaper report of Clark's internment in Dulag Luft. (Courtesy of A.P. Clark/United States Air Force Academy)

Lt.Col. Clark Held as Prisoner in Germany

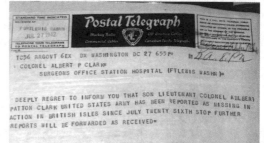

How his parents received the news back home. (Courtesy of A.P. Clark/United States Air Force Academy)

But the Luftwaffe tried to keep matters civilised. The unwilling Kommandant of Stalag Luft III, Colonel Friedrich-Wilhelm von Lindeiner-Wildau. (Courtesy United States Air Force Academy)

And his agreeable subordinate, Captain Gustav Simoleit. (Courtesy of United States Air Force Academy)

The stove in Block 104 under which Harry was tunnelled. (Courtesy of Jimmy James)

Harry's trolley. (Later requisitioned by the Germans and displayed in their 'Escape Museum' at Stalag Luft III. (Courtesy of Jimmy James)

Nevertheless, the Allies continued the fight behind the wire . . . A bogus identity card (for Bub Clark) produced by one of the camp's factories. (Courtesy United States Air Force Academy)

In the meantime, the 'wooden horse'
escapers stage one of the most
audacious breakouts from Germany in
the East Compound. Diagram shows the
tunnel route of Codner, Philpot and
Williams. All three officers escaped to
England in one of the most remarkable
tunnelling feats of the war.
(Courtesy of Desmond Plunkett)

Their success encouraged the once-demoralised prisoners to attempt one of the greatest escapes of them all. The route of tunnels Tom, Dick and Harry out of North Compound. (Courtesy of Desmond Plunkett)

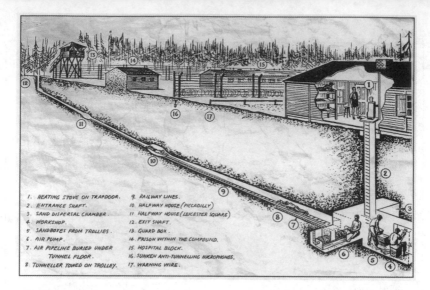

1. HEATING STOVE ON TRAPDOOR.	9. RAILWAY LINES.
2. ENTRANCE SHAFT.	10. HALFWAY HOUSE (PICCADILLY)
3. SAND DISPERSAL CHAMBER.	11. HALFWAY HOUSE (LEICESTER SQUARE)
4. WORKSHOP.	12. EXIT SHAFT.
5. SANDBOXES FROM TROLLIES.	13. GUARD BOX.
6. AIR PUMP.	14. PRISON WITHIN THE COMPOUND.
7. AIR PIPELINE BURIED UNDER TUNNEL FLOOR.	15. HOSPITAL BLOCK.
8. TUNNELLER TOWED ON TROLLEY.	16. SUNKEN ANTI-TUNNELLING MICROPHONES.
	17. WARNING WIRE.

The full extent of Harry, showing the halfway houses Piccadilly Circus and Leicester Square, the ventilation pumps, underground workshops and trolley line. (Courtesy of Jimmy James)

Left: 'There were so many men packed into Block 104 there was actually steam coming out of the windows.' An illustration showing the men waiting in Block 104 on the night of the escape in a variety of disguises. (Courtesy of Jimmy James)

Right: Freedom—for a few precious hours. Ley Kenyon's classic drawing of the men breaking out. 'That was the last I ever saw of Roger Bushell—and some of the finest men I have ever known in my entire life.' Bub Clark. (Courtesy of Jimmy James)

endeavour. The *Jacobsen* was a very small vessel and the hideaways would be sharing it with a complement of German passengers. The men would have to evade a thorough search of the ship before it left harbour and when it arrived in Swedish waters they would have to escape on the pilot's boat without giving the game away to the Germans on board, otherwise the crew would suffer. All three men agreed to do exactly what the Danes told them to.

They were taken on board the *Jacobsen* and hidden in a tiny compartment under the fo'c'sle. While the ship was being searched before it embarked, Williams was cowering in a cramped corner, his eyes within inches of a Nazi soldier's jackboots. At one hair-raising moment the German plunged his hand into the enclosure and began groping around. Williams held his breath and pushed himself backwards as far as he could. Finally, though, the ship set sail. It was an uncomfortable voyage for the British and French as they continued to hide while the Germans strolled around the deck, but after some hours the ship approached Swedish territorial waters. Now, everything depended upon who the Swedish pilot was. If it was somebody sympathetic to the Allied cause, then all would be—almost— plain sailing. If it was a quisling then everybody would be in trouble.

As the pilot boat drew near, Pedersen

breathed a sigh of relief when he saw the face of a friendly captain. He knew him very well—he was a very reliable man indeed. It was a cold winter's day and even colder in the open sea. When the pilot's boat drew alongside the *Jacobsen,* Pedersen was going to make sure all the German passengers would be in the warmth of a cabin on the opposite side of the ship. While they were being distracted by cups of hot chocolate and an unusually garrulous member of the crew, the three escapers were planning to make a run for it only a few feet away. In the event of one of the Germans somehow seeing what was going on, Pedersen had given the order that they land a punch on him—'but not too hard'—to make it look as if they had taken him by surprise too.

In the end it did not prove necessary for such amateur dramatics. The pilot boat drew alongside. The situation was quickly explained by one captain to another. The three men were ordered to leave their hiding places swiftly and board the boat. They did so and it promptly set off full steam ahead for the Swedish coast. On 11 November Williams and Codner disembarked at Stomstad. They said a grateful goodbye to the pilot, and like Philpot before them they were taken to a police cell where they were given a welcome bath and warm meal. Shortly afterwards they were taken to the British Legation in Stockholm. One night they sat down in a cinema, this time to enjoy a film in English. It was James Hilton's classic *Random Harvest* and the two men wept tears of joy for the sentimental vision of England the movie evoked. On 15 November, Williams wrote to his mother in London's Golders Green: 'Dear Mother, Just a line to let you know that I have escaped the "Nazi Hell Camp" and am in Sweden. I am quite fit and shall be in England, I hope, in about a week. Do not worry if I am a bit longer as transport is rather unreliable . . .'

Presently Williams and Codner were both repatriated to Britain. Williams' experiences were put to good use by the RAF. He went on a tour of RAF camps on behalf of MI9, lecturing about escape and evasion techniques. One MI9 officer warned Williams' audiences, however: 'The experiences Flt. Lieutenant Williams describes are not necessarily consistent with MI9 teaching and whilst successful in his case, they may have unfortunate results if attempted as a general principle.' Some time later the news that all three men had got home reached Stalag Luft III. For one night at least there was cheering and happiness throughout the camp.

There was, however, a dark epilogue to the famed wooden horse escape that only emerged after the war. Williams and Codner could not have known as they boarded the pilot boat that they had been spotted by two German trawlers nearby. As their boat made for the Swedish shore, the German trawlers closed in on the *Jacobsen*. To his horror, Pedersen realised the whole thing had been witnessed by German Army officers on board the trawlers watching with binoculars. Soon afterwards one of the trawlers came alongside the *Jacobsen* and a boarding party of armed guards stormed the Danish vessel. The crew were ordered on deck, some of them pulled out of their beds half-naked. For several hours the men were harshly beaten and battered with rifle butts. They stuck to their story that none of them had known there were escapers on board. The Germans informed them that they would be escorted back to Denmark and the three ships set sail, the two German trawlers circling the Danish ship, the officers keeping a watchful eye with their binoculars once more. Oddly, they did not leave a guard on board. The omission allowed Pedersen to dispose of the incriminating photographs. It probably saved him his life. When the *Jacobsen* arrived in Denmark, the interrogation of the crew continued. Eventually an angry German sergeant told them he was going to shoot the youngest crewman, who was barely out of his boyhood. Pedersen had seen many of his compatriots shot for less. He confessed that he had helped the escapers, but that none of the crew knew anything about it. The Germans didn't believe him, but they couldn't prove it, and with the thankful absence of the photographs they could not pin anything more on the Dane. Pedersen escaped being executed, too, but nevertheless spent the rest of the war in a concentration camp.

The success of the wooden horse escapers taught the members of East Compound a vital lesson. So long as the tunnel entrance could be hidden, then a successful tunnel really could be built. In fact, in the following spring the prisoners began such a tunnel called, for some reason lost in time, 'Margaret'. They were to use the morning and afternoon roll-calls to camouflage their tunnelling activities. In the morning, while hundreds of men assembled for the morning roll-call, a couple of their number would dig a tunnel in the middle of them, and remain for most of the day down the tunnel. In the evening they would emerge during roll-call. The excavated sand was carried away by all the other men, hidden in bags beneath their winter greatcoats. The digging began in January 1944 and Margaret was complete by the following March. Everything was ready for a team of five men to go out when another attempt forced the escape to be postponed. That was through a tunnel called Harry.

CHAPTER SIX

HARRY

The news of the success of the wooden horse escape reached Stalag Luft III shortly after the three men had arrived back in England. When their safe arrival home was announced at morning Appell, a huge cheer went up. The escape of Williams, Codner and Philpot proved to be a huge psychological boost after the devastation wrought by Tom's discovery. The prisoners' morale was raised further by news of the Allies' incursion into southern Italy. The arrival of a contingent of Allied officers who had been involved in the Italian campaign, and had escaped from POW camps in Italy, also cheered them up. For the hungry and weary men of Sagan, the sudden appearance of the comrades-in-arms with tanned faces and tales of victories against the Nazis came as a welcome change. They listened, thrilled at their stories of enjoying weeks of freedom in the Alps hoping to get to Switzerland. Hitler's hated Third Reich, which had held the world in its thrall at the beginning of the war, now appeared to be a less formidable beast. 'Fortress Europe' was quickly crumbling. The once-feared Nazi war machine was on the retreat at sea, in the air and on land. German cities were falling under a relentless Allied bombing campaign. Often the prisoners were treated to the sight of American Flying Fortresses or Liberators high in the sky returning from their sorties. A ripple of applause and cheering would break out across the camp, much to the irritation of the goons. At night it comforted the inmates to hear the soft, distant boom of British air raiders. After Berlin had been subjected to a particularly heavy pounding, an angry Glemnitz marched up to Bub Clark in the South Compound. The two men normally had a cordial relationship, but on this occasion Glemnitz poked his finger at Clark's face and hissed: 'When this war is over, you will rebuild this country, Colonel Clark.' The American officer couldn't help but sympathise with the German, whom he liked and would continue to see after the war. But at that stage of hostilities Clark had seen enough of the Nazis' barbarity not to be too concerned about the methods used to bring it to an end.

The escape season was now effectively over. The winters in Central Europe were so cold that few prisoners wanted to endure the hardship of life outside the wire. Most of them battened down the hatches to enjoy a quiet Christmas, dreaming of their escape plans that would begin once more in the spring, or simply settling down to reading or attending classes and staging theatrical and musical productions. German classes were the most popular, with so many officers preparing themselves for escape. It was generally agreed that October's *Macbeth* was one of the theatre's most accomplished productions. Welcome arrivals around this time were British and American feature films shown at the cinema, among the favourites being the Ginger Rogers and Fred Astaire classic *Shall We Dance?* The atmosphere in Stalag Luft III was rather like that of a private boarding school, albeit a rather austere one at that.

The Germans also relaxed their guard and there were few altercations between captives and captors. There was one amusing incident when the stooge system seemed to have broken down and Glemnitz walked in on Ivo Tonder making a civilian suit. Glemnitz marched out of the compound holding the suit triumphantly. There were one or two absurd escape attempts that harked back to the amateurish efforts of previous times and were authorised by the Escape Committee in a bid to lull the Germans into a false sense of security. Bushell hoped to convince the Germans that the discovery of Tom really had broken the prisoners' will to escape. Bushell himself had put it around that he was no longer interested in escape. He threw himself instead into the world of the camp's theatrical community and was billed to play the role of Professor Higgins in the forthcoming production of George Bernard Shaw's *Pygmalion*.

Much of the innocent camp activity, of course, masked the clandestine preparations that were still going on to make an escape attempt through Harry in the New Year. In fact, Bushell was perpetually talking to Massey and Day about the break-out in 1944, constantly re-evaluating plans and fine-tuning their strategy. He was also working hard on improving his German and had started attending classes to learn Czech and Danish too. Jimmy James continued his Russian and German studies. Despite Glemnitz's momentary victory, Tommy Guest and Ivo Tonder's tailors carried on working on a whole range of civilian and some military disguises. In Block 103, Al Hake's operation manufactured compasses with the assembly-line efficiency of Henry Ford's car factory. Des Plunkett's team of map-makers set about building up a portfolio of highly detailed maps showing potential escape routes tailored towards individual escapers' plans. Tim Walenn's forgery department, now operating from Block 110, continued to churn out an enormous panoply of false papers, passes and ID cards that would be needed by the escapers.

By the time of the break-out a few months later, there would be 250 compasses and 4,000 maps available to the escapers, as well as some

100 handmade suits indistinguishable from those lovingly made by the tailors of Hamburg or Dresden, and 12 German uniforms. That winter saw Dean & Dawson acquire two innovative devices that very much speeded up the forgery process. A tame ferret, who had not been intimidated by Rubberneck, gave the Escape Committee a typewriter and John Travis built a small printing press, which he operated from the bottom of Dick's entry shaft. Dick was now beginning to look increasingly redundant as an escape outlet as it became obvious that the tunnel would have to be prolonged by perhaps as much as 600 feet under the rapidly growing West Compound. Consequently, the tunnel was used to store much of the clandestine material that would be required for the escape. Tommy Guest kept his suits and other completed clothing in the attic of the toilet block. The rest of the escape material—compasses, maps, high-energy food and so on—was hidden behind false walls, a ruse of the Allies that the Germans had still, remarkably, failed to cotton on to.

November brought the first fluttering of winter snow, but it was only in December that the first really heavy snowfall came. The prisoners were cheered up a little by the arrival of additional Red Cross parcels and the showing of the Hollywood film *Bringing Up Baby,* starring Katharine Hepburn and Cary Grant. On the night before Christmas the camp listened in total silence as a bugler played 'Silent Night'. It was not a great consolation for men dreaming of being at home with their families by a warm coal fire, but having to live with the reality of the Silesian snow and bitter east winds that raked the camp. For some, like Wings Day, it was their fifth Christmas in captivity, and hardly an anniversary to celebrate. Most of the prisoners tried to create some sort of festive distraction, organising Christmas dinners and so forth. Most of the men had been saving up supplies to splurge out on Christmas Day. Jimmy James recalls that some of the men entertained themselves by offering 87 per cent proof brew to the German guards. One man, says James, collapsed in the snow after drinking his bottle and was dragged away by the two guard dogs in his charge. Another guard, this time in a goon box, was tossed a bottle of the illicit brew. Later that night he fell out of the watchtower. Despite the diversions, Christmas was not a happy occasion for most of the men. However, when on New Year's Eve they toasted the arrival of 1944 with illicit whisky, the mood was a little more cheerful, because they all knew work on Harry was just around the corner.

By the New Year the Escape Committee had definitely ruled out Dick, thanks partly to the West Compound but also because it had become so cluttered with stored escape material and Travis's printing press. Now it was decided that the carpentry department should be moved there too. All the Escape Committee's efforts were going to be thrown into Harry, which already extended some 100 feet northwards underneath the Vorlager (and directly under the cooler). The Escape Committee calculated that it would only need to be extended a further 220 feet for it to emerge safely behind the tree line. And Bushell was hoping to catch the Germans by surprise by breaking out before the arrival of spring, when the ferrets would be at their most alert, which meant that the men would have to start digging soon.

It was with a feeling of renewed anticipation that work resumed on Harry on 10 January. The trap-door had been sealed so well it took two hours to reopen. Harry Marshall, Wally Floody and Crump Ker-Ramsay took turns to chip away at the cement in the tiled concrete block. Once it was open the men descended into Harry and subjected it to a meticulous examination. They were delighted to discover that the tunnel had weathered the winter much better than they had expected: only four shoring boards needed securing back in place, while the sacks on the ventilation pumps had rotted and needed minor attention. The most difficult repair work applied to the Klim milk tin ventilation pipes. The weight of the tunnel structure had cracked the ventilation line in parts and sand had seeped into many of them, clogging up the air passage. It was difficult to get to them and repair them because they were firmly pressed down by the upright shoring boards. In the event, it took only four days to remove individual sections of the flooring and replace the sections of pipe affected. The Escape Committee was not at all unhappy with this minor programme of renovation, which took only a few days. By 15 January, digging on Harry was resumed.

By the end of the month the tunnellers had constructed the first staging post (called, variously, haulage points or halfway houses) and had christened it Piccadilly Circus. They planned to call the next one Leicester Square and the thought of it spurred them on. Work progressed at the rate of about four to five feet a day. Wally Floody and Ker-Ramsay led the digging teams, which worked until the late afternoon. Inside the tunnel, at the workface, there were a couple of close calls. Wally Floody was buried in a collapse, to be hauled out half unconscious. Another tunneller was given a nasty crack on the head by a bed board that fell from the top to the bottom of the entry shaft, but it was remarkable how few injuries and accidents there were.

The thick blanket of snow that covered the compound presented Peter Fanshawe's sand dispersal teams with a difficult problem. It was clear the sand could not be dispersed in the usual way. Ever resourceful, Fanshawe came up with a solution. The theatre with which von Lindeiner had so thoughtfully provided the camp had been built by the prisoners themselves. It featured tiers of 350 seats, each raised slightly above the other to give all the audience a view of the proscenium. There was nothing at all beneath this voluminous triangular structure, which had been sealed when construction of the theatre had been completed. It was probably capable of holding all the sand excavated from Harry. Creating a secret trap beneath one or more of the seats would not be a problem. Once more the Escape Committee was eternally grateful for Fanshawe's apparently boundless ingenuity.

For his part, Fanshawe needed someone reliable and meticulous to be put in charge of organising the theatre dispersal—not as easy a job as may at first appear. It wasn't just a case of pouring bags of sand down a hole. It was vital that the sand didn't sprinkle out onto the snowy ground on its way to the theatre, leaving the Germans a nice neat trail to follow. The work also had to be completed in darkness, as the light in the winter went at 5 p.m. Shortly afterwards, Fanshawe bumped into Jimmy James as they were both doing their daily circuits around the compound. James had been one of the most enthusiastic diggers, but now Fanshawe wondered whether he might like a change. He asked him if he wanted a job.

'Well, I am unemployed at the moment, as most of us are, and if I have to stick around this place much longer, I'll be permanently unemployable,' said James. 'What's cooking?'

Seat number 13 was chosen to conceal the trap-door. 'Thirteen is supposed to be lucky in some countries,' reflected James, ever the optimist. The seat swung backwards on hinges especially constructed by John Travis. Fanshawe thought they would need two dispersal teams of six men each to do the job every night between the hours of 6 p.m. and 10 p.m., when the Germans banged down the barracks. Jimmy James would be in charge of one; Squadron Leader Ian Cross the other. (Cross had recently attempted a more instinctive form of escape when he attached himself to a truck laden with pine trees and branches about to leave the compound. Unfortunately, Glemnitz saw him, stopped the truck and asked the driver if he would mind driving as fast as he could around the compound. After careering over the tree stumps and bumps of the compound, the truck returned to Glemnitz, who was standing ready to greet Cross, who emerged shaken but unharmed from his hiding place. 'I hope you enjoyed your ride, Squadron Leader, and came to no harm,' said Glemnitz before dispatching him to the cooler.)

Another 70 men were involved in the sand-dispersal operation. The sand was first of all

239

loaded into kitbags at the bottom of the shaft and taken across to Block 109, where the carriers hid the bags under their greatcoats for the walk across to the theatre. Occasionally, if the ferrets could be distracted, it was taken directly to the theatre but usually it had to go by a more circuitous route to allay suspicion. Once in the theatre, the bags were dropped through seat 13 to the workers underneath while rehearsals continued on the stage above. Flight Lieutenant Bernard 'Pop' Green (so called because he was one of the oldest prisoners) soon discovered what a difficult job it was. He was walking across the compound one night with a load of sand when his greatcoat snagged on one of the many severed tree trunks that strewed the compound. The sand spilled out in an untidy mess in the snow.

A further problem with the excavated sand was that it gave off a distinctive odour. The ferrets rarely missed an opportunity to search the theatres and von Lindeiner and other German officers often attended theatrical productions. If they got one whiff of the unusual smell, the game would be up and they would undoubtedly close down the theatre. The theatre was, everybody acknowledged, one of the few genuinely morale-boosting facilities in Stalag Luft III. It would be an awful loss to the men, but under Wings Day's new philosophy of bringing the battlefront to Sagan, the Escape Committee ruled that escape was the main priority, not morale. In the end, Jimmy James came up with an ingenious method of camouflaging the smell by distributing various scents, most notably tobacco, underneath the theatre seats in smouldering tins. Pipe and cigarette smokers were encouraged to patronise the theatre until a haze of smoke hung over the building.

With February came a shock for the escapers. Without warning a posse of Wehrmacht soldiers arrived at the main gate and within seconds they were sprinting towards barrack block 104, led by Rubberneck. By the time George Harsh shouted 'ferrets!' down the corridor, the Germans were in the building barging through every door into every room. Harsh wondered how many seconds it would take them to get to the stove which, presumably, at that very moment was shoved to the side to reveal the gaping hole of Harry's entry shaft. But Harry's Trapführer, Pat Langford, had set a record for concealment. In 20 seconds flat he had slammed the concrete down, swept the floor of dust and replaced the stove and its chimney. By the time Rubberneck stormed into the little canteen area Langford was smiling benignly and everything was in place. The ferrets turned 104 upside down, but didn't find a thing. Alarmingly they paid a great deal of attention to the tiled concrete of Harry's trap. In one sense the fact that they couldn't detect a thing despite such close

241

scrutiny was encouraging. But the episode was worrying all the same for the Escape Committee. The Germans obviously knew the tunnel was from 104. It could only be a matter of time before they found it.

The digging continued and the dispersal teams worked relentlessly—except for a few days in early February when the full moon cast such a dazzling light over the camp that there was no realistic way they could not be seen by the goon boxes. But by then the diggers were well on their way to the 200-feet mark. The dispersal teams were granted a stroke of luck one night when the ferret was distracted for two hours by his contact entertaining him with coffee and biscuits in his room. In two hours the dispersal team managed to get rid of an astonishing four tons of sand. At around about the same time the Escape Committee was delivered another stroke of fortune when von Lindeiner ordered the compound to be wired up to a public address system that would spread throughout the camp. While a German engineer toiled at the top of a pole trying to attach one loudspeaker, the Canadian officer Red Noble was passing by and couldn't help but notice two large coils of electricity wire at the foot of the pole. An insouciant Noble picked them up and sauntered off as the hapless workman looked on in despair. As was often the case in such instances, the theft was never reported. The workman was, presumably, more concerned with his own well-being than whether the Kriegies got their hands on a bit of valuable escape material. And Noble's loot was valuable—nearly 300 yards of waterproof electric cable. It meant the tunnellers could hook into the camp's power supply and dispense with the fat-burning lamps for much of the time.

At the premiere of *Treasure Island* at the beginning of the month, the cast was delighted to observe that the German officers present did not smell a rat. The tunnel itself went almost without a hitch until one of the surveyors noticed what seemed to be a 'clink' in its course. On closer inspection it was discovered Harry had veered one foot out of line. It was impossible to reverse the error because the removal of shoring would risk a collapse and so the mistake had to be rectified over time and the result was that the tunnel veered four feet off course before it continued on a parallel course in the original direction. It was only a minor mishap but, perhaps, it should have rung alarm bells among the surveying team as a precursor of possible trouble to come. However, digging continued apace and by the middle of February the tunnel had reached some 200 feet in length and the diggers were ready to carve out the next staging post, Leicester Square.

*   *   *

While the men dug, the Escape Committee addressed the problem of who, exactly, was going to be allowed the privilege of escaping. Bushell had decided that 200 men were going to make the attempt. That meant that there were going to be a lot of disappointed people. More than 600 prisoners were directly involved with the construction of the tunnel. The contribution of those who had not been 'at the coal face' was just as crucial to the completion of the task: the stooges, the officers involved in laborious sand-dispersal operations, the forgers, map-makers and tailors. In addition to that, there were many other people on the camp administrative staff and involved with the theatre who would surely have helped on the tunnel if their duties had not prevented them from doing so. The Escape Committee decided to seek applications from those interested in escaping. They were not surprised to get 510 requests.

They then set about working out how to select the lucky 200 and in the end the 510 names were put in a hat for a draw to be held on 20 February. However, the Escape Committee decided on a priority system. The first 30 places in the tunnel must go to those who had the best chance of escaping. Almost all of these would have to be fluent in German or other foreign languages. The first 30 would be provided with the very best documentation and disguises that the forgery department and tailors could supply. They would all travel by train and it was vital that they got the chance to get to the railway station first, preferably before midnight, after which there were very few trains until the morning.

The following 20 places would be reserved for the prisoners who had done the most work on the tunnel itself. Again, their names would be drawn out of a hat. The next batch of 20 would be selected in the same way from the prisoners who had worked above ground as stooges and penguins, and in the forgery, tailoring and compass-making departments. The next 30 (who would make up the final group of the first 100) would also be drawn out of a hat, this time from the ranks of those who had failed to get a place in the earlier draws. Finally, the remaining 100 places were drawn from the remaining names on the list. After the names had been drawn out there was one final amendment to the list. Ker-Ramsay suggested that it made sense that every 20th escaper was an experienced tunneller. If anything went wrong at least there would be someone familiar with the workings of the tunnel close at hand and capable of keeping things moving.

Everything seemed to be going smoothly both above and below ground, but the Escape Committee was right to believe that von Lindeiner's security staff were homing in on the tunnel. Despite the best efforts of Jimmy James and Ian Cross, it was impossible to prevent small quantities of sand falling on the ground, and there, in the morning, were the little give-away trails that indicated a tunnel was afoot. Rubberneck's response was to have his ferrets descend on the compound in force and search it repeatedly and relentlessly. All the barracks in the North Compound were subject to spot checks and the blitz of 104 in early February was not the only one. On one occasion Roger Bushell and Wings Day were ordered out of their barracks and strip-searched on the spot. The prisoners, however, were not entirely unprepared for these blitz searches. They were still being helped by the fact that many of the ferrets ignored Rubberneck's injunctions against fraternising with the enemy and they were tipped off in advance of many spot checks. Valenta had a very valuable contact in one of Pieber's men, called Walter. He warned Valenta to expect a sudden check on Block 110 and sure enough the barrack building was searched. Keen Type kept his contact, Marcel Zillessen, informed. Of course, this sort of traffic was two-way. The Germans knew through their contacts with the airmen that they were up to something and something big. Some of the prisoners did not help their cause by being less than discreet in letters home to their families.

Von Lindeiner was concerned to hear the

intelligence reports from his security staff. He knew that the problem of escaping Allied prisoners was beginning to aggravate the Nazi High Command, which was being compelled to divert more and more resources to tracking them down. Von Lindeiner tried always to respect the Geneva Convention but was aware that Berlin's attitude towards escaping officers was becoming less sympathetic. There had been some ugly incidents in other camps. Dulag Luft was no longer the holiday camp of Theo Rumpel's day. In one instance an SS officer had ordered two Luftwaffe guards to shoot an Allied airman in their care. When they refused he took out his gun and shot the man on the spot. The episode provoked the new Kommandant of Dulag Luft to travel to Berlin and protest to the German High Command—but his protest fell on deaf ears.

In early 1944 the authorities issued two orders that had ominous portents for future escapers. The first order, known as 'Stufe Römisch III', came from the OKW. The Oberkommando der Wehrmacht was the supreme headquarters of all the regular armed forces. All the more surprising then that the order stated that future escapers who were recaptured, with the exception of the British and Americans, were to be handed over to the Gestapo rather than the appropriate German military authority. The British and Americans were to be held in military or police jails, while the authorities decided whether to hand them over to the Gestapo or not. The prisoners became aware of this order when an officer, Bill Jennens, found himself alone in the Kommandant's office and to his surprise realised the safe was open. Curiosity getting the better of him, he discovered the order lying there for his inspection. Whether von Lindeiner deliberately staged this episode or not, we will never know. It would certainly be in keeping with his character.

The second order was even less subtle. The 'Aktion Kugel' (Bullet Decree) was a secret order issued by the Gestapo chief Heinrich Müller. It decreed that all recaptured officers, except Britons and Americans, were to be taken to Mauthausen concentration camp and executed before their names were even entered on the camp register. They would simply disappear. The method was disgusting. They would be taken to the camp and ushered to a 'measuring device' supposedly to fit them out for a prison outfit. In fact it contained a hole through which the prisoner would be shot in the neck from behind. But it was not just the SS and Gestapo that concerned von Lindeiner. He was equally worried about the prisoners' fate at the hands of the German public. The intensifying of the Allied air campaign against German cities was producing an ugly mood among civilians.

In the first four months of 1944 the

saturation bombing was intensified. Among some people British and American fliers were no longer seen as bona fide military fighters but branded as 'air terrorists'. The case against the Allied air forces had been reinforced by relentless Nazi propaganda that characterised them (as they did the Russians) as inferior beings who heartlessly attacked women and children. Around about that time the Nazi propaganda minister, Josef Goebbels, asked: 'Who is in the right? The murderers who expect humane treatment after their cowardly attacks? Or the victims of those foul and cowardly attacks who seek their revenge? We owe it to our population, which is defending itself with so much honesty and courage, that it not be allowed to become human game to be hunted down by the enemy.'

As ever the situation was far more complicated than it appeared. Any equivalence between the Allied bombing campaign—launched in desperation, the only way of taking on Germany's brutal might—and the wholesale and calculated slaughter of millions of Untermenschen ('subhuman' races) is an abomination. Bomber Command's policy might have been mistaken and perhaps ruthless, but it was understandable. Also, as ever, the Nazi propaganda ministry was not being entirely honest. Goebbels was labouring under two enormous problems.

The first was the psychological blow that the

air campaign had undoubtedly delivered. Under the onslaught from the air, ordinary Germans were beginning to question their government's policies and there was a distinct possibility of some sort of popular rebellion. Second, Germans everywhere knew in their hearts that they were defeated. The Red Army had reversed German advances in the east and in the west the long-expected 'Second Front' was not far away. It might have been illegal to listen to the BBC, but many Germans did. The enormous build-up of American, British and French troops across the Channel was no secret to most Germans.

Nevertheless, there had been cases of downed aircrews being set upon by lynch mobs only to be saved at the last moment by the Home Guard or Hitler Youth that generally arrived on the scene as soon as a plane hit the ground. (This was slightly odd in itself, since Nazi propaganda actually encouraged people to believe that revenge against airmen was justified.) Von Lindeiner wondered what sort of reception escaped airmen from Stalag Luft III would receive if they were caught by angry Germans and there was nobody there to step in.

When the German Kommandant heard that the prisoners were planning a mass break-out he decided to summon senior officers from every compound to warn them of the dangers. Von Lindeiner said the war could not possibly go on for more than another year and it was folly to take such risks in the circumstances. He wasn't the only one worried. Many of the German staff were genuinely fond of their Allied prisoners and passed on their concerns to them. It wasn't through self-interest alone that Pieber privately warned the Allied officers to avoid a mass break-out. He told them the Gestapo were looking for any excuse to take matters into their own hands but most of the prisoners, in their isolated existence, knew nothing of the change in mood outside the camp. Even the German warnings of courts-martial the previous year had not been taken seriously, few Allied prisoners believed the Germans would shoot them in cold blood. Tim Walenn displayed a commendably gentlemanly view of the enemy when he insisted they would never be so 'unsporting'. Some of the prisoners believed that the rumours they were hearing from the camp staff were part of an orchestrated campaign to dissuade them from staging an escape, which could only reflect badly on von Lindeiner.

The Luftwaffe, as von Lindeiner repeatedly warned the Allied officers, could only guarantee their safety and proper treatment while the prisoners were in its hands. Once outside the wire there was a bewildering array of different criminal and neo-military bodies into whose hands the airmen could fall. Few of them could be trusted to take as indulgent a view of Allied airmen as Hermann Göring did. The most feared organisation was Heinrich Himmler's Reichssicherheitshauptamt (RSHA or Reich Security Main Office). The RSHA's responsibilities ranged from regular police traffic patrols to extermination in the concentration camps. There were many wings of the RSHA, including the Kripo (criminal police), headed by General Nebe, and the Gestapo (which the former was often confused with), headed by Gruppenführer Heinrich Müller. And there was one particular department concerned purely with preventing escapes from prisoner-of-war camps. The man from the department responsible for Stalag Luft III was an SS major called Erich Brunner.

In February of 1944, von Lindeiner asked Brunner to come to the camp. During a short meeting, von Lindeiner is believed to have expressed fears that a mass escape was imminent. Curiously, despite this explicit warning, Brunner failed to reinstall seismograph equipment that had been removed from the camp for maintenance work. (It was an oversight that led to speculation after the war that the Nazi authorities were hoping there would indeed be an escape and that they would use it as an opportunity to make an example of the escapers.) At the same time Sydney Dowse warned Roger Bushell that his contact, Corporal Hesse, had heard ugly rumours about what the Gestapo planned to do with Bushell if he escaped again. Dowse tried to persuade Bushell not to take part in the break-out, but the response was predictable. 'I've worked too long on this,' Bushell told him. 'This time they're not going to catch me.' Bushell was not alone. Most of the potential escapers had thought carefully about the risks they faced.

Ian Cross had discussed the matter with Jimmy James. 'The Geneva Convention makes it quite clear that it recognises an officer's duty to escape, and that escaped prisoners of war are a protected species so long as they don't break the law of the land they are in,' said James. 'If apprehended we should give up in a peaceful fashion and we will be conveyed back to our prisoner-of-war camp.' Many of the prisoners agreed with Des Plunkett, who decided that the havoc they would cause the Germans was more than worth the possible bullet they'd receive in the back. Von Lindeiner's warnings were not falling on deaf ears. They were being carefully weighed up by extremely experienced military men, some of whom had been driven to the verge of madness by incarceration and all of whom took their responsibilities as fighting men very seriously indeed.

It was with delight therefore, several days later, that the X-Organisation received some welcome news. Valenta's tame ferret Walter told him that Rubberneck was going on two weeks' leave from 1 March. Valenta immediately told Bushell, who knew that Corporal Griese's endless searching of the compound was as unpopular with his own men as it was with the prisoners. They were bound to take the opportunity of his absence to enjoy a respite of their own. Shortly after the news, the draw for the 200 places was held. That evening there were 200 souls in Stalag Luft III for whom escape now seemed a very real prospect indeed. Their excitement, though, was tinged with a sense of fear at the dangers to come.

Jimmy James drew number 39. 'I was delighted,' he says, 'and like all the others I was gripped by the mounting tension and excitement pervading the compound.' Some prisoners couldn't help but tell their families back home what was about to happen. 'We are all expecting to be home in a few months,' wrote a remarkably indiscreet Tim Walenn. Others were slightly more opaque, but it would be astonishing if the letters littered with nods and winks escaped the censor's notice.

With Rubberneck's absence imminent, the Escape Committee immediately made plans to intensify digging in Harry. Unfortunately, Rubberneck seems to have been all too well aware of the universal euphoria that his absence would create. On the last day of February he arrived in the compound with

Major Broili and a list of 19 prisoners who were to be dispatched immediately to the satellite camp of Belaria, five miles away. They were all members of the X-Organisation and included Peter Fanshawe, Wally Floody, George Harsh and Bob Stanford-Tuck. Surprisingly, Roger Bushell's name was not among the 19. Presumably, his efforts to dissociate himself from escape activities had paid off. After being marched off to their barrack blocks, the 19 luckless men were not even given an opportunity to return. Instead, their belongings were gathered for them and shortly thereafter they were transported out of Stalag Luft III for good.

Their loss was a profound blow to the escape plans, not least because the hiatus surrounding their announced departure wasted a whole day. Those who had lost escape partners were compelled to make last-minute changes of plans. But the diggers responded to this attempted blow to their morale by redoubling their efforts. Ker-Ramsay took over as chief engineer and over the next ten days the tunnel was to progress more rapidly than it had ever done before. In one day alone 14 feet of tunnel was excavated and shored up, the air pipes fully laid and the sand completely dispersed. In the space of nine days 112 feet had been dug and shored up. By 10 March the tunnel was 348 feet in length, comfortably beyond the 335 feet that

255

they calculated marked the tree-line. The team had left four days in which to build the final staging post and the vertical escape shaft. Remarkably, they built the staging post ten feet long in a single day, leaving them three days to finish the twenty-five foot vertical shaft.

The construction of this vertical shaft was far more hazardous and complicated than the original entry shaft. Given that that had taken some two weeks to build it was extraordinary that the prisoners were contemplating finishing this in less than a quarter of that time. However, they were driven by a desperate desire to complete the job and they were helped by a stroke of luck when a four-foot section of the shaft 'excavated' itself by collapsing into the tunnel below. The task of burrowing upwards was made just a little easier but it was still an onerous and exhausting one. It was conducted by the digger holding above his head a square frame of three boards the size of the tunnel shaft that acted as both a shield and work implement. Each of the boards could be removed. The digger would remove the first and excavate a small amount of sand before replacing the board and removing the next. After the next section of sand had been excavated the third board would be removed and the practice repeated. Thus the digger moved slowly upwards. When a section of five feet had been completed, the walls were shored with the usual method. As the shaft progressed, the roof of the final staging post below was strengthened. At the end of the second day, unbelievably, the shaft had risen 19 feet. The men were probably just six feet away from breaking through the topsoil—give or take a foot or two.

That night Red Noble and Johnny Bull went down the tunnel to work out exactly how much leeway there was. It must have been a remarkable feeling to descend the entrance shaft and push along the tunnel past Piccadilly Circus and Leicester Square and finally to the exit shaft. It was a beautifully engineered construction. Bull had with him a length of old fencing foil with which he was to probe the soil above the shaft. When it met no resistance he would be able to mark exactly how deep the sand was. The rest of the engineering team waited in anticipation in Block 104. Bull and Noble returned within 20 minutes and were both clearly excited. There was less than nine inches between the tunnel and the open ground inside the woods. The entry shaft was 28 feet deep, yet the exit shaft was only 20 feet high. The discrepancy was due, possibly, to the lower level of the ground outside and, perhaps, the tunnel had risen one or two feet as it had progressed. In any case, the discovery had been yet another stroke of luck. Had the team continued digging that afternoon there would have been every chance of the tunnel breaking through prematurely. Noble pointed out that there was also every possibility that a patrolling goon would put his foot straight through the exit trap-door. Quickly, the diggers strengthened it with a far more sturdy timber construction wedged firmly into position.

It was 14 March. The men came out of the tunnel at 9.45 p.m. and sealed the trap-door. Harry would be opened again only on the day the Escape Committee decided they would break out. The next day Rubberneck arrived back in Stalag Luft III and promptly ordered the ferrets to blitz Block 104. For four hours his teams of ferrets turned the place upside down. It was freezing cold outside, but the atmosphere was nerve-wracking as the prisoners recalled the unhappy day last September when Tom was rumbled. Everybody was relieved when the ferrets finally emerged from 104 with no grins on their faces this time. Rubberneck looked in a blacker mood than they had ever seen him before. Harry was safe. For the time being. But it was obvious to everybody that the escape would have to happen sooner rather than later.

The Escape Committee was confronted with an urgent decision. It was madness to attempt to escape on anything other than a moonless night, but the next moonless period was only two weeks away on 23, 24 and 25

March. The arctic weather was unlikely to have improved by then. Many of the men planned to 'hard-arse' it across country— walking without specific plans or schedules, sometimes alone but mostly in pairs, in the hope of snatching any opportunity that presented itself on the way. They would take with them better rations than the rest to keep them going, and warmer clothing to keep the cold at bay. But some of the Escape Committee wondered whether the hard-arsers would really stand much chance in such freezing conditions. Ker-Ramsay and the other tunnel engineers, however, were adamant that Harry should not be left for another month. The warm weather would thaw the snow and who knew how that would affect the tunnel? Some of them had visions of the whole thing collapsing under flood water. Also, the longer they waited the greater the risk of a guard stumbling on the shaft, or even falling through it with its newly strengthened trap-door. Besides, there was the element of surprise. The reason the prisoners had rushed to complete the tunnel was to get out before the Germans increased their security measures at the start of the traditional spring escaping season.

Bushell agreed and it was decided that Friday night, 24 March, would be the provisional date of escape. The night before, Thursday, was not completely moonless. And

Saturday night would leave the escapers who were catching trains at the mercy of Sunday's unpredictable and skeleton railway schedules. Friday night was always a good time for travelling in wartime Germany (or anywhere in wartime for that matter). The trains were crammed with soldiers on weekend leave, their minds only on getting home to their families or sweethearts, not on the look out for escaped prisoners of war. Indeed, the experience of one or two of those who did eventually escape was that regular soldiers were all too keen to ignore any suspicions they might have entertained about their travelling companions. Railway traffic continued throughout the night. It would not be at all odd for large numbers of men to turn up at train stations in the very early hours.

The date was settled. However, it was agreed that the very final decision would not be made until 11.30 a.m. on 24 March, in the event that unforeseen circumstances arose to make the escape too hazardous. That left an extraordinary amount of organisation to be completed in very little time. Documents had to be finished, disguises finessed and cover stories perfected. Papers that required a date stamp would not be stamped until the final decision had been made after 11.30 on the Friday morning.

The plan had always been to get 200 men out, but there was never any realistic hope that this target would be achieved. On the moonless nights in question, dusk came at about 9 p.m., and the sun rose around 5.30 a.m. That gave the men eight and a half hours of darkness, or 510 minutes. Past experience had shown that a man could be got out of a tunnel every two to three minutes. That meant they could aim for between 170 and 255—but that was under ideal circumstances.

The Escape Committee had to factor in unexpected delays and hitches. Many of the would-be escapers would never have been in a tunnel before. Some might be overcome by claustrophobia and panic. Many would be carrying suitcases and other elaborate baggage and were bound to take a little longer. There might be tunnel collapses that would take valuable time to shore up. If they accepted a realistic figure of one man every four or five minutes, between 102 and 128 men might stand a chance of getting out. Nevertheless, Bushell decided that 200 men must be prepared and ready to go, all of them with their disguises, documentation and extra supplies of rations. There was always the possibility that things might run far more smoothly than any of them had predicted.

As the prisoners prepared for the break-out a palpable sense of excitement filled the air and spread to the other compounds. Bub Clark remembered there was a 'buzz' about

261

the camp for several days before the actual escape. It could surely not have escaped the Germans' notice either. Of course it was the lucky 200 who were buzzing with excitement most. The escapers were going to make their way across Germany in a variety of disguises, ranging from smart lawyers, accountants and doctors in middle-class business suits, to scruffy foreign workers and seamen. As 24 March approached they each rehearsed their cover stories, studied maps and brushed up on their foreign languages. Some, perhaps, revised their plans.

'There was a fever of excitement about the place,' says Jimmy James. 'None of the escapers seriously gave any thought to the consequences of recapture after a mass escape on this scale, in the same way that a pilot doesn't think about whether he's going to be shot down before he climbs into his cockpit.' Perhaps that was a valid point of view for an English officer, but some of the other nationalities flying with the RAF had had many sleepless nights wondering what their fate might be if the Gestapo got their hands on them.

The escapers had been given dozens of talks about the various escape routes out of the camp, details of which were provided by those who had been out on parole, tame ferrets or prisoners who had escaped. They knew that there was some sort of heavily guarded lighted compound near the camp that it seemed preferable to avoid. There were several large and small towns near Sagan that would be best to steer clear of too. Towns meant Hitler Youth, Home Guard and security checks. They knew the Oder River was to the north of Sagan and the Berlin-to-Breslau Autobahn to the south. Anyone going to Switzerland was given a pep talk by Roger Bushell. Those escapers going south were taught by Wally Valenta to say in Czech, 'I swear by the death of my mother that I am an English officer.'

Jimmy James was going in that direction, hoping to cross the giant Riesengebirge range of mountains that separated Czechoslovakia from Germany. James was going as one of a party of 12 foreign workers on leave from a local woodmill. His costume was his old RAF tunic, which he had been wearing when he was shot down. Long since bereft of insignia, he had attached civilian buttons in place of the military ones and added to his costume some scruffy Middle East khaki trousers and a hat provided by the tailors. His party would include Johnny Dodge, Johnny Bull and Pop Green, three Polish officers, two Australians, a Canadian and an English RAF man. The plan was for the men to catch an early morning train from Tschiebsdorf, a tiny rural hamlet of less than 700 inhabitants not far from Sagan, which nevertheless boasted a station. They were aiming to travel about 70 miles south to a little town called Boberöhrsdorf, near Hirschberg, on the Czechoslovakian frontier. Squadron Leader John Williams, an Australian, was going to lead the party through the woods as he had already been out on 'parole' walks with the Germans and knew the area better than the rest. Also, the group had been given details of the various paths through the forest by Marcel Zillessen's contact, the ever-helpful ferret, Keen Type. Once at the railway station, a Polish officer called Jerzy Mondschein would take the lead. Mondschein spoke fluent German and he would buy the train tickets and see them through any sticky situations.

Mondschein was one of the Eastern European officers who had not been cheered up by the recent turns of events. German reversals in the east merely meant further encroachments of the Red Army, and it was difficult to know which regime was worse— Stalin's or Hitler's. For months Mondschein had suffered sleepless nights, but now he was faced with the possibility at least of doing something to soothe his flagging spirits. Jimmy James had originally planned to go it alone after Hirschberg, but it had been suggested he team up with a Greek Spitfire pilot called Sortiros 'Nick' Skanziklas, who could take him down the Danube valley to Greece and help him cross over to Turkey.

The Dutch airman Bob van der Stok was

one of the few escapers judged to have a real chance of success. Not only was he a fluent German speaker, he had also lived under the Nazi Occupation and knew what conditions he was likely to encounter. There were many seemingly minor social protocols that could catch an escaped officer out. For instance, train passengers were allowed to sit in station waiting rooms only when they had already acquired a ticket. Those without were liable to be arrested. Identity cards were always required to be shown at certain railway checkpoints, but the checking was invariably perfunctory. Escapers with doubtful documentation who might be tempted to squeeze past the guard would be taking a much greater risk than if they simply held out their card and hoped for the best. Van der Stok was familiar with these protocols and not likely to fall unwittingly into any traps.

Van der Stok was going to go out disguised as Hendrik Beeldman, a Dutch draughtsman taking home-leave from the German electronics firm of Siemens. His disguise had been created by Tommy Guest's men out of a dark-blue Royal Australian Air Force greatcoat, Dutch naval trousers and a beret. The Norwegian airmen Per Bergsland and Jens Muller were also judged to have more hope than most of making a home run. They too spoke perfect German and were familiar with life under the Nazis. Bergsland and

Muller planned to head for Stettin posing as Norwegian foreign workers also employed by Siemens. Bergsland had been provided with false identification as a Norwegian engineer, Olaf Anderson, en route between Frankfurt an der Oder and Sagan. He was kitted out in a respectable business suit and given a suitcase stuffed with German and Norwegian soap and shaving cream. His bogus papers contained instructions to report to Stettin. Muller had a similar cover story.

Their disguises and documentation were as perfect as could possibly be. Both Muller and Bergsland's tunics had been converted into reasonable imitations of civilian jackets. Muller wore a dyed-blue cap. Bergsland had a black tie. Both had highly polished civilian shoes. Both men were also acutely aware that their families faced terrible retribution if they were discovered and took care that their escape gear contained nothing that could possibly be incriminating.

Two of the other plucky Norwegian contingent, Halldor Espelid and Nils Fugelsang, were also aiming for Sweden, as were Cookie Long and Tony Bethell, a young Mustang pilot, who were hoping to travel on freight trains as French workers heading for the Baltic.

Roger Bushell was number 4, and was going out as a French businessman. Bushell spoke fluent French as well as German and so in that respect he stood a very good chance. But he was also the one escaper who knew for certain before he left the tunnel that he was a dead man if the Germans caught him. His disguise was the grey suit that he had smuggled into Stalag Luft III, a dark overcoat, and a trilby hat. He had originally been planning to go out with Bob Stanford-Tuck, who spoke fluent Russian. But since Stanford-Tuck had been sent to Belaria, Bushell's partner was to be Lieutenant Bernard Scheidhauer of the Free French Air Force. Scheidhauer was only 18 when France fell in June 1940. It had always been his ambition to join the air force and he was desperately depressed by the situation his country now found itself in. Once he tried to escape via Spain. A second attempt with a group of young comrades on board a small fishing boat proved more successful. The boat put out from a quiet cove near Brest. After running into heavy weather it was eventually spotted by a British merchantman and the six French refugees were landed in Milford Haven. Scheidhauer first joined the Free French Navy but shortly afterwards was granted his ambition to fly. He won his wings in the summer of 1942 and joined Douglas Bader's old squadron, Number 242, flying Mark V Spitfires. (Bader by then had been a prisoner of war for nine months.) He soon after found himself with 131 Squadron flying sweeps over his native land, often straying over his parents' apartment in Brest waggling his wings in the hope that they realised it was him. Scheidhauer's war in the air finally came crashing to the ground when his Spitfire was hit by flak. He landed it on what he thought was the Isle of Wight only to discover from the farm labourers who rushed to his rescue that he was on German-occupied Jersey. Bravely, for they all could have been shot for what they did next, the islanders helped the pilot dismantle and destroy as much of the valuable aircraft as possible. After 45 minutes, however, the Germans arrived and put an end to their vandalism. Shortly afterwards Scheidhauer arrived at Sagan. Trilingual (in English, French and German) his talents were sorely needed by the Escape Committee and he was quickly press-ganged into the X-Organisation. Since his arrival in Stalag Luft III, he had been one of Wally Valenta's intelligence experts. He knew France back to front. Their plan was to get to Paris as petit bourgeois travelling back to the French capital through Germany. There they hoped to link up with the French underground. Their papers had been produced as close to perfection as possible by Tim Welann's department.

Des Plunkett was number 13, a position he grabbed because nobody else would take it. His partner was Czech fighter pilot Bedrich 'Freddie' Dvorak. They were aiming to head for Prague and, hopefully, have a reunion there with others including Johnny Marshall, Ivo Tonder and Wally Valenta who would travel to Czechoslovakia by separate means. Tim Walenn didn't speak any foreign languages and so was going out as a Lithuanian in the hope that any Germans who stopped him didn't speak Lithuanian either. His partner was the Lithuanian flier 'René' Marcinkus.

Sydney Dowse was number 21. He had been one of the hardest diggers on the tunnel and he had already made two escape attempts. Dowse was going to escape with the Polish officer Stanislaw 'Danny' Krol. Their plan was to head for Poland and link up with some of Krol's underground contacts there. They had false papers as a Dane and a Slav worker respectively. Equally usefully, the ever-resourceful Dowse had obtained a three-week supply of real food vouchers from Hesse, who had also given him a well-tailored suit. Krol's disguise was little more than his uniform and greatcoat with all the distinguishing badges and buttons replaced with civilian ones.

Wings Day was to follow him as number 22 on the list and had what he thought was the most preposterous cover story. His forged papers identified him as an Irish colonel. His story was that he had been converted to the Nazi cause by witnessing the barbarity of the Allied air assault on German cities and was being let out on parole from his POW camp with a Luftwaffe escort. Day had thought the story too ridiculous for words and strenuously protested that he wanted to go out as a Bulgarian. 'But you don't speak Bulgarian,' the Escape Committee had protested.

'Nobody speaks Bulgarian except the Bulgarians and they're 600 miles away,' Wings had retorted, dumbfounded. However, his objections had been overruled.

His companion for the escape was to be Pawel (Peter) Tobolski, a Polish officer wearing the uniform of a Luftwaffe corporal. Tobolski spoke fluent German so there was some hope there at least. Tobolski had married in 1940 but had never met his son, who was born after he was captured and now lived with his mother in Scotland. He was looking forward to seeing the son he had never known. But Tobolski, like the other officers from Eastern Europe, was more troubled than most by the rumours they had been hearing from von Lindeiner's men.

Wings Day wasn't the only one who wanted to go out as a Bulgarian. Gordon Brettell and Kingsley Brown planned to escape as Bulgarian forestry students. This, they reasoned, would give them the ideal cover required if they were to be caught lurking in forests by the Germans. Their plan was to head for the Baltic overland and find a rowing boat that they could row to Sweden.

On 20 March all the escapers had to present

themselves for inspection in their disguises and with their travel belongings to Ker-Ramsay and Marshall. Anybody thought to be taking too much was relieved of his excess baggage. Big suitcases and rolls of blankets could snag on the shoring boards, causing falls and delays. Ker-Ramsay and Marshall demonstrated to each man how to lie flat on the trolley and hold their belongings in front of them, always keeping their heads down. Some of the escapers had worked in the tunnel, but many hadn't. It was important to these that they understood how claustrophobic it might feel down the tunnel, but actually how safe the structure was. The thing the escapers feared most was that one of their members would be consumed by uncontrollable panic.

Not all of the potential escapers were aware of the problem, but one who was, ironically, was Paul Brickhill, the RAF officer who would write the book *The Great Escape*, and inspire the film. Brickhill had drawn a place in the second hundred escapers, but when he was given a sneak preview of the tunnel he got cold feet. He went to Roger Bushell and admitted his feelings. Bushell took him off the list, thanking Brickhill for his honesty.

The escapers also had to present themselves to the intelligence departments that covered the territories they would be escaping through. They were told about what sort of local conditions prevailed from the latest intelligence gathered and given contact details of the nearest underground movements. Thanks to Zillessen's Keen Type, the Escape Committee not only had the timetables of trains that left Sagan station, but also details of border posts on the Czech–German frontier, and the location of berths for ships that went to Sweden from Danzig and Stettin. Not all the escapers were going to go by comfortable trains. Wing Commander John Ellis briefed the hard-arsers on outdoor survival techniques. Bushell gave them the address of a hotelier in Prague who was working with the resistance movement, and a brothel in Stettin frequented by Swedish sailors. The hard-arsers were provided with six cans of high-energy rations. Finally, everybody was handed their maps and compasses.

*   *   *

When the morning of 23 March dawned, a thick blanket of snow covered the compound. The Escape Committee met and postponed the decision for another day. Key to the decision process was Len Hall, a member of the RAF meteorological branch. He told the committee that the next few days would be very cold, but cloud cover would make the evenings very dark. There was a tense debate about the weather. Some of the committee felt that it would be suicide for the hard-arsers and suggested that perhaps the train travellers could break out first, Harry could be resealed, the rest go out in a month or so. Because of the appalling weather conditions the hard-arsers had been given twice as many rations as everyone else. But the prospects they faced in the freezing weather were bleak. Bushell, however, wasn't having any of it. That evening he walked around the compound with Wings Day. As the moment of escape at last approached, Bushell's mind stretched to the implications of recapture for the non-British officers and the prospects of survival for the hard-arsers.

'We've got to go tomorrow,' said Bushell, 'but I hate to make the decision, because very few of the hard-arsers will make it.'

'They wouldn't have much chance anyway,' responded Day. 'About one thousand to one in the best conditions.' Day pointed out that there was no question of any of them freezing to death. They could always hand themselves in if things became unbearable.

'You think we should go tomorrow then?'

'This is an operational war, Roger. It isn't just a question of getting a few people home, because very few will make it. It's just as important to make trouble for the Germans and if we only get half the planned number out then we'll certainly do that.'

That night there was a heavy snowfall while a dress rehearsal of *Pygmalion* took place in the theatre. Flight Lieutenant Ian 'Digger' McIntosh, as Bushell's understudy, paid particular attention that evening. The following morning the Escape Committee met at 11.30 and the decision was finally made. Tim Walenn sped off to date-stamp all the false documents. Crump Ker-Ramsay descended into the tunnel to make his final preparations. Shortly afterwards, in the South Compound, Bub Clark received a message that Bushell was over on the other side of the wire and wanted to talk with him. When Clark arrived, Bushell was shuffling about in the snow. He was brief and to the point. 'We go out tonight,' he said. 'Please don't do anything to screw us up.' Clark assured Bushell that the Americans had no escape plans that evening that would clash with his and would not mess anything up. He then wished him luck.

'And that was the last I ever saw of Roger Bushell,' says Bub Clark, his eyes moistening. 'And some of the finest men I have ever known in my entire life.'

CHAPTER SEVEN

PER ARDUA AD ASTRA

The decision to go ahead with the escape provided at least one prisoner with a break of a different kind. That midday Ian McIntosh was to learn that he would after all be replacing Roger Bushell as Professor Henry Higgins in the theatre production of *Pygmalion*. It's doubtful, however, whether Bushell's understudy relished his unexpected chance of theatrical stardom. Digger McIntosh had been one of the most ardent escape artists and had almost made it to Switzerland in the famed delousing party attempt. Although he suffered from intense claustrophobia, there was no doubt he would have preferred to have been down the tunnel that night. Instead, rehearsals for the current production in the theatre went ahead as normal and the Escape Committee ordered classes, exercise groups and other activities to continue.

Every prisoner in Stalag Luft III sensed something was in the air. 'It's inconceivable,' Bub Clark said of those last few hours, 'that the Germans didn't pick up on the sense of tension.' The letters home of some of the escapers betrayed a combination of homesickness, excitement and fear that they might never see their friends and loved ones again.

In the meantime, the X-Organisation started the final preparations for the escape some of them had waited years for. Those who were going to take part in the escape had to present themselves one last time for inspection. As Tim Walenn's department churned out dozens of date-stamped documents, the Little Xs in each barrack block distributed them to the escapers.

That evening, after roll-call, the inhabitants of North Compound seemed to scatter back to their individual barrack blocks as they usually did. Most appeared to rush back to escape the cold, or attend evening classes to escape the boredom. In fact, over the next few hours before lights out, many of the prisoners were not retiring to their usual quarters but were obeying a prearranged plan to facilitate the escape. The usual residents of Block 104 who were not on the escape list were to stay in other quarters for the evening. In the meantime, the 200 who were on the list were to squash themselves into 104. In order not to raise the goons' suspicions, an intricate plan was devised in which prisoners and would-be escapers were guided around the compound. Marshals waiting discreetly in the shadows of the barracks guided this flow and counter-flow of clandestine traffic.

Shortly after 6 p.m. a few of the escapers

shared a last supper in Johnny Travis's room, among them Roger Bushell and Bob van der Stok. Jimmy James checked his escape kit before having his last meal in Stalag Luft III. 'I wouldn't put a dog out on a night like this,' said one of his barrack-roommates. They had put on a big spread for Jimmy, pooling together as much of their food as they could to celebrate his last night and keep him sustained for the deprivations ahead, but the meal was taken in silence.

'The sense of excitement was tinged by the dark shadow of doom,' James recalls. After checking his escape kit once more, he recalled that he had a stash of cigarettes underneath his bed. He gave them to the others with a good-natured quip to the effect that he could always buy some more in the mess back home. They joked that they would save them for him after he got out of the cooler. Shortly before 9 p.m. James made his way to Block 104 via Block 109, where he had been directed to go first in the complicated traffic scheme that was directing men like him all over the compound. In 104 James was greeted by Dave Torrens, the officer responsible for registering each escaper as they arrived at the block. Torrens sent James to Room 8, which was slowly filling up with the other members of his escaping party. Nick Skanziklas arrived a few minutes later in an overcoat and cloth cap.

The whole of Block 104 was now heaving

with men in an odd assortment of disguises. By the time Les Brodrick arrived in Block 104 it was so crowded that he had to sit on the floor. It was also becoming increasingly stifling as more than 200 men squeezed into a space normally meant for 100. There were so many men packed into the hut that those on lookout duty in other huts were alarmed to see gentle clouds of steam rising out of the windows, and idly wondered how long it would take the Germans to notice this odd phenomenon. Torrens had reason to be alarmed himself when he looked up to see a German guard entering Block 104. He caught his breath— before realising that the German was actually Peter Tobolski—the Polish officer dressed in the uniform of a Luftwaffe corporal—who was to accompany Wings Day in his curious guise as an Irish colonel.

New Zealander Mike Shand was going to hard-arse it cross-country across Czechoslovakia with Len Trent. They didn't really have a plan other than a vague hope of getting to Switzerland via Austria from there. As he awaited his opportunity to leave that night, he was under no illusions. 'I don't think any of us expected to make it to England,' he recalled many years later. 'It was a ridiculous idea with the police and the Gestapo at roadblocks on practically every junction, and in the freezing conditions it would be impossible to make it across country

278

undetected. But we had to do something to hit back at the Germans.'

While the escapers waited in Block 104, Ker-Ramsay and his team of diggers had been down Harry for hours that day making the final preparations for the escape. Among the refinements was a pair of 'curtains' made out of blankets and hung in the tunnel shortly before the exit shaft to stop light and sound percolating out of the tunnel. The tunnel would be jammed with escapers trundling up and down in an endless succession on the trolleys and Ker-Ramsay had installed extra lighting to allay any feelings of claustrophobia some of those new to the tunnel might suffer. Blankets were also laid along the length and breadth of the tunnel to deaden the sound and keep the tunnellers' escape outfits clean. The escape shaft was due to be broken through at 9.30 p.m. sharp. For the officers in 104 the hands of their wristwatches seemed to move far too slowly towards their appointment with destiny.

That night Bub Clark went to bed in the South Compound as usual but slept uneasily. Having been intimately involved in every aspect of the escape plans, he knew that by now Block 104 would be heaving with 200 men barely capable of containing their excitement at the prospect of the adventure to come and freedom at last. He allowed himself a smile when he thought of the variety of disguises they would be wearing. He could imagine what was going on beneath the ground as the chief engineers made the finishing touches to the trolley and ventilation systems and pushed the exit shaft through the soil. He knew that if everything had gone according to plan, the shaft would emerge in the woods, just enough behind the trees to be hidden from the goon towers. He knew that for each man, each moment of waiting would be nerve-wracking, and the instant of breaking out would bring a rush of exhilaration tinged with the peculiar thrill that imminent danger always brought. As he lay in his bunk in the early hours of the morning, Clark half expected to hear the shot that would herald the discovery of the tunnel, but crossed his fingers hoping it did not happen.

*   *   *

At 8.30 p.m. Ker-Ramsay's head finally appeared at the trap-door and he announced the tunnel was ready to accept the first group of escapers. A frisson of excitement spread through the block, but before the escape was declared officially started, Group Captain Massey visited the block and offered them words of encouragement. Since Wings Day was going out in the escape, Massey was taking over as the SBO, a role that they had unofficially 'shared'. Massey pleaded with the men not to behave provocatively towards the Germans if any of them were caught, repeating the warnings that he and Day had received from the Kommandant.

Then the first officers of an advance party began lowering themselves into the tunnel. Johnny Marshall and Johnny Bull led the way. Behind them were Bushell and his escape partner Bernard Scheidhauer; Sydney Dowse and the Czech Flight Lieutenant Wally Valenta, and the South African fitness fanatic Rupert Stevens. It was Marshall and Bull's task to dislodge the reinforced escape hatch, while the others would wait below in the widened chamber at the foot of the exit shaft, with Sydney Dowse ready to tug on the rope and give the signal that the escape had begun. As they made their preparations the prisoners who were to follow began jumping down the hatch. Soon a chain of men lined the tunnel lying flat on their stomachs on the trolleys, each holding their cases in front of them. In all, 17 men were waiting in the tunnel to break out. Crump Ker-Ramsay took up his new position as chief tunnel dispatcher and crouched at the foot of the entrance shaft. At the top of the shaft above him was Henry Lamond, who would control the flow of escapers into the tunnel.

The rest of the would-be escapers were in the barrack block waiting for the moment in a breathless silence but when the appointed time for the break-out came there appeared to be no movement to indicate the escape was under way. Soon everyone above ground in Block 104 was becoming a little restless. Anxious whispers broke the silence. They all wanted to know if something had gone wrong. 'It was getting pretty hot and sticky in that hut,' says Les Brodrick. 'We were all trying to be as patient as we could but we were getting a bit fed up with the delay.'

Jimmy James recalls: 'We were trying to chat to one another as if everything was quite normal, but it was difficult; there was such tension in the air and the atmosphere was stifling. A lot of us began to shed our outer gear.' Ker-Ramsay was at a loss to help them. He hadn't a clue what was going on. The nearest man to him was 100 feet away down the tunnel and communication between either was impossible.

The answer to everybody's question lay at the other end of the tunnel where Bull was struggling with the exit hatch. He couldn't budge it an inch. After an hour of struggling with it, and exhausted by his efforts, Bull edged his way down the shaft to allow Marshall to have a go. Marshall took off his civilian escape gear to keep it clean and clambered to the top of the shaft in his underclothes, but he too encountered an unmoving trap-door. The two men quietly cursed their own good work. The exit trap was as good as set in concrete. Marshall retreated to the bottom, absolutely exasperated. Bull went up and had another go, sweat pouring down his brow as the time ticked away. At 10 p.m. there was a flurry of activity throughout Stalag Luft III as the goons performed their usual evening task of shutting down the compounds. Guards went from barrack block to barrack block, noisily banging down the sturdy wooden 'latches' across each door and slamming the window shutters shut. The men inside 104 sat in hushed silence as the lights in every block were turned off. Slowly, the banging and shouting from outside died down as the Germans returned to the Kommandantur, closing the main gate behind them.

As silence returned in the compound above, Johnny Bull, in Harry, suddenly felt the hatch budge slightly. Clawing away at the edges it began to move more and more before falling into his hands along with a cascade of soil. Ignoring the sand in his eyes, Bull pushed up through the nine inches that rained down into the shaft below him. In the staging post beneath Bull the atmosphere had gone from tense to nerve-wracking. Only those at the head of the tunnel were aware of what the problem was. It was with nothing short of relief therefore that shortly after 10 p.m. Ker-Ramsay felt the gentle breeze of cool air wafting past him. The exit must have broken through. A sense of relief spread along the tunnel and up the entrance shaft to the men waiting above. There was a wave of silent euphoria but after the initial excitement, the time continued to tick away without the expected sense of movement happening. The tension quickly returned. The eyes of everyone in 104 asked the same unspoken question: what was going on? It was even more frustrating for Ker-Ramsay, who continued to be in the dark even though he could sense something was happening a hundred yards or so in front of him.

What was going on was an urgent whispered discussion in the chamber at the base of the exit shaft. Bull had gingerly poked his blackened features out of the hole only to be confronted with a startling revelation. The hole did not emerge comfortably inside the line of trees as the surveyors had planned. Instead it was at least 25 feet short and broke the ground directly behind a goon tower only 45 feet away. There were no trees between the sight line of the guards either in the watchtower or on the perimeter path, which was even closer to the exit hole. Bull looked with alarm at the sentry in the watchtower clearly silhouetted against the cold night sky. Beneath the huddled guard the camp was a vision of whiteness, covered in a thick layer of snow and bathed in pools of bright light from the perimeter fence. The only source of comfort was that the area in which the hole broke through the ground was in the shadows. From there, though, the escapers would still have to scurry across 25 feet of completely open ground before finding any cover. However, Bull also noticed in the woods nearby a 'ferret fence'. These were the little fences behind which the ferrets hid while they were spying on the camp during the day. There were dozens of them around the compounds. The sight of this conveniently placed one gave Bull an idea. He scurried down the shaft to tell Bushell the mixed news.

At the base of the exit shaft there were whispered curses before the men had a hurried discussion to review their options. They were not all that worried about the goon box as the guards stationed in it would be looking at the compound. It was the perimeter guard patrols that were the problem. They could postpone the escape and dig the extra three yards or so in a few days, but it would mean waiting until the next full moon period and Bushell had already voiced his concerns that the Germans might have discovered the tunnel by then. Besides, many of the escapers' forged papers had been dated for this particular weekend. Postponing the escape would mean the forgery department working overtime to replace them in time for next month. Bushell quickly decided delay was not an option.

Bull pointed out to him that the ferret fence

on the fringes of the wood offered some degree of protection from the perimeter guards' prying eyes. A control officer could be stationed there at the end of a rope leading from the tunnel. He would keep his eye on the goon box and the perimeter guard patrols. A tug on the rope would indicate it was safe for the next man at the top of the exit shaft to proceed. The escapers would make their way first to the ferret fence and from there a further 70 yards into the woods, guided by another rope to a rendezvous point. It had its risks, but none of the men could think of a viable alternative. It was now obvious to everyone that with the delays and potential for even more delays nowhere near 200 men were going to break out, but if a significant number were to get away they had to start moving fast. The officers at the base chamber reluctantly nodded their agreement. They would get as many men out as they possibly could. Each escaper would pass on the new instructions verbally to the next man, but to be on the safe side Bushell scribbled a note explaining what to do and this note was pinned to the chamber wall. The word was shortly being whispered back along the tunnel along with a demand to send the rope down to the exit shaft.

After it was passed frantically from man to man, it finally arrived at the foot of the exit shaft. Wrapping it around his arms Bull set off up the ladder one more time, Marshall quickly behind him. One after the other, the men stuck their heads out of the tunnel into the cold Silesian air. After a quick look at the goon tower and the perimeter fence, they hitched themselves out of the hole and dashed towards the woods. It was 10.30 p.m. and the Great Escape had begun. It was the culmination of 12 months of back-breaking toil, meticulous planning and ingenious workmanship. And as the men made their sprint for freedom they carried with them the hopes and dreams of hundreds of men left behind the wire. Valenta, Bushell and Scheidhauer edged up the ladder and waited. Presently, Valenta felt the reassuring tug of the rope and lost no time in leaping out of the hole. In the woods he met Marshall. Shortly a breathless Bushell arrived grinning from ear to ear. Shaking hands the men excitedly bade their farewells, Valenta taking off with his escape partner Marshall, while Bushell took over the role of control officer. Scheidhauer arrived minutes later. Bushell and he waited until they saw the figure of Rupert Stevens silhouetted against the whiteness of the distant camp. The exchange of roles was repeated and the men said their farewells. Bushell and Scheidhauer disappeared into the blackness of the forest. Shortly after them came Des Plunkett and his partner Freddie Dvorak. Halldor Espelid and Nils Fugelsang were hot on their heels. These were the men who were all judged to have the best chance of escape. They had the best disguises and the best documentation. But the meticulousness of the preparations had already gone to waste even before the escape had begun. The men had mostly missed their trains and now faced the worrying prospect of all having to get on the same train. After a hurried conference in the depths of the woods it was decided that one way to assuage the problem was by all of them at least trying to arrive at the train station separately. They decided they would leave the woods in pairs, at five-minute intervals.

The sensation of movement was beginning to be felt in the tunnel. At the base of the entrance shaft Ker-Ramsay suddenly felt a tug on the rope. He breathed a sigh of relief and in a stage whisper passed on the good news to the men above. Once more a wave of relief spread through 104.

'It was an exhilarating moment,' recalls Jimmy James, 'but there was fear too, certainly in the pit of my stomach and, I suspect, most of the others'. None of us knew what to expect and we were all hoping for the best but preparing for the worst, although of course none of us quite realised what the worst would be.'

The escape was under way—albeit an hour later than planned. A little more slowly and a little less surely than hoped for, the escapers

288

edged their way along the tunnel.

As the Escape Committee had predicted, everything did not go without a hitch. One problem was immediately presented by one of the most important members of the X-Organisation. Tim Walenn turned up without his red moustache but with what appeared to be a trunk big enough to carry a kitchen sink in. It was not the modest bag Ker-Ramsay had inspected the night before. Ker-Ramsay was aghast but could hardly send back such a distinguished and dedicated escape artist. Instead, a compromise was arrived at whereby the trunk went on the first trolley, and Walenn followed behind. The two men shook hands awkwardly in the confines of the chamber and promised to stand one another drinks at the RAF Club in Piccadilly in a few weeks' time.

Walenn wasn't to be the only transgressor. Others turned up having either forgotten or simply disregarded the rules regarding baggage. Cases got wedged in the tunnel or fell off trolleys, blocking the way. Sometimes the escapers had to reverse along the tunnel and start again. It was becoming apparent to everyone that things were going seriously slowly. Far from getting out at the rate of one man every two or three minutes, it was taking up to 12 minutes a go in some instances. The men's nerves were beginning to fray and many of them were getting edgy. Tempers flared and

Ker-Ramsay began to take a less-than-good-natured view of officers who turned up with outsized baggage. At one stage a rope pulling the trolleys broke, taking several valuable minutes to repair. Then came more mixed blessings as it became apparent that the RAF had chosen that night to pay one of its visits. Thousands of feet above ground, 800 aircraft of Bomber Command began pulverising Berlin.

It was about 11.45 p.m. when the prisoners suddenly heard the familiar wail of air-raid warning sirens. Although Berlin was more than 100 miles away, any city that might act as a beacon for the bombers was blacked out, and Sagan was no exception. Within seconds the lights in the tunnel flickered out and the escapers on their trolleys experienced that most frightful of conditions: total blackout. The Escape Committee had anticipated the problem and had fat lamps on hand. But it took a long time to get them all lit and some of the escapers did panic. Wings Day was number 20 and was waiting in 104. He had been just about to go down the entrance shaft when the lights had gone out. It was another 35 minutes before the traffic controller gave him the go-ahead. Gratefully, he disappeared down the shaft. Sydney Dowse was even more grateful. He had been at the base of the exit shaft far longer than expected and his partner, Danny Krol, who suffered badly from claustrophobia,

290

had already gone. At the sight of Wings Day he thanked goodness that it was finally his time to get out. He had no idea whether he would find Krol in the woods, but at least the escape chain was moving once more, even though it was moving very slowly.

The power blackout had at least brought one welcome side-effect. It had also thrown the perimeter lighting and searchlights above ground into darkness. That was not entirely good news because whenever this happened the Germans always redoubled their guard and sent their men with sniffer dogs into the compounds. However, on this particular occasion the lookouts positioned at the barrack windows throughout the North Compound could not see any intensification of guard activity. Perhaps the German guards had concluded, like Jimmy James's roommate, that it would be cruel to put even a dog out on a night like that. For a few precious minutes the men found themselves exiting the tunnel at a much faster rate. This came to a conclusive halt when what everybody had feared would happen came about. Tom Kirby-Green's suitcase snagged on one of the shoring planks. The trolley jerked to a halt. There was a moment's nervous silence and suddenly Kirby-Green was buried in a fall.

It took an hour of frantic work to pull out the RAF officer and repair the damage, and no sooner had it been fixed than the electricity came back on and the tunnel lit up. Any advantage the men might have derived from the enforced darkness of the air raid had been thrown away. It was not until 1 a.m. that the last of the 30 'priority' suitcase carriers had finally broken out. Had the escape gone according to the most optimistic plans those 30 would have been well on their way to Sagan station by 10.30 p.m., and by now some 105 men would have been out in the woods.

The indefatigable Jimmy James, number 39, was waiting a little less than patiently at the tunnel entrance, dwelling on similar thoughts. He had expected to get out at midnight and by 1.30 a.m. was beginning to wonder if he would ever get a chance. Nevertheless, in his guise as a humble mill worker, James had no choice but to wait for his turn with his escape partner, the Greek fighter pilot Sortiros Skanziklas. When the traffic controller finally told James it was his turn to go he was thrilled. It had been four years since James had been incarcerated and he'd worked hard on this and many other escape attempts.

He eagerly jumped down the entry shaft and climbed down to the bottom. Settling himself on his trolley he set off for the haulage post as cheerfully as a commuter on the London Underground heading for the real Piccadilly Circus. James's progress along the tunnel was one of the smoothest ones. Swiftly switching trains at Piccadilly Circus he was on his way to

Leicester Square only moments later. One more changeover and like a real train approaching a terminus the trolley began to slow its pace. When he reached the rough 'muffler' blanket at the end of the tunnel he pulled it aside and found himself in the exit chamber.

When he got to the top of the ladder the sight of the stars above him had added significance for James. *'Per ardua ad astra,'* he said to himself, reciting the RAF motto. 'I climbed out into the frozen whiteness,' recalls James, 'The goon box towered above me and I could see the sentry on the perimeter path.' There was no time to lose as James sped off towards the trees, thinking his every movement sounded like the crack of a pistol shot. James later recalled that his procession through the tunnel had been remarkably swift. 'It was quite an easy way to escape, actually.'

But James was the exception to the rule. The progress overall was painfully slow, not least because there was a minor tunnel collapse only minutes after James had departed. Two of the shoring boards had been ruptured by one of the blanket carriers. It took 30 minutes to repair the damage, but then there was another rupture following that caused by exactly the same reason. That took another half hour to repair. Men continued to turn up with inappropriate kit. Johnny Dodge arrived wrapped up so warmly against the cold that he could not possibly have got through the tunnel. Summoning up as much politeness as he could muster, Ker-Ramsay told the senior officer that he would have to lose a jersey or two.

Ker-Ramsay was irritated to see that the 'blanket brigade' of hard-arsers who were going to be toughing it across country had repeated the transgressions of the suitcase carriers. Many were carrying bundles of blankets that were too big for the tunnel, or had stuffed so much food into their tunics that they became wedged in the shaft. Ker-Ramsay was exasperated and repeatedly warned men that they risked being thrown to the back of the queue. The escape continued to be plagued by small tunnel collapses and rope breaks as the men's nerves got the better of them and they made elementary mistakes. And the bundles of blankets wrapped around men's shoulders continued to cause the bulk of the problems. They were repeatedly snagging on shoring planks. The rate of escape had gone down from one man every 12 minutes to one man every 14 minutes. In the end Ker-Ramsay had no choice but to ban them. It would mean the hard-arsers would be thrown to the mercy of the minus 30 degree temperatures outside wearing little more than their ragged greatcoats and surviving on rations that were barely enough to keep an inactive man healthily fed. It is a sign of the men's professionalism that they accepted the diktat without a murmur of complaint. Les Brodrick, with his escape companions, a youthful Canadian flier, Hank Birkland, and a British RAF man, Denys Street, emerged into the freezing night with hardly enough protection for a cool summer's evening, let alone the coldest German winter in 30 years.

It was hardly compensation that after that the escape rate went up to one man every ten minutes. They were all way behind schedule. Fewer than 50 men had escaped by 2.30 a.m. It was perfectly clear that many of the men above in Block 104 were not going to get an opportunity to escape. Reluctantly, Ker-Ramsay ordered the last 100 to go to bed. For the rest of the evening the unlucky ones lay dreaming of what might have been. Some were utterly dejected. Others cheerfully seized upon the opportunity to tuck into their extra supplies of rations, or if they were in a more generous frame of mind, offered them to those men lucky enough to be still in with a chance of escaping. With dawn rapidly approaching, barely 60 to 70 men had got out.

In Block 104 yet another hard decision was made. Tim Newman, number 87 on the list, was told that he would be the last man allowed down the tunnel. Red Noble and Ken 'Shag' Rees, who were down the tunnel acting as haulers, were told to take themselves off once Newman had gone. The Escape Committee clung on to the remote possibility that the tunnel exit could be covered up and remain undetected for them to use it again. They had no idea that the exit had developed into a gaping black hole with a path of sludgy snow leading to the woods in plain view of the goon towers as the feet of the fleeing escapers had melted the snow surrounding it.

On the other side of the wire events were about to take an alarming turn for the worse. George McGill was taking his turn as the traffic controller behind the ferret fence in the woods when he was relieved by Roy Langlois. The Channel Islander was about to give a tug on the rope when he noticed a dark silhouette descending down the watchtower steps. It was 4.30 a.m., and not time for the guard to be changed. Langlois watched the figure intently. With mounting alarm, he saw the guard walking directly towards the exit hole. The German was only feet away when he stopped, opened his greatcoat, squatted down and began to answer the call of nature. The dark hole was directly in front of him. Langlois held his breath. The guard seemed to take an eternity before he finally stood up, turned around and made his way back to his post. When he had settled himself back in his position facing the camp, Langlois tugged on the rope, unsure as to whether he had actually witnessed the scene or perhaps had imagined the whole thing.

The slow momentum of the tunnel traffic continued. As 5 a.m. approached the sky was turning from black to an ominous dark grey with tinges of red sunlight touching the horizon. It was only a matter of time before the dawn light would make any further escapes out of the question. Number 76, Squadron Leader Lawrence Reavell-Carter, and number 77, Flight Lieutenant Keith Ogilvie, had just emerged from the tunnel and ran towards the woods. Waiting for them was Tony Bethell, the young Mustang pilot and Reavell-Carter's escape partner. Langlois was still acting as traffic controller and had just signalled the all-clear to Len Trent, number 79, in the tunnel when his eyes caught another out-of-the-ordinary sight from the direction of the camp. One of the perimeter guards appeared to be walking away off course, apparently directly towards the tunnel exit. If he continued to maintain the same course he would walk straight into the New Zealand officer Mike Shand, who at that very moment was dashing across the snow between the ferret fence and the woods. Langlois urgently tugged on the rope to warn Shand and Trent. Both the officers dived to the ground, their heads buried in the snow, unsure as to what the danger was.

Reavell-Carter was watching from the woods with some concern too. The guard was walking directly towards the exit hole. But it was clear from his movements that he had not noticed anything unusual. He seemed simply to have decided to take a different route for a change. Then Reavell-Carter's concern turned to outright alarm when he saw that the sentry had seemed to notice something. The goon stopped in his tracks before purposefully unslinging his rifle. Quickly, he began stalking his way towards the hole in the ground, which all night long had been emitting a giveaway stream of steam into the freezing air. Shand cocked his head sideways and saw what was happening, promptly deciding he had nothing to lose and to make a run for it. He leapt to his feet, and ran for the woods. Keith Ogilvie, who was waiting on the fringes of the trees, made a dash for the safety of the interior too. By now the German sentry was standing directly over Len Trent, although in the blackness he did not know it. Instead he was distracted by the unexpected burst of movement in the shadows around him. Quickly gathering his wits about him, he lifted his rifle and aimed to shoot at the disappearing figures of Shand and Ogilvie. Seeing all this, and alarmed, Reavell-Carter jumped to his feet and ran out of the woods with his hands above his head. 'Nicht schiessen! Nicht schiessen!' he cried (Don't shoot! Don't shoot!). Reavell-Carter waved his hands about madly to distract the goon. Langlois emerged from the shadows to join in. Now the German really was taken completely by surprise. Not knowing what else to do, he let a single shot off into the air above Mike Shand's head.

The loud report jogged Len Trent to his senses and he too warily stood up with his hands above his head, almost next to the astonished goon. Shand continued running, apparently unaware of the risks Langlois and Reavell-Carter had taken to save his life. He disappeared into the woods hard on the heels of Ogilvie. The German desperately began to shine his torch around him, wondering if there were even more Allied officers littered around the ground. As the beam flickered over the alarmed faces of the escapers, one by one he picked out each of the dark figures emerging from the gloom. Langlois, Reavell-Carter and Trent continued to cautiously hold their hands up, not wanting to make the slightest move that would provoke the guard. Slowly it dawned on the German that he was standing in the middle of a huge black patch of melted snow. He edged warily forward and his light found the tunnel exit, the torch beam settling on the features of Bob McBride, number 80, caught at the top of the ladder. McBride could do little more than smile weakly. At the sight of him the goon pulled out his whistle and blew. It was only a tinny little sound, but it echoed around the woods and across the North Compound like the harbinger of doom.

Everybody in the North Compound looked up when they heard the dull but unmistakable sound of a rifle shot in the distance, and every head in Block 104 turned in the direction from which the shot had come. Shortly after came the awful sound of the whistle, followed by a deathly silence that seemed to last minutes or more. Quickly, though, a rising crescendo of urgent noise emitted from the direction of the Kommandantur. The men could hear the sound of dogs barking and angry German curses. The sounds grew louder and more distinct. There could be no doubt in anybody's mind now that the game was well and truly up.

In the tunnel, however, Tim Newman, believing he would be the last man out, had just bade Ker-Ramsay goodbye and was rattling off towards Piccadilly Circus. He continued on his course despite Ker-Ramsay's shouts to come back. Perhaps he hadn't heard them, or the shot from outside. Ker-Ramsay resolved the situation by jamming his legs against the frame of the tunnel supports and pulling the rope that was attached to Newman's trolley. When a puzzled Newman arrived back at the foot of the entry shaft the senior officer explained what had happened. The two men scrambled back up the entrance shaft as quickly as they could. The priority now was to prevent any casualties and get rid of all incriminating material. When Ker-Ramsay emerged into the barrack he ordered all the escapers to destroy their false identity cards and other forged papers. He told the men to try and hide whatever other escape gear they had wherever they could. He then promptly disappeared back down the shaft to organise the evacuation of those stuck in the tunnel. His worst fear was that a panicked German guard might spray machine-gun fire down the shaft. There were five still down the tunnel, including Muckle Muir and Red Noble, all desperately scooting back towards the entrance shaft. Another officer, Shag Rees, was the last out and he tried to describe to Ker-Ramsay what he could see of the action at the top of the tunnel exit from his vantage point at the base, which was not very much.

As he was doing so, an Allied officer who had been on lookout duty arrived at Block 104 out of breath. He had just seen a party of Germans emerge from the guardroom and storm across to where the tunnel exit was. There was no way of telling whether anybody had been injured by the shot. In hasty succession men began emerging from the entrance to the tunnel, some of them in a panic, all of them sweating in their heavy escape costumes. The trap-door and stove were hastily replaced. Another officer arrived to say that it appeared a party of men had been caught at the exit of the tunnel and were being marched off. The men in Block 104 had lit dozens of little bonfires to burn their papers and the air was thick with smoke. After they had disposed of the incriminating evidence some of them hungrily tucked into the remainder of their extra rations. They knew that these would be the first items to be confiscated by the Germans and they weren't going to give them that satisfaction. Half of them expected to be spending the next two weeks on starvation diets in the cooler. Some of the prisoners attempted to jump out of Block 104's windows and make a break for their own barracks until a goon spotted them and let off a round of machine-gun fire.

Oddly, though, it took some time for the Germans to work out which barrack the tunnel had come from. Thus, when their teams of guards flooded into the compound they began flushing out every block. In the absence of any other willing volunteer to go down the exit tunnel, Charlie Pfelz was prevailed upon to undertake the task and he lowered himself warily into the abyss equipped with a powerful torch and pistol. It was not until 5.30 a.m. that a single German guard arrived at Block 104 with a revolver in his hand and an Alsatian dog straining at the leash. Ironically, it was the tame Hundführer who had been such a help to the men over the past year, supplying them with material and information. But he was now plainly bewildered by what he discovered. The

302

corridor was full of smoke and a score of wild faces were staring at him. Fortunately, his dog seemed to take after his master and apparently bore no ill-will against the Allied officers. He took the initiative and settled down on a heap of discarded greatcoats in the corridor. The Hundführer clearly thought this was a sensible course of action in the circumstances and, after ordering everyone to stay exactly where they were, settled down with the dog. It was not for another hour that a more formidable detail of Germans would arrive in force at Block 104 and when they did the full anger of Colonel von Lindeiner would soon be made apparent.

Outside the wire, the shivering figures of Roy Langlois, Bob McBride, Lawrence Reavell-Carter and Len Trent were savouring their last moments of freedom before a complement of goons arrived to escort them back into the camp. They were thrown for temporary detention into the guardhouse. With only two distracted guards to look after them, the four would-be escapers took the opportunity to surreptitiously dispose of their own incriminating documents in the embers of the burning stove. They were in the middle of this process when the door burst open to reveal Colonel von Lindeiner and Captain Hans Pieber.

The Kommandant was apoplectic with rage, all the more so when the four men refused, as

303

politely as they possibly could, to answer any of his questions about the break-out. Captain Pieber looked visibly distressed and it seemed to the men that he was genuinely sad when he told them that they would probably be transferred to another camp. The uncomfortable confrontation ended with von Lindeiner predicting the Gestapo would extract a terrible revenge for the night's proceedings. 'You have no idea what you have done,' he raged at them as they parted company, the Allied officers being marched off to the cooler, the Kommandant making his way across to the North Compound with Pieber, Simoleit and several other members of his security staff in tow. Among them was a twitchy Rubberneck, who looked as if he would be quite happy to let the Gestapo extract whatever revenge they wanted on the Allied officers.

By now, in Block 104 Ker-Ramsay could hear scratching noises underneath the stove. Either he had failed to account for one escaper, or the goons had traced the tunnel back to its origins. There was nothing he sensibly could do other than ignore it for the time being and wait for the inevitable arrival of Colonel von Lindeiner's men. That took a long time in coming, but at 6.30 a.m. the compound was filled with the sound of roaring engines and squealing tyres as dozens of Luftwaffe guards arrived in a convoy of motorcycles and half-tracks. They were all wearing steel helmets and toting sub-machine guns, which was quite unnecessary in the circumstances, but was clearly intended to let the prisoners know that they meant business. Presently, four heavy machine guns were positioned at each corner of the hut. Shortly after they had assumed their positions, von Lindeiner arrived with Pieber and Rubberneck. A bevy of other ferrets and security officers stood around.

The doors of Block 104 were flung open and the men entered in a state of agitation, uncharacteristically with their revolvers drawn. Von Lindeiner had still not calmed down from his confrontation with the four escapers in the guardhouse. His face was bright red and he could hardly speak coherently. He was heard warning that he personally would shoot anyone who gave trouble. The Allied officers had never seen him in such a mood and any pleasure they may have derived at the trouble they were causing the Germans was tempered by the obvious distress they had caused this evidently decent man. He ordered the lot of them out of the barrack block, where they were told to strip to their underwear.

A light snowstorm had developed outside, but any of the prisoners who dawdled found themselves being unceremoniously marched off to the cooler. Two prisoners who made light of the situation were sent in the same direction. Shag Rees and Red Noble were involved in a nasty confrontation with Rubberneck, who looked as if he would happily shoot the two of them there and then. After a few tense moments the prisoners backed down and stripped off as they had been told to do. Many of those who had been due to escape managed to discard their compasses in the snow and quietly ate their maps and other clandestine material. But they were to discover that any item of clothing that possibly looked as if it was a civilian disguise was snatched off them by the Germans and piled in a big heap.

Soon the whole camp was standing outside in the snow, a shivering mass of pale naked bodies. The tension between the two sets of men gradually began to subside as time passed and tempers cooled. The RAF officers were persuaded finally to open Harry's trap-door and let the hapless Pfelz out. He emerged with a grin all over his face—not, the officers suspected, in relief at the end of his ordeal, but at the thought of the discomfiture Rubberneck was about to find himself in when he gleefully informed the Kommandant of the sheer scale of the tunnellers' achievement. At 8.30 a.m., a thorough count of the whole camp was made, the Germans using photographs to identify who was still in and who was no longer there. When this had been completed the full extent of the escape became known, and the Germans knew the identities of the 76 officers who had broken out. As in any closed community it was impossible to keep a secret in Stalag Luft III, and soon the news was being whispered from prisoner to prisoner. It provoked many smiles of satisfaction and some muted cries of joy. But at that particular moment none of the prisoners dared taunt the Germans with their delight as they might have done in the past.

For Colonel von Lindeiner the news was disastrous. He immediately knew he would face a court-martial—or conceivably a far more unpleasant fate. Reluctantly, but urgently, he ordered his officers to telephone the information to various authorities in the region and, of course, Berlin. Local railway stations were warned to be on the look-out for escaped prisoners. Aerodromes were put on notice to be vigilant. Every civilian, whether on foot, or travelling by car or bicycle, within a radius of 50 miles of Sagan was to be stopped, searched and interrogated.

At the nearest civilian police headquarters, the chief of the Breslau Kripo, Obersturmbannführer (Lieutenant-Colonel) Max Wielen, decided the break-out merited a Kriegfahndung (general alert), before quickly upgrading the emergency to a Grossfahndung: a national hue and cry and the highest level of alert in Germany. Wielen was directly answerable to Heinrich Himmler's Reichssicherheitshauptamt headquarters in Berlin. Besides the ordinary police, the Gestapo and SS, Home Guard and Hitler Youth detachments, as well as Wehrmacht soldiers, were drafted in to search for the escapers. Seaports and railway stations were alerted and border patrols were reinforced.

It was to be claimed that the alert was to involve, in one form or another, as many as five million German civilians, police officials and military personnel over the next months. This figure is most likely an overstatement, but there were undoubtedly many thousands, if not hundreds of thousands, of Germans thrown into the task of hunting the escaped Kriegies down when they could have been doing something more useful for the war effort. It is not an exaggeration to say that when the Führer learnt of the escape he flew into one of the wildest of his rages. He would be presented with a report on the debacle at Berchtesgaden, his Bavarian Alpine retreat, over the weekend.

Finally, as the sun rose over Stalag Luft III, a group of more malfeasants from Block 104, singled out by von Lindeiner and his staff, was marched off to the cooler. At the guardhouse, however, Captain Pieber was informed that there was not room in the cooler for all of them. Consequently, most of them were returned to their barracks cold, hungry but grateful for the little mercy that had been bestowed on them. None of them yet, however, realised just how lightly they had got off. As von Lindeiner made his way back to his offices in the Kommandantur he knew that for him, the war was well and truly over.

CHAPTER EIGHT

THE FÜHRER'S FURY

Roger Bushell and Bernard Scheidhauer were the first to arrive at Sagan station. It was shortly before 11 p.m. and it was comforting to see that, as usual, the booking hall and platforms were milling with civilians and soldiers on leave or in transit. They quickly booked two tickets on the Berlin to Breslau express train and melted into the crowds. Des Plunkett and the Czech RAF officer Freddie Dvorak arrived at the station only a few minutes later to find a working party of Russian prisoners blocking the entrance. To add to their confusion the subway entrance to the station had undergone some minor alterations and its appearance was somewhat different to what the escapers had been led to expect in their intelligence briefs.

The two RAF officers were beginning to panic as they wandered about in the mêlée trying to look inconspicuous. As the minutes ticked away, they desperately tried to work out where the entrance was. Their search was interrupted when Sagan's air-raid sirens burst into their familiar low, oscillating wail. A mile or so away the men in the tunnel at Stalag Luft III were about to be plunged into the darkness that brought them such mixed blessings. The same applied at Sagan station. The commotion made Plunkett and Dvorak feel a little more comfortable. And as everybody dashed to find cover it soon became apparent where the station entrance was. The two men raced towards it, and finding themselves in the ticket hall walked quickly up to the counter. Their relief was to be short-lived. The clerk refused to issue them tickets, directing them instead to go straight to the air-raid shelter in the subway. A minor altercation broke out and at one stage the men were alarmed to be confronted with an armed German soldier who appeared to be telling them to do as the ticket clerk had ordered. The fracas came to a sudden halt as a train showed up and there was a general lunge forward of passengers desperate not to miss it. The German soldier was distracted and without a second thought the RAF officers made a run for it, pushing past the ticket barrier with a crowd of other passengers who would rather risk being bombed than miss the only chance they might have that weekend to see their families.

Plunkett and Dvorak reached the train as it was screeching to a halt. When the conductor stuck his head out of the window and demanded to know what the commotion was all about, they told him there was an air raid on and he immediately ordered the train to continue on its way. The officers joyously

311

jumped on board as the train gathered speed again. It was only after they had squeezed themselves into one of the crowded corridors that the men realised they were on the Berlin-to-Breslau express. Now they had to overcome the problem of having no valid tickets for their journey.

As they were quietly discussing their predicament, Plunkett was mildly alarmed to feel somebody squeezing his hand conspiratorially, and when he looked up he was delighted to see Roger Bushell's familiar features. Bushell had boarded the train further down the platform with Scheidhauer. Big X was evidently checking to see how many other escapers had made it. He didn't say a word, but after shaking Dvorak's hand too, he continued walking down the corridor. Plunkett and Dvorak were wondering how many of their comrades were on the same train. In fact they were the only four, the rest who had meant to be on trains were wandering around in the confusion and mayhem that surrounded Sagan station.

Johnny Marshall and Wally Valenta were not far behind Plunkett and Dvorak and they too were puzzled by the apparent change in appearance of the station entrance and had been stumbling around before the sudden arrival of Bomber Command over Berlin threw the place into confusion. They also had an altercation with a clerk who told them it was against regulations to board a train during an air raid. But unlike their comrades who had arrived a few minutes earlier, Marshall and Valenta hadn't any opportunity to jump a train and instead decided to retreat to the woods to reconsider their strategy. They had planned to get a train to the Czech border town of Mittelwalde and get across the frontier on foot from there. They would then either join up with the local underground, or continue on to Yugoslavia, where they could join Tito's partisans. Being among the priority escapers they were both well equipped. They had 200 marks between them and perfectly produced bogus papers that identified them as Czech workers. However, perhaps taken aback by the number of German guards they had seen in the booking hall—many of them recognisable faces from Stalag Luft III—neither of them cherished the idea of hanging around the booking hall until 1 a.m., when their next potential train arrived. They decided they would have to make their way to the Czech border on foot. Although it was some 80 miles they thought they stood as good a chance on foot as taking the train. They would not be alone in arriving at this hard decision.

Sydney Dowse and Danny Krol arrived at the same conclusion shortly afterwards. They had tickets to Berlin, where they were going to stay before heading for Stettin, but they had been separated when Krol's attack of claustrophobia got the better of him in the tunnel and he could no longer stand the endless delays. The two men had agreed to rendezvous in the woods as soon as the controllers permitted Dowse to break out. But Dowse's position in the tunnel was constantly put back and when he finally stumbled out it was only by a miracle that he actually found Krol. It was long after their scheduled departure and they too did not like the idea of hanging around Sagan station for the next train to Berlin with a bunch of Kriegies on the run and a bevy of familiar goons. Instead, they decided they would take the simple measure of simply following the tracks of the railway line east all the way to Poland. It would be an arduous journey, but at least they had Dowse's three-week supply of real food vouchers to live on and Krol's Polish to get them out of any sticky situations.

Bob van der Stok thought his game was up almost the minute he had escaped when he ran into a German soldier in the woods. The German wanted to know what he was doing. Van der Stok explained that he was a foreign worker looking for the railway station but after hearing the air-raid sirens thought it would be safer to hide in the woods. He was relieved when the German seemed to take him at his word. He pointed towards a path that would lead him directly to the station. When he arrived at the booking hall in the station van der Stok discovered other escapers milling around—most looking vaguely anxious, all trying to avoid one another's gaze.

Meanwhile, the station continued to fill up with more escapers, who were all being confronted with difficult decisions, thanks to the disruption to their plans. They had all arrived hopelessly behind schedule and had missed their trains. Wandering about the booking hall a little self-consciously they tried to avoid one another's gaze with different degrees of success. Most self-conscious of all was Wings Day, who arrived shortly before 1 a.m., a little apprehensive in his disguise of an Irish colonel's uniform. Wings was hoping against hope that the presence next to him of Peter Tobolski in his Luftwaffe corporal's disguise would offer the reassurance necessary to any suspicious German. But when he looked around he could see almost nothing but familiar faces. Gordon Kidder and Tom Kirby-Green were there; as were Dennis Cochran, John Stevens, Bob van der Stok and Johannes Gouws. It seemed to Day that the whole of the X-Organisation was occupying the booking hall.

Shortly after Wings Day arrived, another Berlin to Breslau express screeched into the station and the escapers in the booking hall breathed a quiet sigh of relief. The men began filtering through the ticket barrier. However, it was not quite such plain sailing for van der

Stok. The Dutchman was in for one more close encounter with the enemy. On the platform he fell into conversation with a girl who said that she was one of the censors at Stalag Luft III and was looking for escaped officers. Miraculously, she did not suspect him as being one. Van der Stok made his excuses and joined the other men as the booking hall emptied of those escapers bound for Breslau, among them Gouws, Kidder, Kirby-Green and Stevens. After the train left, a dozen or so other escapers remained nervously in the booking hall due to depart from Sagan. By 2 a.m. their numbers had been boosted as more and more Allied officers arrived. Two of the Norwegian contingent—Jens Muller and Per Bergsland—were bound for Frankfurt an der Oder, as were Gordon Brettell, René Marcinkus, Henri Picard and Tim Walenn. Their train came just after 2 a.m. and they all departed without incident. Now three train-loads of prisoners were making their way to freedom and it was beginning to seem as if all the delays and frustrations of earlier in the night were starting to pay off.

Wings Day and Tobolski were among those left in the booking hall. Wings remained uncomfortable in his unwanted disguise but was reassured somewhat by the fact that some Stalag Luft III guards who had been hanging around the station, obviously on leave, had not appeared to pay him the slightest bit of attention. More to the point, they had boarded their trains and were now gone. Perhaps, reflected Wings, the Escape Committee was right after all and the most unlikely cover stories were the best. There were a handful of other escapers still waiting at Sagan with Wings, also destined for the Reich capital, among them the Norwegians Halldor Espelid and Nils Fugelsang. It was well past 3 a.m. before the Berlin train arrived to whisk them away into the night. Soon the Sagan booking hall no longer hosted the clandestine travellers, who seemed not to have attracted the slightest amount of suspicion among most of their German travelling companions, the station officials and even the prison camp guards. The only other train travellers from Stalag Luft III would be the 12 escapers posing as woodmill workers on leave, but they would be departing from the small country station of Tschiebsdorf, not far from Sagan, from where they would get a local train to Boberöhrsdorf on the Czech border.

However, before the woodmill-leave escapers would have even begun their journey out of the woods, escaped men were already being recaptured. It was not long before Wally Valenta and Johnny Marshall were beginning to regret their decision to leave Sagan on foot. Neither of them was equipped for a journey across country and the sight of them wandering around at that time of the night quickly drew suspicious gazes. When they were challenged in a village not far from Sagan, the game was up immediately. It was a serious blow for two escapers who had both been judged to have a better-than-average chance of making a home run. Sadly, it would prove to be a more serious blow for the Czechoslovakian flier than his English companion.

It was around midnight that the first express train arrived in Breslau bearing the first two pairs of escapers to have made it away. Plunkett and Dvorak had studiously avoided Bushell and Scheidhauer for the remainder of the journey from Sagan. When they got off at Breslau they were still without tickets and were in a quandary about what to do about it. Alarmingly they noticed that Gestapo agents were standing by the ticket barriers. They had no idea whether this was a special precaution because the escape had been found out or whether it was standard procedure. It soon emerged that they were less of an obstacle than first imagined. As the crowd of passengers approached the barriers an argument broke out between one man and a ticket collector. In the ensuing commotion the Gestapo agents were distracted enough not to bother as two shifty-looking civilians slipped behind their backs with their collars up. They found themselves in the booking hall beyond and took a surreptitious peek around to see if they could see Bushell or Scheidhauer. Neither of the other men seemed to be there. Plunkett and Dvorak's connection was at 6 a.m. so they settled down for a long wait, hoping the Gestapo agents would limit their attention to the ticket barriers.

At 2.30 a.m. the second express train arrived carrying the second group of escapers including Gouws, Kidder, Kirby-Green, Stevens and van der Stok. By then Plunkett and Dvorak were sitting on their cases half asleep. The other men wandered around the booking hall attempting to avoid one another. Roger Bushell finally turned up but there was no sight of his partner, Bernard Scheidhauer. When Plunkett quietly enquired what had happened to him, Bushell explained with a wink that Scheidhauer had bumped into a French woman and the two had repaired to her apartment to discuss how she could help them with their escape.

Back at Sagan, the Tschiebsdorf escapers began emerging from Harry at around 1.30 a.m. First to get out of the tunnel were the two key members of the group. The Australian John Williams would be their guide out of the forest and to Tschiebsdorf. Williams was familiar with the area, having reconnoitred it while out on parole. From Tschiebsdorf the Polish RAF officer Jerzy Mondschein would take the lead, he being judged the most likely-looking woodmill worker to buy the escapers' tickets at the station. The group had agreed to rendezvous in the woods. As the night progressed the other members of the group gradually assembled: Johnny Dodge, bereft of the jumpers Ker-Ramsay had told him to shed, and Pop Green; Tony Kiewnarski and Kaz Pawluck; Rusty Kierath and Jim Wernham; Doug Poynter and Johnny Bull; Jimmy James and Nick Skanziklas. They were all assembled in the forest by 3 a.m. when they finally set off, skirting around the Russian and French compounds, before heading in a south-easterly direction through the woods. They hoped to find the railway line that would lead them directly to Tschiebsdorf, but it was hard going picking their way through the trees, and desperately cold. Williams was clearly bewildered—hardly surprising, really, since a brief trip out on parole in the daylight isn't much preparation for a trek through a forest covered in snow in the middle of a moonless night. For several hours the railway line proved elusive. Eventually, with less than an hour to spare, they stumbled upon it and traced its course back southwards to find the station.

It was nearly 6 a.m. when they finally arrived at Tschiebsdorf, exhausted and shivering from cold. Jerzy Mondschein went to get the tickets while the others waited in the booking hall. Mondschein showed the ticket-

320

master his leave pass and requested the 12 tickets. But the ticket-master was a little taken aback by the slightly unusual request and repeatedly asked Mondschein if he was sure he wanted 12 tickets, much to the Pole's irritation and discomfiture. The other escapers in the booking hall looked on, a little concerned, as the ticket-master disappeared into his office. During the course of these anxious moments an elderly farmer and his wife entered the station, took one look at the motley crew of men and promptly retreated from the room. However, much to everybody's relief, the ticket-master eventually emerged and issued them with the 12 tickets just in time to clamber on board the train. They appeared to be the only people on it, so it was perhaps not surprising that their sudden appearance at the ticket office had raised eyebrows.

As their train trundled its way slowly through the countryside to Boberöhrsdorf the first group of escapers destined for Berlin were arriving in the capital. Jimmy Catanach, Arnold Christensen, Halldor Espelid and Nils Fugelsang had had an uneventful journey from Sagan. It was the early morning of Saturday, 25 March, when they disembarked from their train. They were all astonished—and a little gratified—to see the number of office blocks and apartment buildings gutted by bombs and incendiaries but didn't have time to take in the disintegrating sights of the Reich capital. They

321

had to get a connection to Denmark and when it arrived on time they boarded, hoping the trip would be as uneventful as the one from Sagan. By now, of course, the alarm had been raised in Sagan. What was unlikely was that the hue and cry would have reached local Gestapo agents and the units of the Home Guard and Hitler Youth.

As that group was departing on the journey northwards, Wings Day and Peter Tobolski were arriving in the capital. Their train journey had also gone without incident. Once they disembarked they headed directly for the address they had been given by the Escape Committee of a Danish member of the underground. They discovered that he was a generous host and treated them to a minor banquet, which was comforting after the deprivations of Sagan. However, the contact appeared either unwilling or incapable of helping them. The two men decided he might be more of a hindrance than a help to their plans. After Day helped himself to some of the man's civilian clothes, they gave him the slip and embarked on a tour of the German capital to explore for themselves other possibilities of escape. They too were surprised at the level of destruction the Allied air raids had wrought on Berlin. After weighing up the options they decided to head for Stettin the following day, Sunday, where Tobolski's sister lived.

In the meantime, Des Plunkett and Freddie

Dvorak had got their 6 a.m. connection to a little town called Glatz. They disembarked shortly before Glatz (which would probably have had ticket-collectors and Gestapo checkpoints), getting off at the little country station of Bad Reinerz, and planned to complete the journey to the border on foot. Their endeavours very nearly came unstuck when Plunkett went into the toilets to answer a call of nature. It had been hours since he had been able to relieve himself and when he did so at the urinal he proclaimed in English: 'That's better!' There was a German soldier standing next to him. The man looked at Plunkett. The RAF officer was left with little choice but to make an unseemly retreat into the hall outside. Bizarrely the German did not follow him.

The train carrying the woodmill-leave escapers to Boberöhrsdorf turned out to be a very slow one indeed, stopping at every station along its route and picking up more and more passengers. When the train finally arrived at Boberöhrsdorf the escapers were surprised and relieved to find no ticket checks at all at the station. There was just a gap in the fence that separated the road from the platforms. Still, the men agreed there was no time to spare. They had to operate on the presumption that the alarm had by now been raised and it would only be a matter of time before legions of Home Guard and Hitler

Youth were on their tracks. The men began to bid one another farewell and wish one another 'good luck'. From now on they would go their separate ways in pairs or alone.

Jimmy James and Nick Skanziklas were going to try and get to Czechoslovakia via the appropriately named Riesengebirge (the giant mountains). They left the road almost immediately and set off across country before climbing up the snow-covered foothills. It was heavy going, the men slipping on the icy slopes, scrambling upwards, clinging on to tree roots and one another for support. On the higher slopes they were waist deep in snow. The temperature was almost 20 degrees below zero and the men were freezing in their thin clothes. James, who had endured several Canadian winters, was marginally better equipped than Skanziklas, but it was an awful ordeal for both men. They found a manger that offered some shelter and desperately tried to warm up by building a fire out of twigs. The task, though, was impossible and they decided to plough on, regardless of the cold.

After climbing one peak and descending into a valley of the River Bober, they ascended once more only to be confronted with a bleak scenario of endless wintry peaks at the top of their next climb. Thankfully, though, Hirschberg was at least visible in the distant east, but Skanziklas pointed out that the Czech border was at least a further 40 miles away. By now the two men were perishing with cold—neither could face the prospect of walking 40 miles. They decided they had no alternative but to risk walking along the road to Hirschberg and try to get a train from there to Czechoslovakia. They arrived in the town and quickly made for Hirschberg West railway station, a little buoyed by their relatively easy experience so far. They shouldn't have been so confident. As they approached the ticket office James saw out of the corner of his eye a policeman and a civilian official register their arrival. The two men tried to ignore them and walked confidently towards the ticket office, but the officials walked directly up to them and confronted them.

'Papiere,' the policeman demanded in a not-very-friendly fashion.

Still trying to appear confident, the escapers presented their bogus papers. After a perfunctory inspection the German said: 'Komm mit.' (Roughly translated: 'C'mon' or 'Come with me'.)

James protested. 'Our papers are in perfect order,' he said before adding desperately, and somewhat pathetically, he admitted many years later, 'You can't do this, my old mum's expecting me.'

They were marched off to the local police station in front of a gathering crowd of curious onlookers. The two men were destined for the local headquarters of the Kripo. They were made to stand under armed guard while their captors disappeared inside a small outer office. When they emerged it was to place a piece of paper in front of both men and demand they write their names down. Both RAF officers by now realised it would be futile to continue the pretence. They wrote their names down and were told to sit down in a passageway. It would be the beginning of an uncomfortable time for both of them in different ways.

Recalling his feelings many years later, James said he could only feel an immense sense of disappointment. He had been in captivity for the greater duration of the war. It is idle to speculate whether his mind shot back to that moment in Barth, with Death Shore, where he missed his opportunity of becoming one of the first RAF prisoners to make a home run. Given the remorselessness with which he had pursued freedom, it would be hard for even his enemies not to sympathise with him. As the hours passed, more escapers arrived in the Kripo building. It would not be long before they were reunited with the rest of the woodmill-leave group.

*   *   *

Pop Green's greatest asset was his age. Few people would think anybody as old as him would be an Allied officer. However, it proved no use. Leaving the station at Boberöhrsdorf he intended to circumnavigate the town rather than walk through it, not being equipped with any German that could get him out of a confrontation. Green tried various routes but quickly realised that it was probably impossible to do so without arousing suspicion. He decided instead to walk directly through the town. It would be his undoing. He had hardly made it up the main street when he was challenged by someone, no doubt by now aware that Allied airmen were on the loose. Why had he not travelled directly to Hirschberg? the man demanded. Green tried to come up with an appropriate excuse, but it was unconvincing. A phone call was placed to Hirschberg and before long Pop Green was in police custody.

Johnny Dodge's and Jim Wernham's escape was almost as short-lived. After leaving the main group at Boberöhrsdorf they made several futile attempts to buy railway tickets. They fell foul of regulations that restricted travel in border zones and of which they were blissfully unaware. Like so many of the other escapers, Dodge and Wernham found they had no alternative but to make it on foot, trudging through thick snow, cold, wet and dispirited. Later that afternoon they arrived at a small station near Hirschberg and decided to try their luck once more. They were relieved to see that the official who was impassively inspecting their bogus Yugoslav passes did not suspect anything. But then, just as he was about to hand them back, a Yugoslav worker standing nearby addressed them in Serbo-Croat. Neither man had ever heard the language before. When they failed to respond, the ticket inspector realised something was amiss. Within minutes, they were under arrest.

Tony Kiewnarski and Kaz Pawluk made it to Hirschberg but were arrested that afternoon also, in the centre of town. Like Pop Green, Doug Poynter hung around Boberöhrsdorf and found a hiding place that he could shelter in until later in the day. Cold and hungry he eventually boarded a train to Polaun. As the train was crawling its way along the line, Poynter realised two policemen and a Hitler Youth were checking everybody's papers. He held his breath as the policemen inspected his forged papers that identified him as a French worker. They were about to hand them back to him, satisfied, when the Hitler Youth pointed out a minor blemish. Poynter was immediately put under arrest and sent to Hirschberg police station.

Jerzy Mondschein and Johnny Bull had no better luck. After parting with the main group at Boberöhrsdorf they were shortly reunited with Rusty Kierath and John Williams. The four men decided to make a go of it together, trying to climb over the Riesengebirge like Jimmy James and Nick Skanziklas. They were

328

caught by a mountain patrol. Shortly afterwards they were in Reichenberg Prison, in Czechoslovakia, before being sent to Hirschberg to join the rest of their group.

* * *

At Sagan, Paul Royle and Edgar Humphreys were among the last to leave the tunnel, emerging into the darkness outside the camp at about 2.30 a.m. Their plan was to hard-arse it all the way to Czechoslovakia following the course of one of the Nazi's new Autobahnen. But it took them the best part of Saturday to find the highway and it was apparent when they did that the thick banks of snow either side would not allow them to comfortably skirt the road. Instead they would have to walk along the edge, ducking and diving whenever a vehicle appeared. It was a hopelessly inefficient way to travel. By the time they were challenged by some local Home Guard, they had hardly covered any distance.

Les Brodrick was another hard-arser, who set off through the forests of Sagan with Henry 'Hank' Birkland and Denys Street. They crossed the main road undetected and continued through the woods until light dawned when they had agreed they would have to stay put until darkness came again. They occasionally heard the voices of forest workers nearby but nobody came near them. Whoever they were they did not appear to be searching for escaped Allied officers, which offered a degree of comfort. But it was deathly cold in the woods, and it took an effort of immense will for the men not to give up and hand themselves over to the workers. Remarkably, they survived until darkness and continued their escape but the going was slow. The snow seemed to get thicker and the forest seemed to be getting denser. None of them thought they were making much more progress than a few hundred yards every hour. They were all tired and frozen to the bone. 'The only thing that kept me going,' says Brodrick, 'was the memory of stories I'd read about Arctic adventurers when I was a child. I remembered the most important thing to do was keep moving because if you fell asleep in the snow you would never wake up.'

*   *   *

By the late afternoon of Saturday, 25 March, only hours after the break-out, the escapers being held at the Hirschberg headquarters of the Kripo were beginning to realise just what a stir they had created in the Third Reich. Their jailers had about them the contemptuous air of men who were going to teach the Allied fliers a lesson once and for all. As they awaited their interrogation, the officers squirrelled away their escape maps and other incriminating evidence behind a filing cabinet. Jimmy James was the first to hear his name called out. He found himself in a large room confronted by a 'small, bald-headed, mean-looking man in horn-rimmed spectacles' behind a desk. There was a typist and an interpreter. It soon became apparent that the man knew about the tunnel.

His interrogator began firing a string of impatient questions at the RAF officer. He demanded to know what time James had left the tunnel, to which the RAF officer replied, with all honesty, that he had no idea. He wanted to know the number who had escaped with him, to which James replied a little disingenuously that he had no idea about that either. When James was asked what his number in the break-out had been, he refused to say on the grounds that it was a military operation and as a British officer he was not required to disclose details of military operations.

This provoked the German official into a sour laugh. 'Boy scouts!' he sneered and then, hoping to ruffle the RAF man, said that he did not look like an officer.

'Where did you get those clothes?' he demanded.

'They are my uniform,' replied James.

'They are civilian clothes,' retorted his inquisitor.

Already, presumably, the German officials had discussed their strategy for justifying what they were about to take part in.

The mean-looking man continued to quiz James, asking questions about the construction of the tunnel. James refused to reply to any of the questions and refused to sign the transcript when it was presented to him. In a rage, the interrogator led him off down a short passageway and threw him in a dark cell. Having not slept properly for two days, James promptly fell asleep. He had no idea how much time had passed when he was awoken with a start. It was the same man again. James was led back to the office but this time it was full of SS and Gestapo officers wearing smart black uniforms with red swastika armbands. It was an ominous sight.

The interrogation began again, the mean little Gestapo agent attempting to browbeat James into submission. The RAF officer was acutely aware of the sinister presence of the SS men and Gestapo in the shadows but he stood his ground, only to be led outside once more into the original corridor where his seven comrades were huddled. Shortly afterwards, each man was manacled to a police officer by a chain and they were led out into the snow-covered streets to Hirschberg jail, where they were all thrown into a small, dirty cell. Despite the bare stone floor, James, once more, fell into a deep but fitful slumber.

By Sunday 26, Hirschberg jail was playing host to eight of the escapers, all of whom had been on the woodmill-leave party. They were: Johnny Dodge and his partner Jimmy Wernham; Jimmy James and his partner Nick Skanziklas; Pop Green and Doug Poynter; Antoni Kiewnarski and Kazimierz Pawluk. The chief warder, or Meister, of the jail was another mean-looking Nazi, with cold, blue eyes staring through rimless glasses. It was freezing cold inside the jail as well as out, and their grim surroundings were not calculated to raise their spirits. One small compensation was that their meals, such as they were, arrived courtesy of a pretty young Polish girl. 'Even the forbidding presence of the Meister could not detract from the pleasure of my first contact with the opposite sex for four years,' recalled James in his memoir *Moonless Night*.

The men, led by Johnny Dodge, tried to cheer themselves up by singing popular ditties. The Polish officers tried to engage in conversation through the bars of the cell windows with some women prisoners who were being held two floors down. At one point the British officers decided to strike a defiant tone and demanded that they be granted some rudimentary supplies, such as soap and razor blades, that escaped POWs were entitled to. Their modest requests only served to inflame the Meister's superior, who sent back the message that they would make do with what they had. The men were, however, allowed brief daily exercise, walking around the small courtyard of the prison. They all wondered why they were not being sent back to camp, which was the normal procedure.

*   *   *

On that same Sunday, Roger Bushell and Bernard Scheidhauer were approaching the town of Saarbrücken. As they approached the town limits early in the morning, they encountered a Gestapo checkpoint. They were apprehensive but confident their papers were watertight and their German perfect. And indeed they managed to bluff their way through, but then, at the last minute, they fell for one of the oldest tricks in the book. A Gestapo agent wished the Frenchman, in English: 'Good luck.'

'Thank you,' replied Scheidhauer, also in English.

Without further ado the two men were taken to Gestapo headquarters in Saarbrücken, where they were interrogated by the Gestapo chief of Saarbrücken, the sinister Oberleutnant Dr Leopold Spann.

Back at Sagan, Les Brodrick, Henry Birkland and Denys Street had hardly progressed at all in the forests surrounding the camp. That Sunday morning the men had arrived at a clearing. They hid in the only bush cover they could find and in the distance saw some other people. For all they knew, they could have been escapers too. By then their clothes were wet through. They were so cold they had practically lost all sensation in their hands and feet. Night came and they continued walking through the woods but by now Birkland, the youngest of the three, was beginning to show signs of mental breakdown. He was talking to himself and mumbling incoherently. He started to stumble and lost the will to keep moving. The two others tried to persuade him to keep on the go, but he had clearly lost all control over his mental powers. Street decided that, whatever the risks, they would have to seek cover for the night. Fortunately, they found some buildings in the woods. Street could speak German and quickly devised an (unlikely) cover story. When he knocked on the door the man who answered it seemed to believe him. However, after retreating inside he returned with four armed soldiers. Brodrick admits the RAF men were frankly relieved. 'We were dying on our feet,' he recalls. 'At that point I think I would have done anything for a bit of warmth.' The men had travelled less than two miles from the camp.

*   *   *

That Sunday Adolf Hitler received a report on the debacle at his retreat, the Berghof at Berchtesgaden. Present were the air

Reichsmarschall Hermann Göring, the SS chief Heinrich Himmler and the toadying head of the armed forces, Feldmarschall Wilhelm Keitel. By that stage in the war Göring was not one of Hitler's most popular senior commanders, the Führer judging that the Luftwaffe had failed him in almost every respect. Nevertheless, the jovial Reichsmarschall was possessed of such a thick skin and boundless self-confidence that he was oblivious to the contempt of his leader. He firmly put the blame for the Sagan debacle on the shoulders of the prisoner-of-war camp inspectorate, the OKW bureaucracy that ultimately came under Feldmarschall Keitel's command. In fact, the inspectorate had nothing to do with camp security, only inspecting the camps and administering them. For most of the war most air force prisoners had come under Luftwaffe control—at the specific insistence of Reichsmarschall Hermann Göring.

However, the obsequious Keitel appears to have been more anxious than Göring to placate Hitler. The Führer was in an ugly mood and demanded that when the airmen were recaptured they should all be summarily shot. Göring objected lamely. Not, probably, out of the old sense of chivalry that had motivated him in the early years of the war, but because even he knew that the war was coming to an end and such a drastic move would finally implicate the Luftwaffe, and himself, as war criminals alongside the worst of the Nazis. Given that the Luftwaffe had sorely let Hitler down and that he raged almost daily at the Air Force's incompetence, Göring no longer wielded a great deal of influence with the Führer. However, Himmler surprisingly came down on the side of the air Reichsmarschall. The killings would create an international outcry, he objected. It is instructive to reflect that while the fate of 76 Allied officers prompted such a flurry of soul-searching, millions of Jews were being driven to their deaths without a second thought. It is also instructive to note that Himmler, like Göring, had his eye on the end game. He too knew the war was not going to last much longer. Comically, in retrospect, both men actually believed that there would be a place for them in the new Germany of the future. Neither man had the slightest understanding of the loathing in which the Nazi regime was held by the rest of the world.

In the end Hitler agreed to a compromise. At least half of the Allied officers should be shot. The figure of 50 appears to have been settled upon at random. To his eternal credit, the head of the OKW prison inspectorate, General von Graevenitz, objected strenuously to the plan when it was presented to him by Keitel. 'Escape isn't a dishonourable offence,' he told him. 'That is specifically laid down by the [Geneva] Convention.'

Keitel, however, was unmoved. The fawning Feldmarschall was desperate to please the Führer. 'I don't give a damn, we discussed it in the Führer's presence and it cannot be altered.' Keitel told him an example had to be made of these men. The majority of the escapers had probably already been shot, he informed the General casually, and incorrectly.

After the war, Graevenitz's deputy, Major-General Adolf Westhoff, told interrogators: 'Keitel was considerably excited about the escape of these eighty people [including the four caught at the tunnel exit], due probably to the fact that he had been reproached by the Reichsführer [Himmler] and the Reichsmarschall [Göring]. He said that it was incredible that this sort of thing should have occurred and it must not be allowed to continue.' General von Graevenitz resolved that if any of the escapers fell into his men's hands they would be returned directly to Stalag Luft III. He discreetly passed the message on to his underlings, and General von Graevenitz was to be proved true to his word. Ultimately, the dirty work fell into the (mostly) unwilling hands of the Gestapo.

The following morning, Monday, 27 March, Himmler contacted the head of the Reichssicherheitshauptamt (RSHA), Ernst Kaltenbrunner, and informed him of the

Führer's order. It was what was known as a 'Hitler Order': an order issued directly by the Führer himself and under no circumstances to be disobeyed. Himmler informed Kaltenbrunner that he was to issue what became known as 'the Sagan Order.'

The Sagan Order stated:

> The increase of escapes by officer prisoners of war is a menace to internal security. I am disappointed and indignant about the inefficient security measures. As a deterrent the Führer has ordered that more than half the escaped officers are to be shot. Therefore I order that Department V [the Kripo—the Kriminalpolizei] hand over to Department IV [the Gestapo] more than half the recaptured officers. After interrogation it should be made to seem that the officers are being returned to their camp but they are to be shot en route. The shooting will be explained by the fact that the recaptured officers were shot trying to escape, or they offered resistance, so that nothing can be proved later. Amt IV will report the shootings to Amt V giving the reason. In the event of future escapes my decision will be awaited as to the procedure to be

adopted. Prominent personalities will be excepted; their names will be reported to me and a decision awaited.

Kaltenbrunner delegated responsibility for organising the murders to two of the most ruthless Nazis of the Third Reich. Heinrich Müller was the head of the Gestapo (Amt IV or department 4 of the Reichssicherheitshauptamt); General Artur Nebe, the head of the Kripo (Amt V). Müller instructed Nebe to choose the names of those to be killed. Nebe had plenty of blood on his hands. In an early incarnation he had been a commander of one of the SS 'task forces' (Einsatzgruppen) operating in Russian territory taken by the Germans in 1941. The job of these notorious units was to 'liquidate' influential civilians likely to oppose the Reich—in truth, a thinly veiled euphemism for prominent Jews and Communists. Nebe himself claimed his own task force was responsible for more than 45,000 killings, many of them, possibly, women and children. Yet the task of selecting for execution the 50 airmen was one that would apparently distress Nebe.

*   *   *

In the very early hours of Monday, 27 March,

Paul Royle and Edgar Humphreys were taken to the jailhouse at Tiefenfurt, not far from Sagan. Shortly afterwards they were joined by Marshall and Valenta, followed by Albert Armstrong. At daylight they were taken under armed guard in a police van to Sagan. All of them were looking forward to the comparative comforts of the prison camp, even if it meant spending two weeks in a freezing cooler cell. They were a little disappointed therefore that the police van ignored the road that led to the camp and continued towards the town itself. At this stage, though, none of the men had any reason to feel undue concern. The van pulled up outside Sagan police station and one by one the prisoners were interrogated before being thrown into a cell. As the day progressed the police station filled with more and more escaped officers, most of them hard-arsers. Les Brodrick, Denys Street and Henry Birkland were among the first to arrive.

By that Monday Jimmy Catanach, Arnold Christensen, Halldor Espelid and Nils Fugelsang had made it to the Danish border at Flensburg. There their escape came to an abrupt end. They were arrested at a police check. A similar fate awaited Gordon Brettell, René Marcinkus, Henri Picard and Tim Walenn. They were stopped at a checkpoint at Schneidemühl and taken to a prison camp at Marienburg. After their civilian clothes were taken from them they were sent to Danzig

341

Prison.

In Hirschberg, on the same Monday morning, Johnny Dodge was the first to be summoned away. He had no idea where he was going to, but the fact that he was singled out meant perhaps that the local Gestapo had been informed of his supposed links to the British Prime Minister. Dodge was his usual irrepressible self when he bade farewell to the others. That afternoon, the names of four others were read out: Kiewnarski, Pawluk, Wernham and Skanziklas. If any of the men seemed worried, none of them showed it. It was with the usual bluff good-nature that they said 'goodbye' to the remaining three RAF officers, Pop Green, Jimmy James and Doug Poynter. It was the last time they would see their Air Force comrades.

That night in Sagan, the captured prisoners in the local police station were roused in the middle of the night and unceremoniously bundled into another van. There were now 19 escaped officers in the police station and it was full to capacity. This time they were taken to the prison in the town of Görlitz, where once more they were put in small cells, this time four men sharing each cramped space. The men were now beginning to be worried about what exactly was going on. By now they would normally have expected to have been returned to the hands of the Luftwaffe. Unaccountably they had been left in the hands of the sinister little men of the Kripo. Presently, more and more recaptured officers began arriving at Görlitz Prison. Among them Tony Bethell, Mike Casey, Cookie Long and Mike Shand. Tony Bethell and Cookie Long's attempt to ride the railway lines to Stettin had soon floundered. All the trains they encountered proved to be going far too fast to jump on, and they had no alternative but to walk. They made it as far as the village of Benau, where they walked straight into a member of the Home Guard. Mike Shand had been on the run for four days, walking by night and hiding by day. He was finally caught by a couple of railway workers while he was waiting to jump a freight train. Al Hake and Johnny Pohe arrived suffering from frostbite, but their jailers made no attempts to offer them medical treatment. Once more, this unusual breach of protocol worried the men. By Wednesday, 29 March, there were 35 RAF officers in Görlitz jail.

On that same day in Hirschberg the Meister came for Pop Green and Doug Poynter. Jimmy James was all alone. It was only now that James began to feel ill at ease. The manner in which the men were being parted didn't seem to make sense. Perhaps they were not all going back to Sagan? Perhaps they were all going to be sent to different camps? Shortly afterwards, James was removed to another cell in the centre of the prison, the only light coming in through a grubby glass skylight.

* * *

In Görlitz, over the forthcoming days the recaptured prisoners would be taken— sometimes alone, sometimes in pairs—across town to the Gestapo headquarters for interrogation. It was now that the men were beginning to realise something sinister was afoot. Some were told that they would not be returning to the care of the Luftwaffe because the Air Force was transparently incapable of minding its charges. Others were coldly told they would not be seeing their loved ones again. One man was told he would be sent to a concentration camp.

The rest of the escapers, who were gradually being recaptured, continued to turn up at jails in dribs and drabs all over occupied Europe but mainly in Germany. Gordon Kidder and Tom Kirby-Green reached Breslau, but were arrested after taking a train to Czechoslovakia. Both men were taken to a local prison at Zlín on 28 March, where they were interrogated. Dennis Cochran almost reached Switzerland, only to be arrested near the border on 30 March.

By 29 March almost all of the airmen had been accounted for and Nebe began the task of selecting who would die. He had asked an assistant to prepare a pile of index cards with the details of each man. As Nebe sifted through the pile, he was said to be in a state of considerable agitation as he examined them, emitting quiet sighs of anguish as he made his mind up who to spare and who to condemn. 'This man is very young, he can live.' 'This man is for it.' He appears to have tried to save the youngest men, or those who were married with children. Finally, he handed the larger pile to his assistant and instructed him to send the orders out. (Nebe is a curious character in the footnotes of the Third Reich whose wartime career illustrates the terrible ambiguities and moral compromises that war, and tyranny, force on human beings. Several months after the Sagan escape, Nebe would be implicated in the Stauffenberg plot to assassinate Hitler. He was tortured by the Gestapo for two months but refused to give away any names of his co-conspirators. Eventually, he shared the same fate as the 50 airmen.)

On the early morning of 29 March the first murder was to be carried out. Roger Bushell and Bernard Scheidhauer were being driven along the Autobahn to Kaiserslautern in the company of Spann and Emil Schulz, the Kriminalsekretär, when they met their fate, the full details of which would only emerge after the war. Squadron Leader James Catanach was to be delivered to an even crueller fate.

Over the next few days the recaptured airmen began to get their first real inkling of what was going on. Early in the morning of 30 March, a convoy of squealing Gestapo vehicles came to take six of them away, mostly East European RAF officers. The guard in the prison unconvincingly tried to feign ignorance of their fate. The next day, more RAF officers were taken by the Gestapo, including Birkland and Valenta. On 2 April, however, the remaining prisoners were comforted to see four familiar Stalag Luft III Luftwaffe guards arrive. They took away four of the men, including Paul Royle, who was told as he was leaving that he was 'one of the lucky ones'. Successive groups of prisoners were subsequently taken away by the Luftwaffe including Tony Bethell, Les Brodrick, Dick Churchill and Mike Shand. Cookie Long was among the last to be taken away. But it was the Gestapo who turned up for him, not the Luftwaffe.

There were still several men on the run but they too would shortly find themselves thrown into Gestapo cells. Tony Hayter was caught on 4 April in France, not far from the Swiss border. By 6 April Danny Krol and Sydney Dowse had almost completed their marathon journey along the railway line. The Polish border was just a few miles away and the men planned to try and cross it that night. They found a barn to shelter and rest in but were surprised by a farmer. They tried to convince him they were Polish workers and he seemed to believe them, but shortly afterwards he turned up with a Hitler Youth and two members of the Home Guard. The RAF officers were taken to the local jail, where the Gestapo turned up to interrogate them. After they had been put through the same routine as the other prisoners, Dowse was told he was going to be taken to Berlin for further questioning while Krol would be sent back to Sagan. Krol was alarmed when his friend told him this. 'You mustn't let them separate us,' he said imploringly. 'I'll be finished if they do.' Dowse told him not to worry. It was the last he ever saw of Krol.

Des Plunkett and Freddie Dvorak had very nearly escaped. After their near-brush with disaster at Bad Reinerz, the two officers set out on foot across country towards the Czech frontier, the snow sometimes waist deep. They finally made it to the small hamlet of Novi Hradek in Czechoslovakia. There they revealed their true identities to a friendly hotelier who offered to put them up but warned them that the hue and cry was already out for them. Shortly afterwards they were on their way by train to Prague with the details of another hotelier friendly to the resistance. He organised for them tickets on a train that would take them across Germany to Switzerland. It was 7 April when they set out on their journey, taking advantage of the Good Friday holiday crowds. So far they had survived a close encounter with one possible border guard and an interrogation at the hands of a suspicious policeman. Then their luck ran out. On the first leg of the journey, Plunkett and Dvorak stopped at Domazlice, where they checked into another hotel. But they became convinced the inn-keeper was suspicious of them. Rather than continue on their journey, they decided to double back to Klatovy in the hope of throwing him off the scent. It proved to be a fatal mistake. At a police checkpoint in Klatovy it became apparent that Plunkett did not have the correct travel permit. The two men were thrown in the local jail, where they were soon to be subjected to the attentions of the Gestapo.

Wings Day and Peter Tobolski left Berlin on March 26 by train for Stettin, where the Polish officer had a sister married to a German. However, they were disappointed to discover that she was too afraid to offer much more than the most cursory help. She allowed them to shelter at the bottom of her garden for the night and left them some bread, eggs and milk. The next day they managed to find some French prisoners of war prepared to help smuggle them on a ship bound for Sweden. They were hiding on board the ship when the German police arrived to arrest them on

29 March. They had been betrayed by one of the Frenchmen. After spending four days in a local prison the two men were separated. They saluted one another as they parted, both men acutely conscious of what fate probably awaited Tobolski. But Wings Day was far from sure what fate he would face as he found himself being taken to Gestapo headquarters in Berlin. There he was confronted by Artur Nebe himself, the head of the Kripo and the man who had decided which of the 76 would live or die. After a desultory interrogation, Nebe told Day that he was being sent to somewhere he would not escape from again. Without giving him any further clues, he was dismissed and two Gestapo men drove him out of the city through its northern bomb-flattened suburbs. It was 3 April.

Jimmy James continued his unwelcome stay at Hirschberg jail for several more days. On his brief exercise walks he learnt that most of the other occupants were citizens of occupied countries who had committed crimes against the Reich. Most expected to be executed sooner or later. James began to ruminate about his own fate as he watched the comings and goings of sinister Gestapo agents. It was not until 6 April that the doors of his cell were flung open once more and he was invited to step out. He was confronted by the police inspector he had first met at the police station after his arrest. The man told him he was to be removed from the jail and James was marched down the streets to the railway station, ignorant of what his ultimate destination would be. He was accompanied on the railway journey by another Gestapo inspector. He refused to enlighten him about his destination but at a fork in the tracks the German indicated that the other route led to Sagan. James understood he was not going back to Stalag Luft III. When the men boarded a northern-bound train at Görlitz he knew he must be bound for Berlin. Sure enough, some hours later the train pulled into the capital. Like the others James was astonished by what he saw. The city lay in ruins before him, flattened by the twin efforts of Bomber Command and the American Eighth Air Force. 'There was not a pane of glass to be seen and most of the windows were boarded up,' he recalled. Ironically, it was now in the heart of the Reich that James's German guard offered to release him from his handcuffs if he gave his word he would not escape. He did. It was quite apparent that escape was not in the least likely.

He was still puzzled by his intended fate. James was taken to the headquarters of the Gestapo in Berlin, where after a short interlude he was sent once more on a car journey through the bombed city in the company of two SD officers, members of Hitler's elite intelligence and security division.

After a while, the car left the suburbs behind and entered a dark pine forest. Presently, the car came upon a high wall, camouflaged in dull black and green, with electrified wire running along the top and sentry posts at varying distances. There was something chilling about the place, and James's feelings of apprehension were compounded when one of the SD officers said to him: 'Well, Herr James, no more tunnelling for you—it is impossible to escape from here.'

James was taken through a guardroom into this unknown building. Inside was a small area surrounded by high walls, within which was a further compound surrounded by electrified wire and containing two wooden barrack huts. James was marched into one of these where he was greeted by a tall English officer in horn-rimmed spectacles. 'Welcome to your new home,' he said, introducing himself as Peter Churchill. They shook hands and Churchill took James to the end of the barrack block where he was met by a familiar sight.

'Hello,' grinned Wings Day. James felt a spasm of relief, though he still had no idea where he was.

'Is this Colditz?' he asked Day.

'No,' replied the older officer. 'I wish to hell it was. This is Sachsenhausen concentration camp and the only way out of here is up the chimney.'

CHAPTER NINE

THE ONES THAT GOT AWAY

At Stalag Luft III some of the recaptured prisoners began to trickle back into the camp. The first were Pop Green and Doug Poynter. The news of their recapture came on 29 March when Sagan police station telephoned von Lindeiner's office and told them they were ready to be returned to the Luftwaffe's care. But the Kommandant told his aides to reply that if they had wanted so much to be out of the camp, they could stay out. The policeman, a little taken aback, explained as tactfully as he could that they would 'have a hard time of it' if the Kommandant didn't accept them back. Von Lindeiner's curt response was that they could have a hard time of it for all he cared. It took the intervention, ironically, of an SS interrogating officer to have the two men returned to the camp. The goons told them: 'You are two of the lucky ones.' They did not explain what they meant and there was an ominous cloud hanging over Stalag Luft III. One RAF officer, John Casson, was friendly with one of the goons. He was left distinctly unsettled when the German told him that he was glad he hadn't been one of the escapers because the ones that got out faced an

352

unenviable fate.

It was something of a reassurance when more of the recaptured prisoners began turning up at the camp. Among the early returns were Tony Bethell, Les Brodrick, Dick Churchill, Johnny Marshall, Keith Ogilvie, Paul Royle, Mike Shand and Tommy Thompson. Some were sent for their mandatory two weeks' solitary confinement in the cooler, although since it was now usually full to capacity, the majority were directed back to their barracks. Von Lindeiner didn't seem to care what happened to them. Gone now, for the time being at least, was the chivalrous display of gallantry that had marked his stewardship of the camp in the early days. In the days immediately following the escape, he appeared to the prisoners to be spending a great deal of his time supervising the destruction of the tunnel. This time it was filled with raw sewage and sealed at either end with almost three feet of hard concrete. In fact, von Lindeiner was also spending much of his time fielding angry questions from the SS, Gestapo and Reich officials in Berlin and contemplating his own fate.

On 26 March, two Luftwaffe officers arrived at Stalag Luft III with a writ accusing von Lindeiner of incompetence and relieving him of his command. Three days later he collapsed with severe heart palpitations. Thanks to the timely intervention of a doctor, von Lindeiner recovered. Shortly afterwards the colonel retreated to Jeschkendorf Manor to recuperate and prepare for his defence. Presently, the prisoners were told that Colonel von Lindeiner had been relieved of his command. He had offered to resign three times but on each occasion had been turned down. During his 21 months as Kommandant of Stalag Luft III there had been 262 escape attempts, 100 involving tunnels.

The new Kommandant was yet another officer in the chivalrous mould of Major Rumpel and Colonel von Lindeiner. Colonel Braune appeared equally uneasy in his role as a 'common jailer' but, presumably, he, like his predecessors, had little choice in the matter. By now any casual joshing about the escape had long gone and the men were seriously concerned about the fate of those comrades still missing. On 6 April, Hans Pieber turned up in the North Compound and requested that Group Captain Massey accompany him over to the Kommandantur to meet with Colonel Braune. When Massey asked what it was about, Pieber replied hesitantly: 'I cannot say.'

Massey arrived in the Kommandant's office to find a quiet and distracted Colonel Braune and an uneasy Gustav Simoleit. Massey was accompanied by Squadron Leader Philip Murray, who would act as interpreter. Pieber and Simoleit remained in the room, standing a little uncomfortably, their eyes unable to meet the gaze of the English officers. Braune came swiftly to the point.

'I am instructed by the German High Command to state that 41 of the escapers were shot while resisting arrest.'

'How many were shot?' asked Murray, in disbelief.

Braune appeared distinctly uncomfortable. 'Forty-one,' he said, unable to look the RAF officer in the eye.

Murray translated the statement for Massey, whose eyebrows shot up as he listened.

'Ask him how many men were wounded,' he demanded.

'I am only permitted to say by the German High Command that 41 of your men were shot while resisting arrest,' he replied solemnly.

Once more Massey demanded to know whether any of the men had been wounded.

'I am only instructed to read from the communiqué,' said Braune.

Massey angrily ended the conversation by demanding a list of the names of the men shot. He was not to be satisfied for another week. Pieber was shamefaced as he conducted the British officers back to their compound. Very soon everybody in Stalag Luft III knew their worst fears had come true.

At sundown on 15 April a German guard entered the North Compound and attached a list to the bulletin board. It contained the names not of 41 escapers who had been shot, but 47. The Kriegies gathered around in dismay and disbelief. It would be another month before the final three names were added to the list. The day after, in London, Britain's Foreign Secretary, Anthony Eden, revealed to the House of Commons the details of the escape and the murders that followed it. It would be another two months before Eden appeared in the House again to issue a statement about the affair.

> It is abundantly clear that none of these officers met his death in the course of making his escape from Stalag Luft III or while resisting capture. The Gestapo's contention that the wearing of civilian clothes by an escaping prisoner of war deprives him of the protection of the Prisoners of War Convention is entirely without foundation in international law and practice. From these facts there is, in His Majesty's Government's view, only one possible conclusion. These prisoners of war were murdered . . .

Eden ended his statement vowing that the British government would track down those responsible after the war and bring them to 'exemplary justice'. It was a statement and a promise that made headlines in Britain and touched a chord around the world. It was only with the hindsight of years that some historians wondered whether the undoubtedly heinous crime had been taken somewhat out of context. Every day for the past several years thousands of Jews and the wretched Untermenschen of Hitler's bogus racial theories had been consigned to Himmler's gas chambers. The British government paid scant attention to their fate—or to the disgraceful conditions that many ordinary British servicemen suffered at the hands of the Germans. It seemed to some that some elements of the British hierarchy, in common with von Lindeiner and Braune and Rumpel, were lost in a world where the lives of the well bred and high born were valued more than those less fortunate.

Over the next two months the urns and boxes containing the cremated remains of the 50 were returned to Stalag Luft III. By then Colonel von Lindeiner was at Jeschkendorf Manor preparing for his case. He had the formidable might of the Nazi regime against him and it was difficult in the circumstances to muster a defence. It was a very stressful time for him, but the old colonel found time to think about his former prisoners. He paid for the materials and equipment necessary for them to build a memorial to the 50. On 16 September, von Lindeiner answered an urgent knocking at his door. It was one of his subordinates who had remained loyal to him. He warned him that an order for his immediate arrest and incarceration had been issued in Berlin. Von Lindeiner thanked his visitor and advised him to leave at once. Von Lindeiner did not tell his wife. He packed a bag of toiletries, expecting a knock on the door in the early morning.

The expected knock on the door before dawn did not come, but von Lindeiner and several other members of the Luftwaffe Kommandantur at Sagan were court-martialled on 5 October. The accused included Pieber and Broili, several hapless soldiers and a civil servant. The Reich sought 18 months' imprisonment for the colonel in a bid to send out a signal to other camp Kommandants judged to be too lenient towards their prisoners. In the end they got 12 months' imprisonment in a fortress. Von Lindeiner managed to avoid that penalty by taking a leaf out of some of his prisoners' books. He feigned mental illness and was admitted to an army hospital.

In Stalag Luft III relations between the prisoners and their German guards had reached an all-time low. The goons began shooting at prisoners after little or no provocation resulting, sadly, in the death of a non-commissioned officer in April. Massey told his men that they must take the German warnings seriously and virtually all escape attempts were ended, which was not such a difficult decision given that an Allied victory was by now almost certain. Later on still, some guards confirmed to the men that it was now official policy for all escaped POWs to be shot. Not all escape attempts ended, however. The X-Organisation continued, now under the leadership of Wing Commander John Ellis. Crump Ker-Ramsay and Norman Canton were the chief tunnellers and Alex Cassie took over Dean & Dawson. They started another tunnel, called George, from underneath the theatre, although it was decided that they would only use it if things became a little sticky with the Germans.

Massey was repatriated to England, via Switzerland, on medical grounds. Before he went he urged his men not to do anything silly. His replacement was Group Captain D.E.L. Wilson of the Royal Australian Air Force.

In September the Nazis circulated their infamous poster. It read: 'The escape from prison camps is no longer a sport!' It said that certain zones in the Fatherland had been designated 'death zones' and any unauthorised persons entering them would be shot on sight. 'Stay in the camp, where you will be safe!' implored the poster. In fact, at about the same time it appeared, the prisoners were to be informed via their underground contacts with MI9 that escape was no longer regarded as an officer's duty.

By November, George had reached under the wire, but further work was postponed until the following spring. By December, work on the memorial to the 50 victims just outside the camp had been completed and shortly after its completion Stalag Luft III witnessed what must have been one of the most extraordinary episodes of the war. On 4 December a memorial service was held. Among the small group present were senior officers of the Luftwaffe Kommandantur and an honour guard made up of German soldiers, Group Captain Wilson, and 15 officers representing each of the nations of the dead. The service was attended by two members of the Swiss Legation, representing the protecting power, and was presided over by an Anglican and a Roman Catholic cleric. At the end a bugler from North Compound sounded 'The Last Post' and the German honour guard fired a volley of shots into the cold Silesian sky. There can have been few more moving tributes paid during the Second World War from one side to the other.

*　　*　　*

As the Escape Committee had predicted, it was the German speakers who ended up having the easiest ride, particularly the indigenous European ones.

In contrast to many of the other escapers,

Per Bergsland and Jens Muller encountered hardly any problems. At Sagan station they had boarded the 2.04 a.m. express train to Frankfurt an der Oder without any ado. Following them shortly afterwards were Gordon Brettell, René Marcinkus, Henri Picard and Tim Walenn. The train arrived at Frankfurt at 6 a.m. where Bergsland and Muller alighted. (The others had already got off at Kustrin.) At Frankfurt the two Norwegians aroused no suspicions and they were left to idle the hours away unharassed. At 10 a.m. they boarded a train to Stettin, arriving there shortly after 1 p.m. In Stettin they headed directly for an address in the Kleine Oder Strasse distributed to the Baltic escapers by Roger Bushell. To their horror it turned out to be a brothel for Swedish seamen and they didn't have the sort of money to squander in such a place. They made their excuses and left. It was only by a stroke of good fortune that the men subsequently made contact with a sailor who promised to help them. He arranged for them to be smuggled onto the docks next to a ship that was bound for Sweden, instructing them to hide near a large stack of crates until he gave them the all clear. Unfortunately, that was the last they saw of him and they were left to watch the ship depart, in utter frustration. They only managed to extricate themselves from the docks by convincing the guards at the gate that they were electricians on shore leave from another Swedish ship, whose name Bergsland had memorised. It was a risky ploy and they were unlikely to have got away with it had they not been able to speak in good German with Scandinavian accents.

Bergsland and Muller laid low that night, checking into an innocuous-looking hotel, and using the familiar ploy of spending the rest of the day in the anonymity of a cinema. When night fell, they made for Bushell's brothel once more. This time they struck lucky, meeting a couple of Swedish seamen who offered to smuggle the Norwegians onto their ship that night. Again, it was a gamble. The escapers hadn't got the necessary documents to present to the German guards who would be waiting at the gates, but the Swedish sailors convinced them that the Germans were not always as thorough as they should be. The four men approached the docks affecting the posture of mild drunkenness after a night out on the town. To the surprise of the Norwegians the Swedes proved right. The German guards didn't bat an eyelid and accepted their story that they had simply left their papers on board before leaving that night.

The Swedish sailors showed them to an enclosure in which the anchor was kept where they could squeeze themselves in and hide. The only problem now was that it would be a day and a half before the ship sailed. However, the Swede shipmates kept bringing little bits of food to pass the time away. It was uncomfortable for the men and disconcerting whenever strange feet approached their hiding place. They knew, too, that the ship would be searched by the Germans before it was allowed to depart. They just crossed their fingers that the search would not be a thorough one. Ultimately, the ordeal they had feared came in the form of the sound of two pairs of jackboots making their way methodically around the foredeck. Bergsland and Muller held their breath as the two German soldiers shone their torches around the compartment in which they were squeezed. At one stage, one of the Germans began feeling his way around the compartment in which the anchor chain was coiled. His hands probed the recess carefully and almost poked Bergsland in the eye.

Thankfully, the German did not register anything unusual and the two men continued to another part of the vessel. To their intense relief, shortly afterwards the Norwegians listened as the ship's engine spluttered into action. At about 7 p.m. on the evening of 29 March the ship slipped its moorings and began making its way out of the harbour. Four hours later it docked at Göteborg, Sweden, and the men were effectively free. Erring on the side of caution, they waited until the following day when the ship steamed into Stockholm before disembarking and handing themselves over to the British Consulate. It was six days to the day that they had broken out of Stalag Luft III. They didn't know it then, but they were the first Great Escapers to make a successful home run. Sadly, they would be part of a very exclusive group.

*   *   *

Bob van der Stok was the only other escaper to make a home run. Again, it was undoubtedly his linguistic abilities and familiarity with occupied Europe that helped him gain his freedom. He was, however, at large for many more weeks than the two Norwegians. Van der Stok had made the decision to escape on his own. He thought a partner was more likely to be a hindrance than a help. After his alarming encounter with the German guard in the woods around Stalag Luft III, and the girl on the platform who said she was looking for escaped officers, van der Stok had no further unpleasant surprises. He left on the same 1 a.m. train for Breslau as Gouws, Kidder, Kirby-Green and Stevens. After it pulled into Breslau without incident the Dutchman purchased a ticket to Alkmaar in the Netherlands. The journey would require three changes.

He arrived in Dresden later that day at 10 a.m. and, faced with some 12 hours to kill before his next departure, he had a look around one of the most beautiful medieval cities in Europe before sheltering in a picture house. At 8 p.m. he boarded a train to Hanover, where there would be an hour's wait before continuing the journey into Holland, crossing the border at Oldenzaal. This would be the most perilous part of van der Stok's escape because he knew the border checks would be exhaustive. As he had feared, at Oldenzaal, just before the frontier, the train was stopped and everyone was ordered off. The passengers were made to line up in a queue in front of a desk at which a Gestapo clerk inspected their papers. The agreeable feeling of freedom and anonymity that he had experienced in Dresden was quickly disappearing. Van der Stok now felt very conspicuous indeed as the line edged its way slowly forward. It was inconceivable that the tunnel had not been discovered by now. He knew his photograph would have been circulated to every Gestapo bureau in the country. The wait was torturous and as van der Stok felt his pulse quickening he could only have hoped that his alarm did not show up in beads of sweat. Finally, it was his turn to face the inspector.

'Papiere,' demanded the Gestapo man.

Van der Stok handed over his train tickets and bogus papers. The Gestapo man flipped the Ausweis over between his fingers.

'Wohin?' (Where to?) he demanded.

'Alkmaar,' replied van der Stok.

With only the slightest of hesitation, the German initialled the pass and handed it back to van der Stok. The RAF escaper returned to the railway carriage and collapsed in the seat, a heap of nerves as he recalled later in his 1987 memoir *War Pilot Orange*. But it was not over yet—and he knew it. It was not beyond the wit of the Germans to discover that in the early hours of the morning after the escape a Dutchman had purchased a ticket from Breslau to Alkmaar. There was a risk the Gestapo would be waiting for him at the station when he got off. As the train pulled into Utrecht, the station before Alkmaar, van der Stok decided to get off.

Although van der Stok had spent part of his student life in Utrecht he did not feel at home because the Nazi occupation had changed the city beyond recognition. Van der Stok made his way towards the home of one of his former professors, one of the few men he knew he could trust. The professor was delighted to see him and invited another professor who had known van der Stok over to meet him. The three men reminisced for several hours. The professors told their former pupil of how the German occupation had progressed. Van der Stok told them about flying for the RAF in England and being incarcerated in Stalag Luft III. Eventually, they arranged a safe house for him in Amersfoort.

After Jimmy James's bleak introduction to Sachsenhausen, he was cheered up slightly, if that was possible in the circumstances, to find that one of his co-captives besides Wings Day was the indomitable Johnny Dodge. There was a mixed bag of prisoners in their compound, Sonderlager (Special Camp) A, including two Irishmen who may or may not have been Nazi collaborators, and a handful of White Russians who had fought with the Germans against the Red Army. There were several Polish RAF crew and a couple of Italian orderlies. The Italians were detailed to clean the officers' rooms and cook for them. They proved to be masterful cooks, able to work wonders with the meagre rations the men had to share, but it was apparent to the newly arrived Stalag Luft III contingent that it was going to prove difficult knowing whom to trust. It became clear, too, that the small compound next to their own seemed to be reserved for some important prisoners (Prominenten) whom the Germans wanted to keep under wraps and were planning, no doubt, to hold as hostages when the enemy armies arrived at the gates of Berlin.

The first Englishman to greet Jimmy James on his arrival in Sachsenhausen had been Peter Churchill. Now the men discovered that

Churchill had had an illustrious war indeed. He was a member of the Special Operations Executive (SOE) which had been set up by the British Prime Minister and Peter's namesake to 'set Europe ablaze'. Peter Churchill was a fluent French speaker who had lived in France and so became an obvious candidate for clandestine operations in that country. He had been caught by the Nazis on his fourth mission across the Channel with the legendary spy Odette Sansom. The courageous Frenchwoman had returned to her country with Churchill to help the Resistance sow havoc and confusion in occupied France. The two had been separated on capture and both tortured horrendously. But both stuck to their story that Peter was Winston Churchill's nephew and Odette was Peter's wife. Not knowing what to believe, the Gestapo erred on the side of caution and sent Churchill to Sachsenhausen as a potential 'Prominenter'.

The British officers found themselves among a colourful cast of characters. Lieutenant General Piotr Privalov was the highest-ranking officer in the Sonderlager, a Tsarist and former university lecturer who had become a highly decorated soldier, having taken part in a number of military adventures. He had been captured by the Nazis while he was in command of an army corps at Stalingrad. Privalov was a modest and quiet soul, in complete contrast to one of his more boisterous compatriots.

Major-General Ivan Bessanov was a former commander of a fighting section of the Russian NKVD (the People's Commissariat for Internal Affairs—the Communist secret police), captured by the SS. Bessanov, a crude but clever man, had saved his neck by posturing as an anti-Communist. The Nazis held him as a potential head of a puppet state and there in Sachsenhausen Bessanov remained even as the Red Army was punching its way towards the German capital, and the chances of Berlin ever ruling Moscow had long since gone. Bessanov still had great ambitions for himself. The British officers were regularly treated to the general's foul-mouthed lectures about what he would do with Russia once Stalin was deposed.

A week or so after James arrived, the British contingent was reunited with Sydney Dowse, who had been under interrogation since his capture but whose spirits seemed undimmed by the experience. The British officers were vaguely puzzled as to why they had been selected for special treatment out of the 76 escapers from Sagan. Johnny Dodge was obviously there because of his family connection—no matter how tenuous—to Winston Churchill. That was the same reason for Peter Churchill, although in reality he was not directly related to the British Prime Minister. Wings Day had been selected, perhaps, simply because he had been the SBO for most of the war and had proved such a thorn in the flesh of the Germans. But why Sydney Dowse and Jimmy James? Dowse had some fairly distinguished German family connections in the dim and distant past, but James was the modest son of an Indian tea planter. Maybe it was his record of persistent escaping that had condemned him. If so, he was soon going to show the Nazis that sending him to a notorious concentration camp with the implicit threat of death over him was no deterrent.

The Sonderlager was separate from the main concentration compound but British officers were taken into the main camp once a week for a shower. It was the first time any of them were able to witness at close quarters the full obscenity of the Nazis' killing machine. Emaciated figures in striped pyjamas were regularly beaten and humiliated by their SS guards. A gibbet stood in the centre of the camp, a sinister reminder of the fate that awaited anybody who dared defy his SS masters. Every day the men saw the soul-destroying sight of starving and helpless prisoners being led to the execution area and gas chambers. Every day the crematorium chimney belched its foul smoke into the sky. The frequent rattle of machine-gun fire indicated the death of another poor soul attempting to escape. As the British officers lay in bed at night they listened to distant screams of agony as the SS guards gave vent to their unspeakable sadism.

Within days of Dowse arriving, he and James were discussing possible ways of getting out of this hell on earth. The Germans, with their unwavering faith in the power of bullying and bluster to intimidate people had, as usual, miscalculated. The unpleasant surroundings that the men found themselves in did nothing to diminish their desire to score a bloody blow for freedom against their barbaric oppressors—no matter what the cost. They had quickly concluded a tunnel was the only plausible way out. Yet it was only after Wings Day had had a particularly unsatisfactory encounter with the uncouth Kommandant of Sachsenhausen that he gave the men the go-ahead to plan an escape. The Kommandant had treated Day with contempt and a total lack of respect. He told him sneeringly there was no possibility of escape from his camp so they may as well give up and resign themselves to captivity—or whatever else the fates might have in store for them. The exchange brought out the fighting spirit in the Senior British Officer. Wings returned to the Sonderlager determined to prove the little Nazi wrong. He told James and Dowse they could start digging.

* * *

Sonderlager A directly abutted an empty compound next door that the Germans had not finished building. Helpfully, they had left a ladder in it, in full view of the officers. The men would only have to dig about 120 feet to get underneath the wire into the neighbouring unfinished compound. Once in, it would be child's play to pick up the ladder and scale the 15 feet of unguarded wall beyond, which was the only obstacle to the outside world. The soil underneath Sachsenhausen was hard, which would make tunnelling difficult but at least the tunnel would not require complicated shoring. The tunnel would only need to go five feet under, sinking to about twice that to get under the wire. The trap, they decided, would have to be dug from a corner of the room Dowse and James shared. The tunnel would be a primitive affair with no ventilation or lighting, but the lack of these luxuries, desirable as they were, would at least hasten the digging operation. The men would just have to work in complete darkness, breathing in their own foul air, edging forward like moles.

The escapers had another advantage unwittingly handed to them by their captors. The Germans in their arrogance, and believing that the inmates would be so terrified of the consequences of recapture once more, made the mistake of leaving them to their own devices all day long. There were no ferrets, no emergency Appells, no sudden barrack checks.

Dowse and James could happily dig away without the slightest fear of discovery. The only big problem was keeping the tunnel a secret from the prisoners in the compound whom they weren't sure whether to trust or not. They swiftly decided that the only men who could be trusted were the Stalag Luft III officers and the two Italian orderlies. The Italians had to be trusted—there was no alternative, because they cleaned their rooms out every day. So with the two Italians recruited as stooges, the men cut a trap in the corner of the room in the hope of excavating a tunnel below. They were immediately disappointed to discover that under the trap there was very little room to disperse the soil. As a result, many difficult weeks had to be spent underneath the barrack block digging dispersal trenches, with the men working in shifts.

Despite all the factors in their favour it was a mammoth undertaking. The tunnel would be a third as long as Sagan's Harry. But instead of a team of 600 toiling away for 12 months, the only active workers in Sachsenhausen's X-Organisation were Dowse and James, and their only equipment consisted of a kitchen knife and some spoons. Nevertheless, the two men began the arduous task, digging one at a time in two-hour shifts. While one was under the barracks the other made sure he was conspicuous above it. It was murderously slow progress.

At least their morale was boosted virtually every day by the spectacle of Hitler's Third Reich crumbling before their very eyes. Sachsenhausen was close enough to Berlin to give the men a grandstand view of the American daylight bombardment of the city. The officers stood in awe as day after day wave after wave of American Flying Fortresses nd Liberators wheeled over their heads, unleashing their deadly loads on the burning Reich capital below. Halfway through the dig, the men were cheered to hear that the Normandy Landings had been a success. American and British armies now had a firm foothold on Hitler's Fortress Europe in the west and, with the Russians bearing down on Berlin from the east, it could only be a matter of time before the Nazis capitulated.

However, that July the men received some news that was not quite as welcome. Courtesy of a German newspaper they read Anthony Eden's House of Commons speech. What none of them could know, but each suspected, was that their own escape partners had been among those executed by the Gestapo. Yet such a possibility merely strengthened the men's will to hit back at an enemy whose abject depravity they could now see for themselves every day all around them. Wings Day summoned a conference to discuss whether they should continue with the escape.

It was the shortest conference of an 'escape committee' in memory. James and Dowse continued to dig. Peter Churchill did not feel he could help because he thought if he was found out he would almost certainly be shot. Day and Dodge wanted to contribute, but the older men couldn't have worked as fast or as nimbly as the younger officers, and it was vital that they kept an RAF presence above ground or the guards might smell a rat.

That same month there were two new arrivals in the Sonderlager. The first, in the form of Nikolai Rutschenko, posed a potential risk to the escape bid. A former Leningrad University lecturer who had become an officer in the Red Army and been involved in a string of extraordinary military actions, Rutschenko appeared a nice enough man but was put in the room next to the trap and his bed was directly above the tunnel. The men weren't in any position to trust Rutschenko at first, who could very well have been a German plant, given where they had chosen to billet him, and so they had to work very quietly. The second new arrival, however, was a positive plus to their tunnel efforts. He was yet another Churchill—this time the renowned and much-decorated Colonel Jack Churchill. A flamboyant commando leader who always led his men into battle with bagpipes, Churchill had been captured on an island off the Yugoslav coast. The Germans, again assuming he might be related to the British Prime Minister, assigned him to the Prominenten of Sachsenhausen. No sooner had he arrived than Churchill volunteered to help the men build their tunnel. By then they had only just finished the preparatory work of digging dispersal trenches under the barracks. Just as Churchill arrived they were ready to sink a shaft and begin the actual tunnel.

In the meantime, that other Great Escaper was still at large. Bob van der Stok had been in Amersfoort for almost a month. He had discovered that the local resistance movement was unable to help him: it appeared that they had been hit hard by recent Gestapo arrests and they seemed to question whether van der Stok was who he said he was. Eventually, he decided to strike out on his own and try and retrace the route he had taken to escape to Britain in 1940. The resistance gave him directions to a safe house in Maastricht and smuggled him across the Maas River into Belgium. In Belgium, van der Stok found himself alone and without money. Desperate, he walked into a bank and claimed that he had lost his wallet. If they allowed him to phone his uncle in Antwerp, he felt sure he would forward him some money. The gamble paid off. His uncle wired him some funds and gave him the address of a wealthy friend where his nephew could stay. Van der Stok found himself spending the next several weeks in comparative luxury in the Brussels suburb of Uccle. His uncle's friend was the director of an insurance company and lived in a house that boasted a tennis court, which van der Stok was invited to make liberal use of. Unfortunately for him, though, the local resistance in Brussels was also reluctant to help. Once more the Nazis had made inroads into the resistance movement. There had been arrests, torture and executions. Nobody was to be trusted; least of all a bright young man who seemed to have friends in high places and a less than convincing cover story. Van der Stok was on his own again.

Delighted though he was to have found such a haven of luxury after so many years of deprivation, van der Stok was nevertheless anxious to get back to Britain and continue the fight against Nazi Germany. His host arranged for him to go to Paris with all the appropriate travel permits. There van der Stok headed south for Toulouse and from there to the small town of St-Gaudens, where he had been given the name of a contact by the Belgium underground. He had been told to go to a café but had forgotten the name of the establishment. His contact had merely told him that it would be impossible for a Dutchman to forget the name. So van der Stok found himself wandering around St-Gaudens for hours looking for a café name that would jog his memory. Finally he saw it: Café

L'Orangerie. How could he have forgotten it? After presenting himself to the mistress of the Café L'Orangerie he was given a change of clothing and taken to a farmhouse several miles out of town. Van der Stok was now in the hands of the Maquis, the French Resistance. His new home was refuge to several fugitives, including an American, a Canadian and 13 German Jews.

The next day van der Stok listened as the maquisards gave the group directions about how they were all going to escape. They would walk in darkness towards the Pyrenees, climbing in single file towards a pass in the mountains. Anybody who ran or fell out of line would be shot on the spot. The escape would be financed by everybody handing over their money. The refugees put their hands into their pockets and produced all the currency they had. That night they set off. It was a tortuous trip. The weather was freezing cold. The wind became more icy the higher the men and women progressed. Eventually they found a resting place for the night at a farmhouse in the foothills of the mountains. They were all hungry and exhausted. The following day there was a disaster. Van der Stok volunteered to accompany one of the maquisards and the American down to a local village where they would acquire supplies from a café. When they arrived there they found the place had been discovered by the Germans. Several cars full of armed German soldiers descended on the café, machine-guns blazing. The three men escaped unhurt but the group was ordered to quickly transfer to the safer environs of the ruins of a castle. The following morning the group was led over the mountain pass. Once more it was an exhausting experience. On the other side of the mountain, the maquisard pointed to a green mountain pass in the far distance.

'On the other side of that pass is Spain,' said their guide. 'You must make your own way from here.' And with that simple gesture, the man was gone. The group decided to separate: the German Jews sticking together; and the military officers taking a different route. Some hours later van der Stok was in Spain and heading for the British Embassy in Madrid. He flew back to England via Gibraltar. Within two months van der Stok was back in Britain and soon commanding 322 (Dutch) Squadron of Spitfires flying sweeps over Holland.

*   *   *

By early September the tunnel in Sachsenhausen had advanced 110 feet. The men checked the newspaper weather forecasts and saw that the next moonless night was on 23 September. They had two weeks to prepare for the break-out. Jimmy James and Jack Churchill were going out together. James still had his Sagan break-out kit and Churchill had modified his service uniform to make it look like civilian clothing. But the coarseness of their disguises was no impediment. They were planning to jump freight trains all the way to the Baltic and well-tailored suits would not be the order of the day. Wings Day and Sydney Dowse had civilian suits 'lent' to them by the Italian orderlies. They were planning to try and get to France and link up with the underground. Johnny Dodge was going out alone. His plan was simply to walk west and hope to encounter the Allied line.

When 23 September came the five men crawled through the tunnel. There was a slight hiccup due to faulty calculations that meant that James and Dowse had to dig a few extra feet, but after a short delay the men emerged into the disused compound. There they found the ladder had remained faithfully in its place where it had been for the past six months. Within minutes the RAF officers were clambering over the walls of Sachsenhausen concentration camp. All five of them stood at the foot of the wall, hardly able to disguise their excitement—or to beleive the breathtaking simplicity with which the last stage of the escape had been executed. They shook hands and wished one another 'good luck' before disappearing into the night. Once more they had defied their captors. This time they did so in the certain knowledge that recapture must surely mean death.

The escape of the five British officers from Sachsenhausen astonished the Germans and prompted yet another Grossfahndung. Posters describing the men and demanding that they be apprehended on sight appeared all over occupied Europe. The notice was broadcast on the radio, twice.

By early October the five Sachsenhausen escapers had been recaptured. Wings Day and Sydney Dowse were the first to be caught, having progressed no further than the outer suburbs of Berlin. They were sheltering in the cellar of a bombed-out house when a suspicious woman betrayed them to the police. Their reception shortly afterwards back at Sachsenhausen was as they had expected. Instead of being taken back to their old barracks in the Sonderlager, they were taken to a notorious prison block or bunker called the Zellenbau (cell block) where they were each dispatched to separate cells. The men knew little about the Zellenbau other than that few of its inhabitants ever emerged from it alive. The next stop, they could only presume, was undoubtedly the gas chamber. The two men were actually chained to the floor of their cells, a seemingly needless cruelty, especially for Day, who had badly injured his knee. The Germans offered him no medical attention and he was in a great deal of pain.

In the meantime, Johnny Dodge had

managed to make it all the way to Rostock, walking along the railway line and catching a freight train for 20 miles. He finally holed himself up for four weeks, first in a hayloft and then in a pigsty, which may have brought back wry memories of Roger Bushell's first failed escape from Dulag Luft's malodorous goatshed. Dodge had decided the safest bet was to sit it out and await the liberation from the Russians, which could surely not be far away, but he was betrayed by a farmer and handed over to the police. The policeman told him that he had known of his presence for some time and would have been happy to leave him there. Like almost everybody else in Germany he was just longing for the end of the war. Now that Dodge had been betrayed it was more than the policeman's life was worth not to do anything about it. However, the policeman promised to do Dodge one favour. He accepted from him a list of the men who had been in Sachsenhausen and promised to try and get it to the authorities in London.

Jimmy James and Jack Churchill were the longest on the run, having made it to Poland, where they fell into the hands of the Home Guard. They too were not expecting a warm reception back at Sachsenhausen and found themselves in the Zellenbau—though not treated half as badly as Wings and Dowse. In James's cell the only amenities were a bucket for a toilet and an iron bunk. The only light came from a barred window seven feet up. He lay down on the mattress. 'I felt curiously detached,' he recalled in his memoir, *Moonless Night*, 'and began to contemplate what might remain of my life, and what may lie in the life hereafter, with the sanguine hope that my latter period on earth might shorten my stay in purgatory.'

The RAF man's reverie did not last long. Within hours he was rudely awakened by his SS jailer to be informed that it was strictly forbidden to lie down on the bed during daylight. The man was SS Warrant Officer Kurt Eccarius, known as the 'Beast of the Bunker', who was exposed after the war as a sadistic torturer of the worst kind. As Eccarius screamed at James, the Kommandant of the camp stood in the background looking at the prisoner with contempt in his gimlet eyes framed by rimless spectacles. He didn't utter a word as Eccarius slammed the door on James and left him in peace once more.

The following morning James was reunited momentarily with Churchill when he was taken down to the communal washroom and to his great delight also found Dowse and Day. They could only communicate in hushed whispers and so at the time James knew little of the other men's experiences at the hands of the Nazi authorities. Later he was to discover that after their return Day was repeatedly interrogated, first by an officer of the SD, and then by what appeared to be a kangaroo court of Kripo and other police, presided over by some sort of lawyer. However, the fact that the police were present gave Day a little comfort. During hours of relentless questioning it was clear that they were trying to get the British officer to incriminate himself as a spy or saboteur, and hand them the excuse they needed to execute all five men. They told him it was a well-known fact that British POWs were in constant contact with British Intelligence. They pressed him to admit that he had been in touch with the underground movement. Wings, despite his exhaustion and the acute discomfort caused by his knee injury, was wary of every trap that was being laid for him and didn't admit a thing. Instead, he repeatedly expressed his outrage at their disregard for the Geneva Convention. It was a classic confrontation that has gone on in police cells since time immemorial: one side trying to wear the other down with a combination of sympathetic understanding and threats; the other resisting the overwhelming temptation to throw in the towel.

Seeing that they faced a formidable opponent, the inquisitors adopted a different approach. Over the next week Wings was subjected to four more interrogations, two with an SD officer who tried to casually coax a confession out of him deploying the matey, conversational approach that had become a feature of Dulag Luft interrogations. Once more Day did not allow himself to fall into any traps. Finally, he was returned to the kangaroo court.

He later admitted that he was at breaking point. They had succeeded in wearing him down. He was exhausted, becoming confused by their pedantry and in pain. He decided there was no other option left but to go on the offensive. Wings stood up and confronted the panel before him. He angrily pointed out he was a professional soldier who had served in two world wars. He had spent the best part of this one incarcerated in various camps and he would do anything he could to escape back to England. It was his duty as an officer and his fervent desire as a human being. There were, he told them, hundreds of German officers in British captivity who at this very moment would be feeling the same way about their plight. If they attempted to escape and were recaptured they would be treated fairly by the Allies. At that Wings collapsed in his chair, unable to muster another word. He was surprised to hear the president of the panel say, benevolently: 'We understand, Wing Commander.'

Jimmy James had also been interrogated by an SS officer, but the experience had not been anywhere near as wearing. Subsequently, he was left to ponder his fate in his cell. He had literally been left there to rot, with no exercise privileges and a diet of ersatz coffee, black bread and foul soup. At one stage James admits he began to wonder whether death might have been a welcome release from the sheer boredom he was being forced to endure, but he quickly banished such thoughts from his mind. It took an enormous amount of willpower to overcome the bleakness of his situation. All around there was death and pain. Dowse witnessed three men being hung from gallows outside his window one day. All the men were kept awake by the abominable sounds of screaming and torture.

Shortly afterwards, James and the other prisoners were put under a more relaxed regime. They were allowed to read books and German newspapers. Their diet was improved, albeit imperceptibly and they were allowed to exercise in a little walled garden. It was then that they learnt of Wings's disagreeable experience at the hands of the kangaroo court. The men concluded that Day's ill-tempered rant before the panel had probably saved them all from execution, at least in the immediate future. They were all very grateful for his wisdom and strength of character. It might also have helped that Sydney Dowse, under equally harsh interrogation, had told his inquisitors that while he had been a free man he had posted two letters. One to the Kommandantur of Stalag Luft III and the other to the International Red Cross, giving the details of the men's recapture and detention in Sachsenhausen.

The British officers concluded that they were probably being held now as potential hostages along with a score of interesting characters they found themselves sharing the cell block with. There were 100 or so prisoners in all. They included Pastor Martin Niemoller, the one-time U-boat commander turned anti-Nazi clergyman who was perhaps the most potent symbol of the resistance to Hitler within Germany. Another Prominenter was Captain S. Payne Best, the British intelligence chief kidnapped from Holland by the Gestapo. There was an Austrian general, a former German ambassador to Spain, a prominent Polish agent, and the parents of a German agent who had defected to the Allied cause. There were a handful of British service personnel of more than usual value to the Germans. They were all obviously people the Nazis wanted to keep alive, if only to use as gambling chips when the Allies finally arrived at the gates of Berlin, as everybody by now surely realised they would.

The men settled down to await the end of the war like everyone else in the hell that was Sachsenhausen. Johnny Dodge was as indefatigable as ever and his booming voice could be heard singing songs as he exercised in his cell. But Sachsenhausen was a diabolical place and the men were witnesses to a daily toll of slaughter. They were rarely relieved of the sounds of bestial torture practised on the thousands and thousands of prisoners who were sent to Sachsenhausen to be liquidated. Ironically, one of the new prisoners to be sent to the Zellenbau that winter was General Artur Nebe, the man who had decided which 50 of the 76 airmen should die. His curiously anomalous role as a dedicated member of the German resistance movement had finally been exposed when he was implicated in the July 1944 plot to kill Hitler. To Nebe's credit he had survived three months of Gestapo torture without giving anything away. He was not sent to the gas chamber or shot like most of the victims. He was strung up by piano wire to die a long and agonising death, as Hitler decreed all the plotters should do.

Christmas 1944 came and went. The men presented one another with Christmas cards made out of toilet paper and feasted on SS stew. One night they listened to the eerie strains of 'Silent Night' wafting over the bleak barrack block roofs of the death camp. The incongruous sound did not make anybody feel any better, but in the heart of each man it intensified his hatred for the Nazis. At least they had the genuine comfort of feeling the intensification of the Allied bombing raids, the cell block shaking as the aircraft of the United States 'Mighty' Eighth Air Force bombarded the Reich capital. The New Year came, for once the men happy to be in the relative warmth of the cell block and not at the mercy of the bitter German winter outside. February arrived, however, with a note of apprehension. Johnny Dodge unaccountably and mysteriously disappeared. He went without warning and there was no explanation as to his fate from the SS guards. The men were understandably worried. Shortly afterwards they were summoned out of their own cells by the Kommandant. He told them they were going back to Sonderlager but pleaded: no more escaping.

'Next time you will be shot,' were his last words.

In the Sonderlager the men were delighted to find their old friends. Peter Churchill greeted them and told them they had all feared their friends had all been executed. But there was no sign of Johnny Dodge.

⁜   ⁜   ⁜

On the cold February morning that he disappeared from the Zellenbau, Johnny Dodge had indeed woken up to the ominous presence of two SS guards at his cell door demanding he accompany them. And when they marched him out of the building he could have been forgiven for thinking that his time had finally come. The absence, though, of any handcuffs should have been a little reassuring.

For instead of being taken into the main camp to face one of the SS's many odious methods of liquidation, Dodge was introduced to a pleasant young SS officer who informed the major that he was taking him to Berlin. On the journey to the capital in an SS staff car, the young officer gave no clue as to what Dodge's fate would be. To the older man's surprise, however, he was not taken to Gestapo headquarters or to any of the other sinister Reich institutions that flashed through his mind. Instead the car pulled up outside a department store. It was almost a year since the first escapers from Sagan had arrived in Berlin and looked on astonished to see the effect that the massive aerial bombardment had had on the once-great city. Now the sheer scale of the devastation was apparent to Dodge. There was hardly a building standing. Empty shells of apartment and office buildings towered above him. The streets were strewn with fallen masonry and burnt-out vehicles. Palls of black and yellow smoke hung above the ghostly scene.

The SS man ushered Dodge through the doors of the department store, which itself had been bombed and battered but was still standing. He informed him he was to purchase an off-the-peg suit and other items of a civilian wardrobe. Smelling a rat, Dodge demanded to know why. It was only after the SS man assured the British officer that he would not be compromised by wearing the outfit that Dodge selected an agreeable grey suit, crisp white shirt, a fetching tie and socks to match, along with a change of clean underwear. Shortly thereafter Dodge was taken to an opulent apartment, which, he was told, was the home of a senior SS officer and would be at his disposal during his stay in Berlin. By now Dodge was beginning to have an inkling of what might be going on. It was when he was introduced to another Nazi that his suspicions were confirmed.

Dr Hans Thost was a senior member of the German Foreign Ministry. He arrived at the apartment to find Dodge happily ensconced in the apartment, freshly bathed, fragrant (presumably with the SS man's aftershave), and looking very content in his new grey suit. After expressing solicitous concern for the major's comfort, Dr Thost suggested they dine at the Hotel Adlon, Berlin's most exclusive hotel. The Adlon was used throughout the latter part of the war as almost an adjunct to the Chancellery complex for out-of-town VIPs summoned to Berlin, although Dodge had no way of knowing that then. When they arrived at the hotel, Dodge discovered a private room had been reserved for them and in it was another German who was introduced to him as an interpreter. In fact, Paul Schmidt was not just any old interpreter but the Führer's personal one.

'We're sending you home, Major Dodge,' is one version of the events that rapidly unfolded. 'We'd like you to be reunited with your kinsman, Mr Churchill.'

So he was to be a peace emissary to his English cousin many times removed. Dodge had actually met Churchill two or three times, and he rather relished the idea of popping across the Channel on such an important and delicate mission, but he could not resist a wry smile at the conditions he was to lay down for the Prime Minister. Schmidt told him that an unconditional surrender was out of the question, and the Führer would only agree to peace terms if Germany's pre-war boundaries were restored and the balance of power in Europe was maintained. Hitler was not the only senior Nazi to entertain such extraordinary delusions. Himmler had for months been secretly negotiating with the Swedish representative of the Red Cross, Count Folke Bernadotte, in the hope of coming to an arrangement whereby he would rule Germany after the war. And Hermann Göring also believed that he could strike a pact with the Supreme Commander of the Allied Forces, General Dwight D. Eisenhower, whereby he would succeed Hitler as the head of state of the new Germany. None of them seemed to be able to comprehend the magnitude of the free world's hatred of them. Time was well and truly up. President

392

Roosevelt was intent on putting the lot of them on trial for war crimes. Prime Minister Churchill would have been quite happy to have Germany razed to the ground, and every last German with it, as indeed he had often said. Nevertheless, Dodge tried to keep a straight face for fear that they might rescind their tempting offer of freedom at last.

Dodge himself almost became a victim of Churchill's fervent desire to burn every last acre of Germany to the ground. A few days later Thost drove him to Dresden, where the two of them only narrowly missed being caught in the firestorm created by the Allied attack on the ancient city. Thost was taking Dodge to Switzerland, where he finally arrived on 25 April. The two men shook hands, Thost still clearly believing that a deal was possible. In fact, within days Hitler would have committed suicide. His henchmen were already stuffing their bags with Swiss francs and making their getaway plans. The Red Army was about to administer the coup de grâce to Hitler's Third Reich.

Dodge was debriefed by MI6 in the British Legation in Brest and a week later had been flown back by the usual circuitous neutral route to England. He didn't get to see Winston Churchill straightaway as the Prime Minister was too busy overseeing the final annihilation of Hitler's Germany. However, the American ambassador, John G. Winant, eventually managed to arrange a dinner for the two men. Churchill listened with great amusement to the major's tale over brandy and cigars in 10 Downing Street. Two days later Germany agreed to unconditional surrender. The war in Europe was finally over.

EPILOGUE

The days of the Third Reich were numbered after the success of the Normandy Landings. As 1944 progressed there was rarely any good news for Hitler. In the west, the American, Canadian and British armies faced fierce resistance from the defending Germans and their advance toward the Nazi heartland was slow, but it was sure. In the east, the Red Army was advancing remorselessly on a broad front, raping and ransacking its way towards Berlin. All that remained of the German Navy was its formidable fleet of U-boats, but they had been cornered in the Norwegian fjords and were being hunted down relentlessly by the RAF's Coastal Command and the Royal Navy. Many of Germany's cities had been reduced to rubble. Allied fliers were regarded with even more intense hatred than they had been in March. The Allied officers in Stalag Luft III became worried for their own safety. Hints from friendly goons indicated that their captors might consider using the men as hostages or the SS could quite conceivably be ordered by Berlin to wipe them out.

Herbert Massey had been repatriated to England via Switzerland on medical grounds. The new SBO, Group Captain Wilson ordered the men to organise themselves into fighting units, each with a responsibility to perform certain tasks should the worst come to the worst. Some were prepared to disable the goon towers. Others would rush the main gate and occupy the Vorlager and so on. It was a forlorn hope, of course—unarmed and starving men fighting, possibly, against a heavily armed division of SS troops—but the men reasoned it was better to go down fighting than to just accept their fate.

By January 1945, Hitler's Germany was teetering on the brink of the abyss. Indeed, Hitler himself was soon to effectively give up the fight and abandon his field headquarters in favour of the subterranean world of his bunker in Berlin, a city now virtually razed to the ground. There had been rumours all that winter in Stalag Luft III that something was afoot. The prisoners feared the worst and had increased their preparations for a fight. The tunnel, George, which before it was closed down for the winter, extended just beyond the wire, could be opened quickly as an escape route should the need arise. At the end of the month they were told that the entire camp was to be evacuated westward. The news was delivered in the North Compound in the theatre where the players were rehearsing *The Wind and the Rain*. 'Pack up and be ready to move in an hour's time,' they were told. In the American South Compound they were playing (appropriately enough) 'You Can't Take it

With You' when the Senior American Officer arrived and gave them 30 minutes to pack up and be at the main gate. It came as something of a relief to all the prisoners that they were not going to be cut down one by one by the SS, but the conditions they were to face on the long march west would prove horrendous.

It began on 27 January as six columns of 12,500 prisoners were marched out of the main gate under heavy guard. Their destination was Spremberg, near Cottbus, some 40 miles away. Under normal circumstances, it was hardly a great distance for military men to walk. But these men were half-starved and barely clothed. Their rations on the march were even less than in the camp. Bub Clark was so incensed when one man stole another's single potato that he put him on report—and took up the case after the war with Washington DC. His superiors were incredulous and refused to pursue the action. 'They just couldn't understand what one little potato meant to a man,' said Clark many years later. The temperatures were below freezing, producing blizzards, ice and a thick layer of snow that quickly turned into a mud bath nurturing germs and lice. Hundreds of men became ill. Scores fell by the roadside exhausted. Many Allied officers and their German guards died.

Despite the agony of the march, a feeling of comradeship grew between prisoners and guards. They were all in the same boat now.

The airmen carried the rifles and ammunition of some the goons who were too weak to do so themselves. Glemnitz excelled himself, making sure that whatever deprivations the men suffered they would always—with one exception—sleep under cover at night. The local population came out to offer the men little morsels of food and drink in exchange for items from their Red Cross parcels. One village invited the grateful men into their houses for the night, only to have their generosity rescinded by the SS, who threw the Allied officers back into the streets. Incredibly, some of the RAF men's minds were still on escape. Bob Stanford-Tuck and a Polish officer, Zbishek Kustrzynski, stayed behind in a barn one morning when the column had continued on. They slogged through the snow and blizzards to the Russian line and arrived triumphantly at the British Embassy in Moscow shortly thereafter.

At Spremberg the prisoners were dispatched in different directions on cattle trains, which provided a momentary comfort to the weary men. The occupants of North Compound were taken to a decrepit naval POW camp at Marlag und Milag Nord, 37 miles north of Bremen, and not far from the North Sea. It was a miserable place but the proximity to England did a great deal to boost their morale. They could almost feel the breeze from the sea which they knew from

BBC radio reports was now under the complete control of the Royal Navy. The Americans of the South Compound were sent south to Moosburg, near Munich, and the men from the East Compound were taken to a POW camp near Berlin. Each group was clearly being situated at a location where they would be most useful as bargaining chips to their advancing armies.

Then in early April the RAF men at Marlag und Milag Nord were inexplicably ordered out of their camp and marched eastwards to another near Lübeck. They didn't mind it so much when the column was strafed by a pack of RAF Tempests as at least that meant their own side was close. But when the senior officers discovered that the camp they were destined for was infested with lice, they ordered the men to stay put. They commandeered a couple of large commercial farming estates and made them their temporary home, festooning the rooftops with banners proclaiming: 'RAF POWs'. The Germans were too exhausted to do anything to stop them. The end was now in sight. The news of Hitler's death filtered through shortly after 30 April to whoops of delight from the RAF men and, most probably, relief in the hearts of most Germans. On 2 May a British tank of the 11th Armoured Division rolled into the farm, its bewildered occupants soon to be mobbed by a cheering crowd of bedraggled

Kriegies. Five days later Germany capitulated. Shortly afterwards most of the RAF prisoners were flown back to England, where they were deloused before being offered tea and biscuits in a warm if understated welcome by their countrymen.

* * *

For Colonel von Lindeiner, as for many Germans who had been forced into a war they did not want, the experience after hostilities had ended was not quite so happy. Like the POWs of Stalag Luft III, their former Kommandant was caught up in the chaos of refugees fleeing the Russian advance. The army hospital in which he was 'recuperating' was evacuated two days before Stalag Luft III, but the commanding officer of the hospital told von Lindeiner that he could not take him with them. Instead, the colonel made his way home to Jeschkendorf Manor, where, after a brief reunion with his wife, he reported for active duty to the local military authorities. He was immediately appointed second in command of a division defending Sagan against the overwhelming Russian onslaught. When his superior officer was killed in combat von Lindeiner became the commanding officer only to be wounded in action shortly afterwards, on 12 February. He was shot in the shoulder and foot—serious injuries for an elderly man. Fortunately, though, the advancing Soviet soldiers left him for dead and he was able to crawl away from the battlefront to Sagan. Eventually he was admitted to a military hospital at Harz, whereupon he fell into the hands of first the American Army and then the British. He might have expected to be relieved by the experience but to his acute distress von Lindeiner soon learnt that the British were investigating him for war crimes in relation to the 50 murdered airmen.

Von Lindeiner was treated despicably by the British. At one stage of his imprisonment he was left for two days with nothing more than bare boards to sleep on, and no eating utensils. His demands to know what he had done to deserve such squalid treatment fell on deaf ears and he never received a satisfactory explanation. In August 1945, he was dispatched to the London Cage (actually a small Kensington mansion), where German POWs were sent for interrogation after the war. He remained in British captivity for two years, not returning to the British Zone in Berlin until 1947. By then Jeschkendorf Manor had fallen into Russian hands. The von Lindeiners' apartment in Berlin had been destroyed by bombing and his wife's estate in Holland had been confiscated. The colonel's wife had spent the intervening years surviving by teaching music and language lessons.

Many former prisoners wrote to the

prosecuting powers speaking up in favour of the former Kommandant. Some were a little reluctant to do so. Von Lindeiner wrote to Bob van der Stok asking for his help. Van der Stok was sympathetic to his cause but he had returned to Holland after the war to find two brothers had been murdered by the Gestapo, and his father tortured to such an extent that he was blinded. He could not find it in his heart to positively assist anybody linked to the Nazi regime. He wrote back to Colonel von Lindeiner and told him he could not help him, but assured him he would not testify against him. It would be three years before von Lindeiner cleared his name. At his own trial, Hermann Göring said that von Lindeiner was 'not connected' with the shootings.

After hostilities had ceased, the RAF stood by Anthony Eden's pledge to administer 'exemplary justice' to the malfeasants who were responsible for the 50 murders. A team of investigators from the Air Force's Special Investigation Branch (SIB) set about tracking down the perpetrators. It was no easy task. It was some 17 months after the killings in Silesia and many of the minor Gestapo and SS officials involved had disappeared in the chaos of post-war Europe. In any case, many such men had taken their own lives out of fear of the bloody retribution from the Red Army that they knew was sorely justified. Nor did it help that much of Europe was now under Soviet domination. The Communist Bloc powers did not bend over backwards to help the British investigators and sometimes actively hindered them. In some respects they could not be blamed. The murders of 50 Air Force officers paled in comparison somewhat with the Russians' massive civilian and military casualties and the millions of innocents slaughtered at the hands of the Nazis.

Nevertheless, the SIB men persisted. Many of their leads came from the interrogations of Germans suspected of being involved in war crimes conducted in the London Cage under the supervision of Lieutenant-Colonel A.P. Scotland (who subsequently wrote a book about that intriguing episode of his life). For three years the investigators travelled to every corner of Europe to which they were allowed access. Happily, some of the new Communist governments proved more helpful than others, in particular the Czechs. And the investigators were given valuable clues as to where the airmen were killed by the fact that almost all the urns returned to Stalag Luft III identified the place of cremation. As time progressed, though, the size of the SIB team depleted until there were only a handful of people on the case. In the circumstances their efforts proved to be an extraordinary feat of detective work.

The SIB compiled a dossier of 72 culprits who were directly involved in the murders and, given that Himmler had ordered the killings to be carried out in the strictest of secrecy, it was nothing short of remarkable that the team was able to produce detailed re-creations of almost all the killings. They were able to account for all but a tantalising three of the 72 men for whom they went in search. Ultimately, 18 men were brought before the courts and most were prosecuted successfully. The trials began on 1 July 1947 in Hamburg, and eventually resulted in 14 death sentences, although one of the sentences was commuted to life imprisonment. The sentences were carried out, by hanging, in February the following year. Other defendants received hefty prison sentences. One case was dismissed, but that was not the end of the story of the RAF's 'exemplary justice'. One case actually came to court as late as 1967, when the defendant was given two years' imprisonment for his part in the murders.

During the trials, Colonel von Lindeiner was called as a witness. The court wanted to know if before March 1944 he had any direct knowledge of an SS plan to murder escaped officers in the future. Prosecutors were curious about von Lindeiner's meeting in February 1944 with SS Major Erich Brunner, the head of POW security in the area. They wanted to know why Brunner had not checked the anti-escape measures at Stalag Luft III. Allied investigators suspected that the German High Command had wanted a mass break-out to justify a tough crackdown on escapes. Max Wielen, the chief of the Breslau Kripo, had hinted to them that 'the shootings might have been discussed in the camp'.

Von Lindeiner had certainly been agitated after the escape, repeatedly telling the Allied officers: 'You do not realise what you have done.' He had threatened to shoot the men himself and some officers claimed that they had heard him saying the recaptured men would be handed over to the Gestapo for execution. But at the Hamburg trials, von Lindeiner denied any direct knowledge. He said he had merely sensed a distinct change in the climate regarding escaped POWs and had tried to pass his concerns on to the senior Allied officers. This was certainly true. Reminding him that he had taken an oath of loyalty to the Führer, Colonel von Lindeiner was asked what would his response have been had he received a 'Hitler Order' to shoot Allied prisoners of war under his care in Stalag Luft III. He replied: 'In such a case I would take my own life.' Most Allied officers who knew von Lindeiner would find it hard to disbelieve that statement. He might have been on the wrong side, but von Lindeiner was a gentleman.

Sadly, von Lindeiner was one of the few gentlemen to appear before the Hamburg court but, poring over the transcripts of those proceedings, it is difficult not to feel a little sympathy for some of the smaller men and minor minions caught up in an atrocity beyond their control. The men who ended up having to do the dirty work were not the big fish that had orchestrated the outrage. They weren't the masterminds behind the millions of other slaughters of Hitler's reign of terror. Some were, undoubtedly, the worst sort of Nazi psychopaths. The Gestapo agent who shot Tom Kirby-Green, Erich Zacharias, was implicated in at least two other murders and the rape and killing of an 18-year-old girl. Zacharias was a weasel of a creature and, typical of his sort, attempted to claim he had been tortured in the London Cage by the British into making his confession. The majority of the murderers were otherwise harmless souls, weak and compliant men, and often very stupid people. They found themselves caught up in a terrible situation and had little choice in the matter, and neither the wit nor the imagination nor the courage to do anything about it. One interesting aspect of the SIB investigation for historians is that it illustrated (as in the case of SS General Artur Nebe) the curious anomalous position that ordinary and sometimes good people find themselves in under the all-powerful embrace of a totalitarian state. Alfred Schimmel was a case in point. He was ordered to kill Tony Hayter the day after his capture, which happened to be Good Friday, but Schimmel was a deeply religious man and could not square his conscience with carrying out such a dark deed on the holiest day of the year. He resolved this acute moral dilemma by taking Hayter out and having him shot immediately on the Thursday.

Most of the Gestapo chiefs who received the orders to carry out the killings made sure they delegated them to someone else but Leopold Spann of Saarbrücken Gestapo was different. Spann was the man detailed to murder Roger Bushell and Bernard Scheidhauer. He at least was brave enough to do the dirty work himself, along with a Gestapo agent, Emil Schulz. Spann had been killed in an air raid by the end of the war, but the SIB men found out what had happened to Bushell and Scheidhauer thanks to the testimony of the driver who witnessed their last moments. The RAF officer and his Free French counterpart had been taken from the police jail and driven along country roads for about an hour. Eventually, Spann told them they could get out and relieve themselves if they liked. The two prisoners went off into the bushes. Spann and Schulz followed with their guns drawn. When the men began to relieve themselves Spann gave a signal, both the Germans raised their pistols and shot their helpless victims from behind.

The full details were later confirmed by Schulz at his trial. 'Scheidhauer fell on his face,' he testified. 'I think Bushell crumpled up, fell somewhat on his right side and was lying there turned on his back. On approaching closer I noticed the dying man was in convulsions. I lay on the ground and shot him in the left temple, whereupon death took place immediately.' Most of the men were killed in this cowardly and deceitful manner, in pairs or shot alone, but not all. A group including Gordon Brettell, René Marcinkus, Henri Picard and Tim Walenn were taken in a lorry, very much as the film depicted, and machine-gunned down at the top of a hillside.

Wilhelm Scharpwinkel, the Breslau Gestapo chief, was more typical than Spann of the men who were handed the responsibility for killing the Allied officers. A slippery, evasive man, Scharpwinkel ordered the killings of James Catanach, Arnold Christensen, Halldor Espelid and Nils Fugelsang. If Spann evaded the RAF's exemplary justice by getting killed, Scharpwinkel did so by switching sides. After the war he moved to Moscow, where he appeared to be too valuable an asset to the Soviets for them to extradite him to the West. The Russians, though, at least allowed the investigators to interview him, and Scharpwinkel gave them enough information to help them work out exactly what had happened. (Shortly afterwards, the RAF was told by the Russians that Scharpwinkel had died. Had he?) It turned out Scharpwinkel had delegated the job to his deputy Johannes Post and another Gestapo chief, Fritz Schmidt. Post and Schmidt recruited a team of Gestapo men to help them murder the four unsuspecting airmen.

The SIB investigators never found Schmidt, but they tracked down Johannes Post and some of his accomplices. In the men who helped carry out the killings the investigators encountered the familiar phenomenon of postwar denial that existed in Germany. They all insisted they had no idea who the RAF officers were. They had been told they were saboteurs and secret agents—and their executions were therefore entirely 'legitimate'. It was impossible to get to the bottom of whether they were telling the truth or not. But in the ringleader, Post, the RAF investigators found no such ambiguity. Post was an unrepentant Nazi who harboured no regret for his actions.

Post took upon himself the job of murdering Catanach. He detailed the other men to take care of Christensen, Espelid and Fugelsang. The car loads of condemned men then took off from the prison. On the journey Post engaged Catanach in pleasant conversation. After ten minutes or so he told the Australian that he was going to order the car to pull over in a few more minutes.

'What for?' asked Catanach.

'Because I am going to shoot you.'

Catanach couldn't tell whether Post was joking or not, which, of course, is exactly what the German intended. He demanded to know why he was going to kill him.

'Because those are my orders,' replied Post quietly.

The RAF man objected that it was the duty of all officers to escape, but his words fell on deaf ears. He still did not know whether to take Post seriously or not. Post continued his casual conversation and even ordered the driver to take a diversion so that he could drop off some theatre tickets for his mistress. He was anxious that she didn't miss the show that night. When they arrived at a quiet cutting along the roadside, Post ushered Catanach out of the car with his Walther 7.65mm pistol. Presumably Catanach still did not believe Post would do what he had threatened to do, because he seems to have willingly gone along. As he began to relieve himself, the German shot him through the back of the chest and the Australian fell to the ground.

Catanach's body was lying by the side of the road when the other three unfortunate airmen arrived to meet their fate. Seeing what had happened, Christensen, Espelid and Fugelsang made a run for it. Two were cut down and killed immediately. One was only injured. Post walked over to the sprawling body and issued the coup de grâce.

Again, perhaps it is in some grotesque way

commendable that after the war Post did not join the legions of Germans denying that they had ever had anything to do with the Nazi Party. Indeed, many people offered to act as character witnesses for him at his trial. (Post had once saved the life of a British pilot.) He refused, however, to even entertain the idea. 'I could not have been a National Socialist for so many years,' he explained, 'and suddenly put in affidavits from Communists or Jews or Freethinkers.' He described the Allied airmen as Terrorfliegers (terror fliers) and subhumans who deserved to be shot. Post was one of those hanged in February 1947.

Post and Spann were the exception to the rule. Most of the Gestapo agents tried to avoid having anything to do with the executions, going to extraordinary lengths to deputise the work to others. The case of Dennis Cochran is a typical example. He was in the custody of the Kripo at Ettlingen, near Karlsruhe, but it was the local Gestapo that received the instructions to murder Cochran on the morning of 31 March. The chief of Karlsruhe Gestapo was a man called Josef Gmeiner. He promptly deputised the responsibility to a member of his staff, Walter Herberg, who objected but nevertheless went along to Ettlingen police station to pick up the RAF officer with two Kripo men, Otto Preiss and Wilhelm Boschert. Cochran's death followed a depressingly familiar pattern. In his case the car pulled up near a concentration camp and he was taken to urinate by the side of the road by the two Kripo men and Herberg, but Herberg managed to keep his own hands clean. After giving the instructions to Preiss to kill the handcuffed officer, he turned his back and walked away, unable to bear looking at what was to follow. Preiss shot Cochran twice: once in the back, level with where the heart is, and once in the neck. At his trial Herberg testified that he had considered the possibility of letting Cochran escape, but that the ramifications for him would be awful. He had even considered taking his own life, but that would not have saved the life of Cochran. 'I did not see any way out,' said Herberg. Other defendants complained that if they did not carry out their orders, their families faced reprisals. This was undoubtedly true.

Other Gestapo agents resorted to more disingenuous methods to justify their actions. The orders to kill the men were passed from one office to another, the buck being passed down the chain. The Germans were careful to destroy all the paperwork but the SIB investigators in their interrogations of the culprits were able to reconstruct the order which was sent by teleprinter to each individual Gestapo station. Marked 'top secret' they originated from the RSHA, and stated that they were by the order of the Führer and the Reichsführer SS, Heinrich

Himmler. The order expressly instructed that the shootings were to be carried out in such a way that the prisoners did not know what was about to happen. However, Wilhelm Scharpwinkel, the Breslau Gestapo chief who was responsible for most of the Görlitz Kripo jail killings, claimed that he was told beforehand that the prisoners had been condemned to death by the Führer. Scharpwinkel did not carry out the shootings himself, of course, he delegated that gruesome business to others, but he implied that the men lined up and accepted their fate calmly as men condemned to death often do. Scharpwinkel's victims included Mike Casey, Al Hake, Johnny Pohe and George Wiley. Was Scharpwinkel telling the truth? Or was he simply trying to legitimise his actions? We will never know.

It is natural to sympathise with men who had been put in an impossible situation and whose own lives were at stake if they disobeyed orders. Most had every reason to fear that they themselves would face the bullet if they did not do what they were told. Worse still, there was the very real possibility that their families would face reprisals. Most of the 72 culprits had wives and children but the RAF officers had families too. When they climbed into their aircraft and taxied down those wet and windy airstrips in Britain, they were well aware of the fact that shortly thereafter they might be dead. If they were lucky they might simply be riddled by cannon fire and die instantly. Or they might perish in a horrendous fireball. Or be smashed into the ground when their parachutes failed to open, but whatever their manner of death, they would no longer see their loved ones again.

Of course they might have been taken prisoner instead. Many who sat the rest of the war out were grateful to have been saved the prospect of having to go into battle once more. And who can blame them? But many continued to fight the war, as Wings Day vowed they would, bringing the battlefront to the Germans in their prisoner-of-war camps. They were men who endured many months, perhaps years, of extreme discomfort and hard toil, before breaking out and facing an unknown fate at the hands of a barbaric enemy. They did so in the knowledge that their next meeting with the Gestapo might mean a swift bullet in the neck. Or perhaps several weeks of unendurable torture. They did so in the knowledge that they might never see their families again and with a stoic lack of self-pity that is in stark contrast to the weasel words of their Nazi oppressors. The words of Jimmy James, thrown into a cell to await his doom, come ringing back. 'I . . . began to contemplate what might remain of my life, and what might lie in the life hereafter, with the sanguine hope that my latter period on earth might shorten my stay in purgatory.'

Jimmy James's war ended on a note every bit as remarkable as Johnny Dodge's. On 1 February 1945, the Kommandant of Sachsenhausen received an order from Gruppenführer Heinrich Müller to liquidate the entire camp. Thankfully, for the sake of Jimmy James and the other British prisoners, not to mention the other 45,000 starving and brutalised inmates, he rejected the idea as impractical. (Little did James know it at the time, but he had conceived the even more diabolical idea of taking the inmates to a Baltic port, putting them in ships and sinking them.) The British prisoners were blissfully unaware of the machinations going on in Berlin, but the massive destruction of the city around them held out hope that the end was near. On 3 April, a local police inspector came to the camp to inform the British contingent that they were being evacuated south. They found themselves on two buses with the Russian Major-General Ivan Bessanov and Greek generals from the neighbouring VIP compound. The thousands of non-VIP occupants of Sachsenhausen were not in for such a comfortable journey. They were herded like cattle towards the Baltic, where the ships that would take them to their deaths awaited. Pushed and prodded by the SS, the lucky ones

415

survived without food and drink for five days. The less lucky were shot in the back by their repulsive guards.

The British officers from Sachsenhausen found themselves in similarly uncouth conditions after a long journey through the devastation of Germany. Past the pleasant hills of the Bavarian Oberpfalz, near the Czech border, they were confronted with the high fences and barbed wire of yet another concentration camp, in this case Flossenburg. The Kommandant presumed they had been sent there for execution and they were only saved, once more, by the intervention of the friendly police inspector, Peter Mohr. Mohr had already been helpful to Wings Day. He told him that the men were VIP prisoners vital to the Reich as bargaining chips with the Allies. The men witnessed some appalling scenes at Flossenburg before being sent with a party of VIPs to Dachau. From there the party was dispatched southwards past Munich towards the Italian border in a convoy of vehicles closely guarded by a troop of trigger-happy SS men just waiting to unleash their weapons on their cargo of Prominenten.

Among the VIPs were Pastor Niemöller, Prince Frederick Leopold of Prussia and the Mayor of Vienna. Dachau was soon host to many other VIPs being sent there as hostages from all over Nazi Germany. Jimmy James encountered Count Fabian von

Schlabrendorff, who had been prominent in the resistance and implicated in a plot to kill Hitler. Members of the von Stauffenberg and Goerdeler families who had been implicated in the July 1944 plot to assassinate the Führer arrived. They were known as Sippenhäftlinge (family hostages). Others included Wassili Molotov, the nephew of the Soviet foreign minister, Hjalmar Schacht, the former President of the Reichsbank, Fritz Thyssen, the businessman, Leon Blum, the ex-Prime Minister of France, and senior German officers who had refused to carry out 'Hitler Orders' to eliminate innocent people.

But the course of the war was changing rapidly. The prisoners occupied a town in a beautiful part of the Dolomites. They were treated to hearty Italian meals with wine and could come and go as they wished, regardless of the diktats of their SS escort. Soon, some of the German Army officers among the Prominenten were telephoning their old friends who happened to be commanding divisions nearby, asking them to guarantee their safety. Eventually, a group of Wehrmacht arrived and disarmed the SS. They took themselves out of town and were subsequently found to have been hung in the woods by Italian partisans. The Prominenten heard the news of Hitler's death on the BBC. Jimmy James was attending a Mass of thanksgiving in a pretty church at the foot of the Dolomites when the Americans arrived in town. Shortly afterwards, the British party was flown home to England. They passed over the white cliffs of Dover and landed in Hampshire, the first time some of them had been on their native soil for five years. 'We had passed through a nightmare experience of what can happen, in any country, when the forces of totalitarianism prevail,' wrote Jimmy James.

After the war James learnt that he had been a lucky man indeed. After their escape from Sachsenhausen, the five men had provoked Himmler to order that they were all to be handed over to the Gestapo for verschafte Vernehmung (interrogation under torture) and then murdered and classified as 'escaped but not recaptured'. This was exactly the same fate that befell seven British commandos caught in an operation to blow up a hydro-electric station in Norway. Indeed, Himmler not only ordered the British officers to be shot, he demanded the heads of the Kommandant, his deputy, the officer on duty on the night of 23 September, and—in an illustration of just how psychotic the Nazi leadership was—the architect who designed Sachsenhausen. In the end their death sentences were rescinded, but Gestapo agents were dispatched to the camp to kill the British officers.

Jimmy James is in no doubt that only the intervention of the Kripo saved their lives. After the war he had the pleasure of receiving a letter from the inspector in charge of the investigation, Peter Mohr, by then resident of the London Cage. Mohr wrote that the mass escape from Stalag Luft III had no doubt been the greatest as far as volume went but he said the escape of the five officers from Sachsenhausen surpassed Sagan in one way. 'It was the most surprising, and for Himmler the most disagreeable, escape of prisoners that caused great confusion and almost severe consequences for both British and German sides.'

Jimmy James was lucky not to be one of the 50. But it wasn't luck that made him one of the 76, or one of the hundreds and hundreds of other men in Stalag Luft III who fought endlessly to bring the battle to the enemy. It is the choices you take in life that define you and it was James's choice to do what he did. He was joined by scores of other men from all sorts of different backgrounds and from every corner of the globe. They were bank clerks, lawyers, high-school dropouts and mining engineers. They were intellectuals and aesthetes; artists and musicians; adventurers and sportsmen. The one thing they had in common was their love of living and their hatred of oppression. Jimmy James prefaces his own memoir of that time with a quotation from the Gospel of St Matthew, Chapter 10, verse 28:

> And fear not them which kill the
>   body,
> and are not able to kill the soul.

Few words can summarise the spirit that drove the Great Escapers better than those written by St Matthew when the world was still young and had yet to lose its innocence. The Great Escapers are an elderly and frail bunch today, but the young have as much to learn from their experiences as they do from the Bible that has shaped our civilisation.

APPENDIX I

THE GREAT ESCAPERS

This list contains the names of those who broke out of Stalag Luft III in the Great Escape. (Those who were murdered by the Germans have been highlighted in bold.)

Flight Lieutenant Albert Armstrong (RAF)
Sergeant Per Bergsland (RAF)
Flight Lieutenant R.A. Bethell (RAF)
Flying Officer Henry J. 'Hank' Birkland (RCAF)
Flight Lieutenant E. Gordon Brettell (RAF)
Flight Lieutenant Lesley C.J. Brodrick (RAF)
Flight Lieutenant Lester J. 'Johnny' Bull (RAF)
Squadron Leader Roger J. Bushell (RAF)
Flight Lieutenant Bill Cameron (RCAF)
Flight Lieutenant Mike J. Casey (RAF)
Squadron Leader James Catanach (RAAF)
Flying Officer Arnold G. Christensen (RNZAF)
Flight Lieutenant S.A. 'Dick' Churchill (RAF)
Flying Officer Dennis H. Cochran (RAF)
Squadron Leader Ian K.P. Cross (RAF)
Wing Commander Harry M.A. 'Wings' Day (RAF)
Major John B. Dodge (Territorial Army)

Flight Lieutenant Sydney H. Dowse (RAF)
Flight Lieutenant Bedrich 'Freddie' Dvorak (RAF)
Sergeant Halldor Espelid (RNAF)
Flight Lieutenant Brian H. Evans (RAF)
Lieutenant Nils Fugelsang (RNAF)
Lieutenant Johannes S. Gouws (SAAF)
Flight Lieutenant Bernard 'Pop' Green (RAF)
Flight Lieutenant William J. Grisman (RAF)
Flight Lieutenant Alistair D.M. Gunn (RAF)
Flight Lieutenant Albert H. Hake (RAAF)
Flight Lieutenant Charles P. Hall (RAF)
Flight Lieutenant Anthony R.H. Hayter (RAF)
Flight Lieutenant Edgar S. Humphreys (RAF)
Pilot Officer B.A. 'Jimmy' James (RAF)
Flying Officer Gordon A. Kidder (RCAF)
Flight Lieutenant Reginald V. 'Rusty' Kierath (RAAF)
Flight Lieutenant Antoni Kiewnarski (RAF)
Squadron Leader Thomas G. Kirby-Green (RAF)
Flying Officer A. Wlodzimierz Kolanowski (RAF)
Flying Officer Stanislaw Z. 'Danny' Krol (RAF)
Flight Lieutenant Patrick W. Langford (RCAF)
Flight Lieutenant Roy B. Langlois (RAF)
Flight Lieutenant Thomas B. Leigh (RAF)
Flight Lieutenant James L.R. 'Cookie' Long (RAF)
Flight Lieutenant Romas 'René' Marcinkus

(RAF)
Flight Lieutenant H.C. 'Johnny' Marshall (RAF)
Flight Lieutenant Alastair T. McDonald (RAF)
Lieutenant Clement A.N. McGarr (SAAF)
Flight Lieutenant George E. McGill (RCAF)
Flight Lieutenant Harold J. Milford (RAF)
Flying Officer Jerzy T. Mondschein (RAF)
Second Lieutenant Jens E. Muller (RAF)
Lieutenant Alastair D. Neely (Royal Navy)
Flight Lieutenant T.R. Nelson (RAF)
Flight Lieutenant A. Keith Ogilvie (RAF)
Flying Officer Kazimierz Pawluk (RAF)
Flight Lieutenant Henri A. Picard (RAF)
Flight Lieutenant Des L. Plunkett (RAF)
Flying Officer Porokoru Patapu 'Johnny' Pohe (RNZAF)
Lieutenant Douglas A. Poynter (Royal Navy)
Squadron Leader Lawrence Reavell-Carter (RAF)
Pilot Officer Paul G. Royle (RAF)
Lieutenant Bernard W.M. Scheidhauer (Free French Air Force)
Flight Lieutenant Michael M. Shand (RNZAF)
Pilot Officer Sortiros 'Nick' Skanziklas (Royal Hellenic Air Force)
Lieutenant Rupert J. Stevens (SAAF)
Flying Officer Robert C. Stewart (RAF)
Flying Officer John G. Stower (RAF)
Flying Officer Denys O. Street (RAF)

Flight Lieutenant Cyril D. Swain (RAF)
Flight Lieutenant Alfred B. Thompson (RCAF)
Flying Officer Pawel 'Peter' Tobolski (RAF)
Flight Lieutenant Ivo P. Tonder (RAF)
Squadron Leader Len Trent (RNZAF)
Flight Lieutenant Arnost 'Wally' Valenta (RAF)
Flight Lieutenant Robert van der Stok (RAF)
Flight Lieutenant Raymond L.N. van Wymeersch (RAF)
Flight Lieutenant Gilbert W. 'Tim' Walenn (RAF)
Flight Lieutenant James C. Wernham (RCAF)
Flight Lieutenant George W. Wiley (RCAF)
Squadron Leader John E.A. Williams (RAAF)
Flight Lieutenant John F. Williams (RAF)

Key
RAF: Royal Air Force
RAAF: Royal Australian Air Force
RCAF: Royal Canadian Air Force
RNZAF: Royal New Zealand Air Force
RNAF: Royal Norwegian Air Force
SAAF: South African Air Force

APPENDIX II

EXCERPTS FROM THE TESTIMONY OF HERMANN GÖRING RELEVANT TO THE TREATMENT OF AIR FORCE PRISONERS

Testimony of 20 March 1946

SIR DAVID MAXWELL-FYFE (British prosecutor): I want to ask you first some questions about the matter of the British Air Force officers who escaped from Stalag Luft III. Do you remember that you said in giving your evidence that you knew this incident very completely and very minutely? Do you remember saying that?

GÖRING: No—that I had received accurate knowledge; not that I had accurate knowledge—but that I received it.

SIR DAVID MAXWELL-FYFE: Let me quote your own words, as they were taken down, 'I know this incident very completely, very minutely, but it came to my attention, unfortunately, at a later period of time.' That is what you said the other day, is that right?

GÖRING: Yes, that is what I meant; that I know about the incident exactly, but only heard of it two days later.

SIR DAVID MAXWELL-FYFE: You told the Tribunal that you were on leave at this time, in the last period of March 1944, is that right?

GÖRING: Yes, as far as I remember I was on leave in March until a few days before Easter.

SIR DAVID MAXWELL-FYFE: And you said, 'As I can prove.' I want you to tell the Tribunal the dates of your leave.

GÖRING: I say again, that this refers to the whole of March—I remember it well—and for proof I would like to mention the people who were with me on this leave.

SIR DAVID MAXWELL-FYFE: What I want to know is, where you were on leave.

GÖRING: Here, in the vicinity of Nuremberg.

SIR DAVID MAXWELL-FYFE: So you were within easy reach of the telephone from the Air Ministry or, indeed, from Breslau if you were wanted?

GÖRING: I would have been easily accessible by phone if someone wanted to communicate with me.

SIR DAVID MAXWELL-FYFE: I want you to help me with regard to one or two other dates of which you have spoken. You say: 'I heard one or two days later about this escape.' Do you understand, Witness, that it is about the escape I am asking you, not about the shooting, for the moment; I want to make it quite clear.

GÖRING: It is clear to me.

SIR DAVID MAXWELL-FYFE: Did you

mean by that, that you heard about the actual escape one or two days after it happened?

GÖRING: Yes.

SIR DAVID MAXWELL-FYFE: Did you hear about it from the office of your adjutant or from your director of operations?

GÖRING: I always heard these things through my adjutant. Several other escapes had preceded this one.

SIR DAVID MAXWELL-FYFE: Yes, that's right. There had been a number of escapes from this camp.

GÖRING: I cannot tell you exactly whether they were from this camp. Shortly before several big escapes had taken place which I always heard of through the office of my adjutant.

SIR DAVID MAXWELL-FYFE: I want you to tell the Tribunal another date: you say that on your return from leave, your chief of staff made a communication to you. Who was your chief of staff?

GÖRING: General Korten was chief of staff at that time.

SIR DAVID MAXWELL-FYFE: Can you tell us the date at which he made this communication to you?

GÖRING: No, I cannot tell you that exactly. I believe I discussed this incident with my chief of staff later, telling him what I had already heard about it from other sources.

SIR DAVID MAXWELL-FYFE: Who was the first to tell you about it? Was it your chief of staff who told you about the shootings? Do you mean that someone else had told you about the shooting?

GÖRING: I cannot say exactly now whether I heard about the shooting from the chief of staff, or from other sources. But in any event I discussed this with the chief of staff.

SIR DAVID MAXWELL-FYFE: What was the date that you talked about it with your chief of staff?

GÖRING: I cannot tell you the date exactly from memory, but it must have been around Easter.

SIR DAVID MAXWELL-FYFE: That would be just about the end of March, wouldn't it?

GÖRING: No. It might have been at the beginning of April, the first half of April.

SIR DAVID MAXWELL-FYFE: And then you had an interview with Himmler, you have told us?

GÖRING: Yes, I talked with Himmler about this.

SIR DAVID MAXWELL-FYFE: Can you fix that?

GÖRING: Of course I cannot establish this date with certainty. I saw Himmler, and, at the first opportunity after I had heard about this incident, spoke to him about it.

SIR DAVID MAXWELL-FYFE: So you can't fix the date in relation to your coming back from leave, or the interview with your chief of staff, or any other date, or Easter?

GÖRING: Without any documents it is, as I said, impossible for me today to fix the date. I can only mention the approximate period of time; and that I have done.

SIR DAVID MAXWELL-FYFE: You said the other day that you could prove when you were on leave. Am I to take it that you haven't taken the trouble to look up what your leave dates were?

GÖRING: I have already said the 28 or the 29 of March. I cannot tell you. I know only that I was there in March.

SIR DAVID MAXWELL-FYFE: Witness, will it be perfectly fair to you if I take the latest of your dates, the 29 March, to work on?

GÖRING: It would be more expedient if you would tell me when Easter was that year, because I do not recall it. Then it will be easier for me to specify the dates, because I know that a few days before Easter I returned to Berchtesgaden in order to pass these holidays with my family.

SIR DAVID MAXWELL-FYFE: A few days before Easter you went back to Berchtesgaden?

GÖRING: Yes.

SIR DAVID MAXWELL-FYFE: So you had come back on leave some days before that. Before you went to Berchtesgaden you had come back from your March leave?

GÖRING: Berchtesgaden was then at the same time the headquarters of the Führer. I returned from my leave to Berchtesgaden and with my return my leave ended, because I returned to duty. The return to Berchtesgaden was identical with the termination of my leave.

SIR DAVID MAXWELL-FYFE: Well, I can't give you Easter offhand, but I happen to remember Whitsuntide was 28 May, so that Easter would be early, somewhere about 5 April. So that your leave would finish somewhere about the end of March, maybe the 26 or the 29; that is right, isn't it?

Now, these shootings of these officers went on from the 25 March to the 13 April; do you know that?

GÖRING: I do not know that exactly.

SIR DAVID MAXWELL-FYFE: You may take that from me because there is an official report of the shooting, and I want to be quite fair with you. Only 49 of these officers were shot on the 6 April, as far as we can be sure, and one was shot either on the 13 April or later. But the critical period is the end of March, and we may take it that you were back from leave by about the 29 March.

I just want you to tell the Tribunal this was a matter of great importance, wasn't it? Considered a matter of great importance?

GÖRING: It was a very important matter.

SIR DAVID MAXWELL-FYFE: General

Milch—I beg pardon—Field Marshal Milch [Göring's deputy] has said that it was a matter which would require the highest authority, and I think you have said that you know it was Hitler's decision that these officers should be shot. Is that so?

GÖRING: The question did not come through clearly.

SIR DAVID MAXWELL-FYFE: It was Hitler's decision that these officers should be shot?

GÖRING: That is correct; and I was later notified that it was Hitler's decree.

SIR DAVID MAXWELL-FYFE: I want you just to remember one other thing, that immediately it was published, the British Foreign Secretary, Mr Eden, at once said that Great Britain would demand justice of the perpetrators of these murders—do you remember that?

GÖRING: I cannot remember the speech to the House of Commons given by Eden. I myself do not know the substance of this speech even today. I just heard that he spoke in Parliament about this incident.

SIR DAVID MAXWELL-FYFE: I want you to tell the Tribunal just who the persons in your ministry involved were. I will tell you; I think it would be shorter in the end. If you disagree you can correct me.

The Kommandant of Stalag Luft III was Oberst von Lindeiner of your service, was he not?

GÖRING: That is quite possible. I did not know the names of all these Kommandants. There was a court-martial against him and that was because the escape was possible. He was not connected with the shootings.

SIR DAVID MAXWELL-FYFE: No, but he was Kommandant of the camp, and I suppose you had to review and confirm the proceedings which convicted him and sentenced him to a year's imprisonment for neglect of duty. That would come to you, wouldn't it? Wouldn't that come to you for review?

GÖRING: No, only if larger penalties were involved. One year imprisonment would not come to my attention. But I know, and I would like to certify, that court proceedings were taken against him for neglect of duty at the time of the escape.

SIR DAVID MAXWELL-FYFE: In May 1943, Inspectorate Number 17 had been interposed between the Luftwaffe and the Prisoners of War Organisation of the OKW, the Kriegsgefangenenwesen; do you remember that?

GÖRING: I do not know the details about inspection nor how closely it concerned the Prisoners of War Organisation of the OKW, or how it was otherwise.

SIR DAVID MAXWELL-FYFE: I want to remind you of who your own officers were.

You understand, Witness, that your own officers are involved in this matter. I want to remind you who they were.

Was the head of Inspectorate 17 Major-General Grosch of the Luftwaffe?

GÖRING: Major-General Grosch is of the Luftwaffe.

SIR DAVID MAXWELL-FYFE: You told the Tribunal the other day—I am quoting your own words—that you knew from information, you knew this incident very completely and very minutely. You are now telling the Tribunal you don't know whether Major-General Grosch was head of Inspectorate Number 17 of the Luftwaffe.

GÖRING: That is irrelevant. I told the High Tribunal that I heard an accurate account of the incident of the shooting of these airmen, but that has no connection with General Grosch and his inspectorate, for he did not participate in the shooting.

SIR DAVID MAXWELL-FYFE: I will show you that connection in one minute if you will just answer my questions. Was Grosch's second-in-command Oberst Welder? Do you remember that?

GÖRING: I do not know the particulars of the organisation for inspection of prisoner-of-war camps, nor the leaders, nor what positions they held. At least not by heart. I would like to emphasise again, so that there will be no confusion, that when I said I knew about this matter, I mean that I knew how the order was issued and that the people were shot, that I came to know all about this but not as far as this was related to inspections, possibilities of flight, et cetera.

SIR DAVID MAXWELL-FYFE: And did General Grosch, as head of Inspectorate 17, have to report to General Förster, your director of operations at the Luftwaffe Ministerium?

GÖRING: That I cannot tell you without having the diagram of the subordinate posts before me. General Förster was, I believe, at that time head of the Luftwehr, or a similar designation, in the ministry. I concerned myself less with these matters, because they were not directly of a tactical, strategic, or of an armament nature. But it is quite possible and certain that he belonged to this department.

SIR DAVID MAXWELL-FYFE: I put it to you quite shortly and if you don't know I will leave it for the moment. Did you know Major-General von Graevenitz was head of the Defendant Keitel's department, the Kriegsgefangenenwesen, that dealt with prisoners of war?

GÖRING: I first heard about General Graevenitz here, for this department did not directly concern me. I could not know all of these military subordinate commanders in their hundreds and thousands of departments.

SIR DAVID MAXWELL-FYFE: So I take it that you did not know Colonel, now General, Westhoff, of the department under von Graevenitz?

GÖRING: Westhoff I never saw at all, and he did not belong to the Luftwaffe.

SIR DAVID MAXWELL-FYFE: I am not suggesting that von Graevenitz and Westhoff belonged to the Luftwaffe. I wanted to make it clear that I was suggesting they belonged to General Keitel's organisation.

GÖRING: I did not know either; and I did not know what posts they occupied.

SIR DAVID MAXWELL-FYFE: Up to that time you still had a considerable influence in the Reich, didn't you?

GÖRING: At this time no longer. This no longer concerns 1944.

SIR DAVID MAXWELL-FYFE: But you were still head of the Luftwaffe and head of the Air Ministry, weren't you?

GÖRING: Yes, I was.

SIR DAVID MAXWELL-FYFE: And you had, as head of the Luftwaffe and head of the Air Ministry, been responsible for six prisoner-of-war camps for the whole of the war up to that time, hadn't you?

GÖRING: How many prisoner-of-war camps I do not know. But of course I bear the responsibility for those which belonged to my ministry.

SIR DAVID MAXWELL-FYFE: To the Air Force?

GÖRING: Yes, those which were subordinate to the Air Force.

SIR DAVID MAXWELL-FYFE: You knew about the general plan for treatment of prisoners of war, which we have had in evidence as the 'Aktion Kugel' plan, didn't you?

GÖRING: No. I knew nothing of this action. I was not advised of it.

SIR DAVID MAXWELL-FYFE: You were never advised of Aktion Kugel?

GÖRING: I first heard of Aktion Kugel here; saw the document and heard the expression for the first time. Moreover, no officer of the Luftwaffe ever informed me of such a thing; and I do not believe that a single officer was ever taken away from the Luftwaffe camps. A report to this effect was never presented to me, in any case.

SIR DAVID MAXWELL-FYFE: You know what Aktion Kugel was: that escaped officers and non-commissioned officers, other than British and American, were to be handed over to the police and taken to Mauthausen, where they were shot by the device of having a gun concealed in the measuring equipment when they thought they were getting their prison clothes. You know what Aktion Kugel is, don't you?

GÖRING: I heard of it here.

SIR DAVID MAXWELL-FYFE: Are you telling the Tribunal that you did not know that escaped prisoners of war who were picked up by the police were retained by the police and taken to Mauthausen?

GÖRING: No, I did not know that. On the contrary, various prisoners who escaped from my camps were caught again by the police; and they were all brought back to the camps; this was the first case where this to some extent did not take place.

SIR DAVID MAXWELL-FYFE: But didn't you know that Colonel Welder, as second-in-command of your ministry's inspectorate issued a written order a month before this, in 2/1944, that prisoners of war picked up by the Luftwaffe should be delivered back to their camp, and prisoners of war picked up by the police should be held by them and no longer counted as being under the protection of the Luftwaffe; didn't you know that?

GÖRING: No. Please summon this colonel to testify if he ever made a report of that nature to me, or addressed such a letter to me.

SIR DAVID MAXWELL-FYFE: Well, of course, I cannot tell whether your ministry was well run or not. But he certainly issued the order, because he says so himself.

GÖRING: Then he must say from whom he received this order.

SIR DAVID MAXWELL-FYFE: I see. Well, he says that he issued this order, and you know as well as I do that prisoners of war is a thing that you have got to be careful about, because you have got a protecting power that investigates any complaint; and you never denounced the Convention and you had the protecting power in these matters all through the war, had you not? That is right, isn't it?

GÖRING: That is correct, but I take the liberty to ask who gave him this order, whether he received this order from me.

SIR DAVID MAXWELL-FYFE: Well, he would not get it direct from you. I do not think you had ever met him, had you? He would get it from Lieutenant General Grosch, wouldn't he?

GÖRING: Then Grosch should say whether he received such an order from me. I never gave such an order.

SIR DAVID MAXWELL-FYFE: I see. So you say that you had never heard; this was three and a half years after the beginning of the war and you had never heard that any escaped prisoners of war were to be handed over to the police. Is that what you ask the Tribunal to believe?

GÖRING: To any officers or police, I believe gave an order to the extent that if escaped prisoners of war committed crimes, they were of course turned over to the police but I wish to testify before the Court that I never ordered that they should be handed over to the police or sent to concentration camps

438

merely because they had attempted to break out or escape, nor did I ever know that such measures were taken.

SIR DAVID MAXWELL-FYFE: This is my last question: I want to make it quite clear, Witness, that I am referring to those who had escaped, who had got away from the confines of the camp and were recaptured by the police. Didn't you know that they were handed over to the police?

GÖRING: No. Only if they had committed crimes while fleeing, such as murder and so on. Such things occurred.

Testimony of 21 March 1946
Morning Session
SIR DAVID MAXWELL-FYFE: Witness, do you remember telling me last night that the only prisoners of war handed over to the police were those guilty of crimes or misdemeanours?

GÖRING: I did not express myself that way. I said if the police apprehended prisoners of war, those who had committed a crime during the escape, as far as I know, were detained by the police and were not returned to the camp. To what extent the police kept prisoners of war, without returning them to a camp, I was able to gather from interrogations and explanations here.

SIR DAVID MAXWELL-FYFE: Would you look at Document D-569? Would you look first at the top left-hand corner, which shows that it is a document published by the Oberkommando der Wehrmacht?

GÖRING: The document which I have before me has the following heading at the top left-hand corner: 'The Reichsführer SS' and the subheading: 'Inspector of Concentration Camps.'

SIR DAVID MAXWELL-FYFE: It is a document dated the 22 November 1941. Have you got it?

GÖRING: Yes, I have it now.

SIR DAVID MAXWELL-FYFE: Now, look at the left-hand bottom corner, as to distribution. The second person to whom it is distributed is the Air Ministry and Commander-in-Chief of the Air Force on 22 November 1941. That would be you.

GÖRING: That's correct. I would like to make the following statement in connection with this . . .

SIR DAVID MAXWELL-FYFE: Just a moment. I would like you to appreciate the document and then make your statement upon it. I shall not stop you. I want you to look at the third sentence in paragraph one. This deals with Soviet prisoners of war, you understand. The third sentence says:

'If escaped Soviet prisoners of war are returned to the camp in accordance with this order, they have to be handed over to the nearest post of the Secret State Police, in any case.'

And then paragraph two deals with the special position—if they commit crimes, owing to the fact that:

> . . . at present these misdemeanours on the part of Soviet prisoners of war are particularly frequent, due most likely to living conditions still being somewhat unsettled, the following temporary regulations come into force. They may be amended later. If a Soviet prisoner of war commits any other punishable offence then the Kommandant of the camp must hand the guilty man over to the head of the security police.

Do I understand this document to say that a man who escapes will be handed over to the security police? You understand this document says a man who escapes will be handed over to the secret police, a man who commits a crime, as you mentioned, will be handed over to the security police. Wasn't that the condition that obtained from 1941 up to the date we are dealing with in March 1944?

GÖRING: I would like to read the few preceding paragraphs so that no sentences are separated from their context.

SIR DAVID MAXWELL-FYFE: My Lord,

441

while the witness is reading the document, might I go over the technical matter of the arrangement of exhibits? When I cross-examined Field Marshal Slecking I put in three documents, UK-66, which becomes Exhibit 274; D-39, which becomes GB-275; TC-91, which becomes GB-276; this document will become GB-277. [Turning to the witness.] Have you had an opportunity to read it, Witness?

GÖRING: Yes, I have.

SIR DAVID MAXWELL-FYFE: Then I am right, am I not, that Soviet prisoners of war who escaped were to be, after their return to the camp, handed over to the secret state police. If they committed a crime, they were to be handed over to the security police, isn't that right?

GÖRING: Not exactly correct. I would like to point to the third sentence in the first paragraph. There it says, 'If a prisoner-of-war camp is in the vicinity, then the man who is recaptured is to be transported there.'

SIR DAVID MAXWELL-FYFE: But read the next sentence, 'If a Soviet prisoner of war is returned to the camp'—that is in accordance with this order which you have just read—'he has to be handed to the nearest service station of the Secret State Police'. Your own sentence.

GÖRING Yes, but the second paragraph which follows gives an explanation of frequent criminal acts of Soviet prisoners of war, etc., committed at that time. You read that yourself; that is connected with this paragraph number one. But this order was given by itself and it was distributed to the Army, the Air Force and the Navy. And I would like to give the explanation of its distribution. In this war there were not only hundreds, but thousands of current orders which were issued by superiors to subordinate officers and were transmitted to various departments. That does not mean that each of these thousands of orders was submitted to the Commander-in-Chief; only the most decisive and most important were shown to him. The others went from department to department. Thus it is that this order from the Chief of the High Command was signed by a subordinate department, and not by the Chief of the High Command himself.

SIR DAVID MAXWELL-FYFE: This order would be dealt with by your prisoner-of-war department in your ministry, wouldn't it?

GÖRING: This department, according to the procedure adopted for these orders, received the order, but no other department received it.

SIR DAVID MAXWELL-FYFE: I think the answer to my question must be 'Yes'. It would be dealt with by the prisoner-of-war department—your ministry. Isn't that so?

GÖRING: I would say yes.

SIR DAVID MAXWELL-FYFE: It is quicker, you see, if you say 'yes' in the beginning; do you understand?

GÖRING: No; it depends upon whether I personally have read the order or not, and I will then determine as to my responsibility.

SIR DAVID MAXWELL-FYFE: Well, now, the escape . . .

THE PRESIDENT: You were not asked about responsibility; you were asked whether it would be dealt with by your prisoner-of-war department.

SIR DAVID MAXWELL-FYFE: Now, the escape about which I am asking you took place on the night of the 24 to the 25 March. I want you to have that date in mind. The decision to murder these young officers must have been taken very quickly, because the first murder which actually took place was on the 26 of March. Do you agree with that? It must have been taken quickly?

GÖRING: I assume that this order, as I was informed later, was given immediately, but it had no connection with this document.

SIR DAVID MAXWELL-FYFE: No, no; we are finished with that document; we are going into the murder of these young men. The Grossfahndung—a general hue and cry, I think, would be the British translation— was also issued at once in order that these men should be arrested; isn't that so?

444

GÖRING: That is correct. Whenever there was an escape and such a large number of prisoners escaped, automatically in the whole Reich, a hue and cry was raised, that is, all authorities had to be on the lookout to recapture the prisoners.

SIR DAVID MAXWELL-FYFE: So that in order to give this order to murder these men, and for the Grossfahndung, there must have been a meeting of Hitler, at any rate with Himmler or Kaltenbrunner, in order that that order would be put into effect; isn't that so?

GÖRING: That is correct. According to what I heard, Himmler was the first to report this escape to the Führer.

SIR DAVID MAXWELL-FYFE: Now, General Westhoff, who was in Defendant Keitel's Kriegsgefangenenwesen, in his prisoner-of-war set-up, says this, that 'On a date, which I think was the 26, Keitel said to him, "This morning Göring reproached me in the presence of Himmler for having let some more prisoners of war escape. It was unheard of."' Do you say that General Westhoff is wrong?

GÖRING: Yes. This is not in accordance with the facts. General Westhoff is referring to a statement of Field Marshal Keitel. This utterance in itself is illogical, for I could not accuse Keitel because he would not draw my attention to it, as the guarding was his responsibility and not mine.

SIR DAVID MAXWELL-FYFE: One of the Defendant Keitel's officers dealing with this matter was a general inspector, General Rottich. I do not know if you know him.

GÖRING: No.

SIR DAVID MAXWELL-FYFE: Well, General Westhoff, as one could understand, is very anxious to assure everyone that his senior officer had nothing to do with it, and he goes on to say this about General Rottich:

> He was completely excluded from it by the fact that these matters were taken out of his hands. Apparently at that conference with the Führer in the morning, that is to say, the conference between Himmler, Field Marshal Keitel, and Göring, which took place in the Führer's presence, the Führer himself always took a hand in these affairs when officers escaped.

You say that is wrong? You were at no such conference?

GÖRING: I was not present at this conference, neither was General Westhoff; he is giving a purely subjective view, not the facts of the case.

SIR DAVID MAXWELL-FYFE: So that we find that—you think that—Westhoff is wrong? You see, Westhoff, he was a colonel at this time, I think, and now he finishes as a major-general, and he asks that the senior officers be asked about it; he says this: 'It should be possible to find out that Himmler made the suggestion to the Führer—to find that out from Göring who was present at the conference.' Again and again Westhoff, who after all is a comparatively junior officer, is saying that the truth about this matter can be discovered from his seniors. You say that it cannot.

GÖRING: I would not say that. I would like just to say that General Westhoff was never present for even a moment, therefore he cannot say, I know or I saw that Reich Marshal Göring was present. He is assuming it is so, or he may have heard it.

SIR DAVID MAXWELL-FYFE: What he says is, you know, that Keitel blamed him, as I have read to you; that Keitel went on to say to him at General Von Graevenitz's, 'Gentlemen, the escapes must stop. We must set an example. We shall take very severe measures. I am only telling you that, that the men who have escaped will be shot; probably the majority of them are dead already.' You never heard anything of that?

GÖRING: I was neither present at the Keitel–Westhoff–Graevenitz conversation nor at the Führer–Himmler conversation. As far as I know General Westhoff will be testifying here. Moreover, Field Marshal

Keitel will be able to say whether I was there or not.

GLOSSARY

Appell	Roll-call
Ausweis	Identity Card
Autobahn	Motorway
Big S	Code name for head of security in the Escape Organisation
Big X	Code name for the head of the Escape Organisation
Brigadierführer	Brigadier
Dean & Dawson	The Escape Organisation's forgery factory
Dulag Luft	Luftwaffe Transit Camp (Durchgangslager Luftwaffe)
Ferrets	Nickname for German guards specifically detailed to ferret out escape activity
Gestapo	State Secret Police (Geheime Staatpolizei)

Goon	Nickname for the regular German guards
Goon box	Guard tower
Gruppenführer	Major-General
Hard-arser	An escaper planning to travel on foot
Hauptsturmführer	Captain
Hundführer	Guard dog master
Kommandantur	The German administrative compound
Kriegie	Shorthand for Kriegsgefangene (prisoner of war)
Kripo	Shorthand for Kriminalpolizei (plain clothes, criminal police)
Little S	Allied security officer in charge of each barrack block
Little X	Allied officer in charge of escape-planning in each barrack block
Luftwaffe	German Air Force
Oberstgruppenführer	General
Obergruppenführer	Lieutenant-General
Obersturmbannführer	Lieutenant-Colonel

Obersturmführer	Lieutenant
Oflag	Offizierlager (officers' prison camp)
OKW	Oberkommando der Wehrmacht (the High Command of all Germany's armed forces)
Penguins	Allied officers responsible for dispersing sand via trouser leg bags
RSHA	Reichssicherheitshauptampt (the Reich Security Office)
SBO	Senior British Officer
Stalag	Stammlager (other ranks' prisoner of war camp)
Stalag Luft	Air force prisoner-of-war camp
Standartenführer	Colonel
Stooge	Look-out
Sturmbannführer	Major
Trapführer	Allied officer in charge of tunnel entrance trap-door
Untersturmführer	Second Lieutenant

Vorlager   Compound housing
cooler, medical room
and postal room

SELECT BIBLIOGRAPHY

Books

Andrews, Allen, *Exemplary Justice*, Harrap, London, 1976

Brickhill, Paul, *The Great Escape*, Faber & Faber, London, 1951

Burgess, Allan, *The Longest Tunnel*, Bloomsbury, London, 1990

Crawley, Aidan, *Escape from Germany: A History of RAF Escapes During the Second World War*, Simon & Schuster, London, 1956

Durand, Arthur A., *Stalag Luft III: The Secret Story*, Louisiana State University Press, Louisiana, 1988

Foot, M.R.D. and Langley, J.M., *MI9 Escape and Evasion 1939–1945*, Bodley Head, London, 1979

Gill, Anton, *The Great Escape*, Review, London, 2002

Gill, Anton, *The Journey Back from Hell*, HarperCollins, London, 2001

Harsh, George, *Lonesome Road*, Norton & Co., New York, 1971

James, Jimmy, *Moonless Night*, Pen & Sword, London 2001

MacDonald, Callum, *The Killing of SS Obergruppenführer Reinhard Heydrich*, New York Free Press, New York, 1989

Martin, Gwyn, *Up and Under*, Gwyn Martin,

Wales, 1989

Philpot, Oliver, *Stolen Journey*, Hodder & Stoughton, London, 1951; New York, 1952

Scotland, A.P., *The London Cage*, Evans, London, 1956

Smith, Sydney, *Mission Escape*, Hodder & Stoughton, London, 1951; New York, 1969

Smith, Sydney, *Wings Day*, Collins, London, 1968

Vance, Jonathan F., *A Gallant Company*, Pacifica Military History, California, 2000

van der Stok, Robert, *War Pilot Orange*, Pictorial Histories, Montana, 1987

Williams, Eric, *The Wooden Horse*, Collins, London, 1949

Memoirs
The Memoirs of Colonel Friedrich-Wilhelm von Lindeiner (privately published, courtesy of the United States Air Force Academy, Colorado Springs)

Public Record Office Sources
Hamburg Trial of Gestapo Agents and Testimonies
The Official History of the North Compound, Stalag Luft III

Imperial War Museum Sources
The files of Eric Williams

Other Sources
Transcripts of interviews with Albert Clark and Jimmy James conducted by the author for the Learning Channel television documentary *Breakout,* subsequently broadcast as *Escape Stories* in the United States.
Transcripts of interviews with Tony Bethell, Les Brodrick, Sydney Dowse, Jimmy James, Des Plunkett, Paul Royle and Mike Shand for 'Last of the Great Escapers', the *Sunday Express Review*, 23 December 2001.